Travel Air

Wings Over the Prairie

ED PHILLIPS

Above the Crowd,
On Upward Wings Could I But Fly,
I'd Bathe in Yon Bright Cloud,
And Seek the Stars that Gem the Sky.

Charles Sprague

FLYING BOOKS

Eagan, Minnesota 55122

FOREWORD
by Joseph P. Juptner

Civil aviation in its infancy had no industry to speak of and was saddled with a literal flood of cheap, war-surplus airplanes after the 1914-1918 war.

Pilots that chose to continue flying did their best with these machines in spite of their shortcomings. Forced ingenuity in the next few years fashioned many modifications to these airplanes that did improve their capabilities.

To fly continually with any success the pilot also had to be a good mechanic and most learned to be "aircraft engineers" in the process.

Eventually coming to limits of what one could do to improve the "Jenny" or "Standard," there was born a number of new designs. Because of the great size of our nation those in aviation during the early 1920s were widely scattered and few in number, but they did gather occasionally.

They met to get acquainted, renew old friendships, spin a few tales and discuss new theories on aircraft. Being brethren with a common cause, no one felt hesitant to borrow ideas from another airman.

Swept ahead by enthusiasm it was not long before "aircraft factories" were sprouting up all over the land, and one company named Travel Air emerged to make their bid.

In this gathering that made up Travel Air there were all kinds of people — some with artisan skills, some with dreams and some who were the "movers"; ones who got things done.

The owners and pilots of Travel Air airplanes were the company's most avid boosters.

Being among the first to engage itself in the untried business of commercial airplane manufacture, the Travel Air team, under able leadership soon became one of the largest airplane manufacturers in the world.

This book is the story of Travel Air as never told before. . . a behind-the-scenes look into the company in a time when aviation was thrust upon the American scene in a manner that has never been equalled.

Joseph P. Juptner

Copyright © 1982 Flying Books, Publishers & Wholesalers, Eagan, Minnesota 55122

Library of Congress Cataloging in Publication Data
Phillips, Edward

Travel Air
Wings Over The Prairie

82-082791

ISBN 0-911139-00-1

Printed in the United States of America
First edition

INTRODUCTION

Braced against the chill of March 13, 1925, a small group of men watched impatiently as the biplane taxied across the Kansas sod.

Anxiety was building, anticipation clutched at each man's thoughts. They had waited nearly three months for this event, put their money, desire and ambition together to build and fly an airplane. Now the time had arrived for their creation to take wing, and everyone wondered how the ship would fly.

Why was it taking so long? Was something wrong? All the pilot needed to do was check the magneto and controls, then "give her the gun" and be off.

Their questions were answered when the familiar sound of an OX-5 at full throttle ripped through the air. All eyes tracked the trim airplane as it accelerated, bouncing gently with the tail up, gathering speed. Then, virgin wings feeling their first encounter with the air, the first Travel Air was in her element.

Man and machine soared gracefully over the prairie of Wichita's California Section, climbing, turning, locked in the thrill of flight. Soon, her master brought them both down to a smooth landing, ending the maiden flight, but marking the beginning of Travel Air, Inc.

Walter P. Innes, Jr., Lloyd C. Stearman, Clyde V. Cessna, Walter H. Beech, Charles G. Yankey and William "Bill"

Snook had an airplane, a company and enthusiasm suited for success. Stearman gave Travel Air #1 her graceful lines, Beech incorporated redundancy into the controls and comfort for the passengers and pilot.

Cessna fashioned her from design to reality, along with the irreplaceable talents of skilled workers, and Innes helped her to fame with financial wisdom and foresight. Snook directed and assisted in her construction and development.

In the five years following the first flight, nearly 1400 examples of Travel Air quality, durability, safety and performance would uphold the lineage of #1 in the highest fashion. The name Travel Air became synonomous with one of the finest airplanes money could buy, excellence in design and craftsmanship, performance under adverse conditions and, as Walter Beech would declare in 1929, "The Standard of Aircraft Comparison."

This is the story of Travel Air, from humble beginnings to the pinnacle of success in aviation. It is a story of men and machines. Six men launched their dream that day in March, a dream with wings that flew into history.

Edward H. Phillips
October 18, 1981
Wichita, Kansas

Book Dedication: TO THE MEN AND WOMEN OF TRAVEL AIR

ACKNOWLEDGEMENTS

In assembling the information for this work, many people have given the author such assistance and aid that it can be clearly stated that they, and history, have made this book a reality.

Much time was unselfishly given in the furtherance of details on airplanes, persons, events and locations. The patience they all displayed with a subject over 50 years of age and a researcher of lesser number is greatly appreciated.

As with any endeavor of this magnitude, a large number of people are required to add their expertise and knowledge to the making of a historical publication . . . photographers, artists, librarians, public relations personnel, layout technicians and untold others who have made the story of Travel Air possible.

To these good people and those who continually gave encouragement and interest in the project, I am deeply grateful. Every effort has been made to ensure no person has been omitted from the following list, but should this have occurred I am stating here a sincere 'thank you.'

W.C. "Dub" Yarbrough, Mort Van Kueren, Bill Ellington of the Wichita City Library and the staff of the reference section, John Zimmerman, Earl Sayre, Bob Pickett of Cessna Aircraft Company, John Davis, Walt Boyne of the Smithsonian Institution, Phil Edwards, also with the Smithsonian; Ken Wilson, Richard Allen, John Prigmore, Mrs. Roy Edwards, Dean Edwards, Phil Schultz, Mrs. William Barnes, Tom Ramsey, Ted Cochran, Ray Phelps, Bob and Cora Phelps,

Clarence E. Clark, Dan Doyle, Ted Wells, J. Jack Clark, Truman and Dorothy Wadlow, Newman Wadlow, Phillips Petroleum Company and Mr. Bob Finney, Letha Brunk, Morton Lester, Carl Davis, Bill Blakemore and Robert Lansdown, Linda Stone of the Frank Phillips Museum, Mrs. Atlar Meyer-Smith, Mr. and Mrs. Carl Burnham, Mrs. Walter Burnham, Mrs. Ralph Nordberg and Ms. Jane Bingham, Bill Chomo, George Hardie, Jr., Carole Blake and Gene Chase of the Experimental Aircraft Association; Mr. and Mrs. A.M. "Monty" Barnes, Roger Tengwall, Verda Pruner, Eldon Cessna, John Robson, Al Kelch, Jim Rezich, Mike Rezich, Joseph P. Juptner, Fran Rourke, E.M. "Matty" Laird, Kansas State Historical Society, Pat Finley and William M. Watson of the Federal Aviation Administration in Oklahoma City; George Disinger, Mrs. Olive Ann Beech, Mrs. Bette Bulmer, Mrs. Sherry Huenergardt, Bill Thaden, Gordon S. Williams, Peter M. Bowers, Max Prickett, Mike Sheets, Pat Combs, Barbara Harding, Sondra Van Meter, Mike Madewell, Tressa Hales, Mary Hall, Arlen Ray, Kenny Freeman, Jim Zluticky, Bob Parish, Mal Holcomb, Doug Ambler, Donna Irvin, Bill Robinson, and Patricia Hurley of Beech Aircraft Public Relations Dept., The Boeing Company, Walt House, Jack Wecker, Wichita State University Library, Pauline and Jack Winthrop, The Hunter Family and special thanks to Marla Weyand, Bob Resley, Jim Rigg and the Graphic Arts Dept. of Beech Aircraft Corporation.

TRAVEL AIR

CHAPTER ONE
Wichita — The Air Capital

Thousands of Wichitans watched in amazement as Roy Knabenshue manuevered his 40 horsepower dirigible over the crowds. It was October 8, 1908 and Wichita, Kansas was getting its first exposure to the wonder of manned flight. Knabenshue guided his fragile craft performing turns, climbs and descents, thrilling the people below.

It was just the beginning of an association between a city on the plains and aviation, an association that remains today. Knabenshue was followed three years later by Jimmy Ward, Eugene Ely, C.C. Witmer and R.C. St. Henry flying four Curtiss biplanes in Wichita's first "air show."

This four day event was staged by Orville A. Boyle, a produce broker who was interested in bringing aeronautics before the eyes of his contemporaries.

Some 11,500 people paid to witness the four men flying in formation and attempting to set an altitude record. The meet received excellent newspaper coverage from the Wichita Eagle and Beacon papers, but Mr. Boyle received a financial loss of $375 for his efforts.

Everyone was enthusiastic about viewing such an event, and many wondered if this era of "aviating" had any future. It certainly did, and the city would become the womb of many airplane companies.

By 1929 Wichita could boast of 16 airplane factories, 13 airplane and engine service facilities, nine air transportation companies, 13 schools devoted to ground and air instruction and 25 stores of aeronautical accessories and supplies.

In 1919 two companies were formed to put the airplane before the public eye and prove it to be a vehicle of usefulness. The Wichita Aeroplane Service Company and the Wichita Aircraft Company both came into existence for the purpose of getting folks up in the air.

The Wichita Aeroplane Service Company was first to set up shop. A.A. Stratford, owner of the Ponca Tent and Awning Company, joined with Leslie L. Petticord to form the new venture. Petticord had about 400 hours of flying time from his stint with the Air Service. The two men leased 80 acres near Fairmount College (now Wichita State University) and the site became known as Stratford Field.

Original configuration of Laird "Limousine," with two Curtiss OX-5, 90 HP engines. First flown in July, 1921, Matty Laird's airliner was too new and no market existed for it. Ship had top speed of 105 MPH. (Earl Sayre)

Revised "Limousine" after installation of Packard 300 HP engine. Walter Beech later replaced it with 450 HP Liberty. Irl Beach made a forced landing with the airplane near Fairmount College, the biplane being intentionally destroyed later that day. Walter Beech stands next to engine. (Beech Aircraft Corporation)

Using two Curtiss "Jennys" the company planned to act as a sales agent for Curtiss airplanes, give "Air Joy Rides" for $15 and be available for shows at county fairs. An air taxi service "anywhere, anytime" was also offered.

Stratford and Petticord soon split their alliance over an insurance dispute, the company fading into history. But another company was getting into aviation, too. In May and June, 1919 it had organized and filed for state charter by July 5. Businessmen were becoming involved also. J.B. Witt and E.J. Mason, along with Jacob Moellendick founded the Wichita Aircraft Company under the motto "Safety First." Plans called for a school of "fliers," passenger and air taxi service and five hangars on the field, one mile northeast of the city.

Before the end of 1919, the firm was nearly out of business. Financial backing from businessmen was not forthcoming, especially for an endeavor that showed little promise of trade and profit. Few people and even fewer businessmen took aviation seriously.

But Moellendick would hear none of that. He believed one way to put the city on the aeronautical map was to build airplanes there. A bold concept that seemed doomed to failure as so many other enterprises had been. But "Jake" was right — building airplanes was the answer.

He had one important necessity — money, oil money, ready to spend on aviation's future. All he needed was a good airplane design to manufacture. Moellendick was a friend of William "Billy" Burke, an automobile sales agent from Okmulgee, Oklahoma, who also managed an aerial circus company as a part-time business.

Burke had met a quiet, genial, self-taught engineer by the name of E.M. "Matty" Laird during a visit to Ashburn Field in Chicago around 1917. Laird had a natural engineering talent and designed airplanes that flew well on meager power.

Laird had sold Burke the first Model S in 1919. Billy flew it in his National Airplane Exhibition Company. Jake explained his idea of building airplanes in Wichita and convinced Burke to relocate there. On a Chicago trip in late 1919, Burke again met Laird. Matty showed him plans for a three-place, open cockpit biplane he was designing. Burke was immediately interested. Laird's machine offered the first true "break" in cockpit configuration from World War I airplanes, namely that of three positions with the pilot in back and room for two passengers in the front cockpit. Matty's design was just what Jake Moellendick needed. Burke siezed the opportunity and suggested Laird move his small factory to Kansas.

He explained that Moellendick had money and the three men could form a partnership. Laird's new design could be produced and sold all over America, and Moellendick would have his airplane factory.

Matty accepted the proposal and moved south. Burke and Moellendick each invested $15,000 while Laird furnished the design and some equipment for his share. A very small factory was obtained and production was soon underway. Laird flew the first airplane on April 8, 1920. William Lassen witnessed the flight and commented, "it flies just like a Swallow," and the name stuck.

After Swallow production was well underway, Burke suggested a seven passenger biplane be constructed for airline service.

Designed by Laird, the "Limousine," as it was called, was powered by two 90 horsepower OX-5 engines, but these were replaced by a single 300 horsepower Packard. The Packard was in turn replaced by a 450 horsepower Liberty. Dissatisfied with the airplane, Moellendick ordered it flown to Arkansas City, Kansas for storage.

Irl Beach (no relation to Walter Beech) was flying the airplane on a test hop prior to leaving for Arkansas City. The coolant expansion tank in the upper wing burst, damaging part of the wing structure. Beach made a forced landing, called the factory and asked for instructions. "Burn it" was Jake Moellendick's reply. Bob Phelps and Melvin Wheeler were dispatched to the site and stripped all useable parts and the engine from the airplane. Then, after spreading gasoline over her broken form, they set fire to the "Limousine" and watched it burn.

Laird hired Lloyd Carlton Stearman in 1920 after Stearman answered Matty's newspaper ad. Lloyd was working hard building wings and fuselages when in 1921, Moellendick hired Walter Herschel Beech as a part-time demonstration pilot and general employee. Beech cleaned cosmolene from crated engines and attended to customers flying into the Swallow airport on North Hillside Avenue.

Another key employee at Swallow was William "Bill" Snook. He was responsible for much of the factory mangement and found his views on airplane construction allied solidly with those of Beech and Stearman.

By 1923 a growing friction between Laird and Moellendick caused Matty to leave Wichita and start his own airplane company in Chicago. He left in October with $1500 and two Swallows for his four years with Jake's airplane business.

After Laird's departure, Stearman became chief engineer. At age 23 he was put to the task of coming up with an improved biplane. His design talents responded with the "New Swallow" of 1924. An instant success, the biplane's smooth, flowing lines enticed every pilot's eye, and the crowning feature was a graceful, hand-worked metal cowl that fully enclosed the OX-5 engine.

Orders came pouring in. Swallow pilots took New Swallows to many races and speed events, winning considerable sums of money that helped the Swallow Airplane Manufacturing Company stay in business.

Walter Beech developed a talent for sales and increased his piloting skills with Swallow airplanes, while Lloyd Stearman advanced his knowledge and execution of aeronautical design. Experience at both the Laird and Swallow companies helped Stearman, Beech and Snook

in later times. They learned aviation from the ground up and never forgot nor ignored the lessons they learned.

Wichita continued to grow aviation-minded. Airplanes were catching the fancy of the public and evidence of serious attention regarding use of airplanes for transportation was developing.

By the close of 1924, people were beginning to agree that the airplane was useful for more than a weekend sideshow. But the pulse of Wichita's aviation interests meant only one company — Swallow. Sales were good, and so was Moellendick's attitude.

However, Jake's attitude stiffened when Beech and Stearman approached him with a suggestion: change the Swallow's fuselage from wood to welded steel tubing. To Jake, the New Swallow looked good in wood and no change was necessary. It wasn't a novel idea, as Laird used a form of steel tubing in his early designs and European designers were beginning to employ the practice, too.

If steel tubing was to be used, it wouldn't be in a New Swallow. Stearman, Beech and Snook decided to build their own version of a light, commercial airplane, which Lloyd Stearman had been designing.

In December, 1924 the three men had a promising design, a determination to build and sell it, but they needed help.

Stearman knew of Clyde Vernon Cessna in Rago, Kansas, who was a pioneer aviator and had built airplanes since 1911. Cessna had purchased an OXX-6 New Swallow in early 1924 and was very familiar with current aeronautical construction practices.

He would be a valuable ally in the new organization they hoped to start. After discussion with Stearman and Beech, Cessna agreed to join the group. He would be the most important financial source for the venture, as Cessna knew very well that nearly $30,000 would be required to see the emerging company through its first year of existence.

With the addition of Clyde Cessna, the genesis of Travel Air Manufacturing Co., Inc. was complete.

Lloyd Stearman's talent resulted in the New Swallow of 1924. Ship caused great interest in aviation circles, and heralded the new breed of post-war airplanes emerging on the market. (Beech Aircraft Corporation)

Above — Curtiss OX-5 installation in New Swallow. Engine bearers were wood attached to steel tube supports. Walter Beech and other Swallow pilots entered and won air races with Swallow airplanes, winning money and notoriety for themselves and the company. (Smithsonian Institution Photo No. 81-2190)

Below — View of Swallow Field and factory, 29th and Hillside Avenue, 1924. Three New Swallows are parked in the grass. Main factory building is at right in background. (Beech Aircraft Corporation)

CHAPTER TWO
Beginnings

January 26, 1925 was a typical cold day of winter for Wichitans. Kansas winters were usually mild compared to those of the upper Plains states, but occasionally the bitter grip of winter took hold of Wichita and held on for days.

Picking up the morning edition of the Wichita Eagle, the people of Wichita read with interest the continuing story of the "Jazz Girl," a young woman who became hysterical when certain jazz tunes were played. The case was being followed closely, as lawyers tried to prove her mental instability was responsible for her behavior. She was in danger of being "put away" unless her innocence was proven to the court.

Wichitans had been following the case for days, but that wasn't the only news they were interested in. Wichita was located in Sedgwick county, where oil and wheat reigned supreme. The grain and oil market news was always a center of studious discussion and speculation.

But, on a back page near the advertising section a small article appeared. As reported by the Eagle, Wichitans read about the formation of Travel Air, Inc., announced by Walter P. Innes, Jr., spokesman. The new firm would use part of the factory space available at

Where it all began . . . 471 West First Street. Building housed the Kansas Planing Mill Co., where first Travel Air was built. Kansas Gas and Electric owned the facility when this photo was taken in 1929. The structure no longer stands. (Beech Aircraft Corporation)

471 West First Street for construction of a three-place, OX-5 powered biplane, the company's first product.

Innes said that no name for the biplane had been chosen as yet, but plans were underway to place the new model, when finished, in certain downtown hotel lobbies and merchant stores for public viewing. Suggestion boxes for naming the airplane would be placed alongside the machine.

The company planned to produce the biplane in lots of 10 machines, with a five-place, heavy-duty cabin biplane to be added later. Lloyd C. Stearman was chief engineer.

In February, Innes announced that materials for several biplanes were on order, and that construction would begin soon.

An important segment of the article announced company officers. William "Bill" Snook was factory manager, Clyde V. Cessna was vice-president and Walter H. Beech was secretary. Cessna's position as vice-president was one of the terms required by the Rago pilot for his entry into the firm. Clyde had discussed this with Beech and Stearman during their flying visit to Rago in December, 1924.

The presidency of Travel Air, Inc. belonged to Walter P. Innes, Jr., as did the position of treasurer. Innes' holding two offices is not difficult to understand. He was providing cash for the company and wanted close association with the financial workings of the firm. As

both offices were connected from a business standpoint, one man would best serve both capacities for the first four months.

Charles G. Yankey was named as an interested party with the company. He was a Wichita investor who saw the value of backing Travel Air with some funding.

Beech and Stearman also put up cash. Beech invested nearly $5,000 and Stearman $700. Some of this money came from personal savings and earnings while with Swallow; especially the racing rewards in Beech's case.

Clyde Cessna contributed $5,000, and he also loaned wood-working equipment to the company. Machinery was hauled from Rago to the Wichita factory in January, 1925.

Although Travel Air, Inc. was less than one month old, Innes was looking ahead with respect to the future. Not just the future of one company, but of Wichita as an aviation center of the United States.

On February 18, 1925, Innes planned to depart the city for Washington, D.C. to hold talks with the government on air mail contracts. Should the air mail contracts be let, Innes wanted his home town and Travel Air to be remembered to the bureaucracy. His forsight would reap rewards for both.

Nor was Innes alone in this quest. L.S. Seymour, president of the local chapter of the National Aeronautic Association (NAA), agreed with Innes and heartily endorsed his trip. The Wichita Chamber of Commerce was very enthusiastic about the air mail possibilities, and the city was experiencing even more aviation interest than expected.

The most likely air mail route would be from Chicago to Dallas, with Wichita as a major stopover point. Both mail and passenger service were contemplated, so that would draw even more business for whoever won the contract for the route.

Later on, Travel Air's monoplane design would play an important part in the hopes of Walter Innes. The engineers of Travel Air would come up with a design that could provide both air mail hauling with passenger seating in a comfortable environment.

On February 4, 1925, Travel Air received its approved

Above — Aviator, salesman and promoter of flight, Walter Herschel Beech poses for Edgar B. Smith, late summer, 1925. Model A biplane is early production version with revised landing gear, wooden tail skid and full length exhaust stacks that directed offensive fumes away from cockpit. (Beech Aircraft Corporation)

Below — Travel Air No. 1 during fabrication, winter, 1925. Fuel tank is between front cockpit instrument panel and firewall, held 30-1/2 gallons and featured gravity feed. Fuel shutoff valve is below tank, with control running aft to pilot cockpit. Both seats had thick, comfortable padding. Landing gear bolted to lower longeron, and axle was sprung with shock cord. (Beech Aircraft Corporation)

Below — Empennage construction of the first Travel Air. Horizontal stabilizer was steel tube with wood ribs. Spruce was used for vertical stabilizer shape. Elevators were steel tube with stamped ribs incorporating lightening holes. Rudder used very similar configuration. Note three-leaf tail skid, wood turtle-deck and formers, strap hinges of elevator and rudder. (Beech Aircraft Corporation)

Walter Beech flies an early production Model A near Wichita, August, 1925. Generous wing area of 296 sq. ft. shows clearly in this view. Photo was taken by Edgar B. Smith from his Standard, flown by Ted Braley. (Beech Aircraft Corporation)

charter of incorporation from the State of Kansas. The new company was officially recognized as an aircraft manufacturer and down at the West First Street facility construction of the first Travel Air biplanes continued.

There was no possibility for the infant firm to build a factory. Too expensive, to say the least, and Travel Air, Inc. was not exactly overflowing with cash in January, 1925.

But, friends in need are friends, indeed. The Breitwieser boys, Fred, Bert and Earnest were willing to lease space to Walter, Lloyd and Bill to help them build the first Travel Air. The "space" they referred to in their discussion with Beech and Stearman was about 30' x 30' of total working area.

Hardly enough room to fabricate and assemble Travel Air #1, but they would take it. The Breitwiesers owned the Kansas Planing Mill Co., at 200 N. Waco in 1924. Another building would house the planing mill operations, since the boys needed more room to expand their business.

One other advantage for Beech and Stearman was the ready availability of some equipment owned by the Breitwiesers. The company could use this tooling in addition to the Cessna-loaned woodworking machines. The Company planned to buy its own equipment as soon as profits permitted.

All these preliminary steps of financing, personnel and a factory were completed prior to the January 26 Eagle article. By early February all materials for the first biplanes were on order and enroute to Wichita.

By design the original Travel Air biplane was fairly straightforward, with no revolutionary ideas incorporated. But, it did have the influence of Beech and Stearman entrenched solidly from spinner to rudder.

Lloyd's architectural background helped in the basic design of the steel tube fuselage, or "body" as Beech often called it.

The actual choice of steel tubing was 1020 grade commercial tube. It was thin-walled and light, yet Lloyd expected a stress analysis to prove the strength as adequate for his design goals.

One must remember that no government regulations existed to guide the engineer or designer as to safety factors for the completed structure or materials selected for fabrication.

This process was based on known performance of certain materials in actual service and acceptable standards used throughout the United States by manufacturers of airplanes. Hence, Lloyd Stearman knew his design would be strong enough in the fuselage area, but detailed structure testing would still be required to eliminate all doubt.

Travel Air, Inc. had no testing equipment available, but Lloyd knew someone who did. Mr. C.O. Johnson, of the Agronomy department at Kansas State Agricultural College was contacted and he agreed to run specimen tests on the steel.

The batch of sheet and tube steel that arrived at the Travel Air, Inc. workshop was *assumed* to be adequate for the intended use of building an airplane. No material guarantees existed, therefore the specimen tests were essential, and during February Stearman readied the test parts.

In the January 26, 1925 issue of AVIATION, Travel

Air, Inc. was announced to the aviation world. The wording followed very closely that given by Innes in the Eagle newspaper story. Beech was referred to as only a "pilot in the Wichita area," but his flying skills were already winning him a notable reputation.

Stearman, mainly due to his genius with the New Swallow design, was labeled "well known aeronautical engineer" and Clyde Cessna as a "pioneer flier of Rago, Kansas."

Travel Air was careful to release information on the new company in synchronization with magazines such as AVIATION and AERO DIGEST, another popular aviation periodical of the era. Maximum saturation and publicity for the reading public was assured with the greatest impact, an impact that Travel Air, Inc. hoped would lead to the most important commodity they needed but didn't have: sales!

Back at the workshop, Beech and Stearman, along with Snook and other workmen were busy welding up the fuselage and building the wings for the first machine.

No blueprints were used. The time-proven method of floor layout was used, whereby the dimensions as given by Lloyd were marked on the floor of the shop for overall shape. Three-view drawings were also utilized, but detail drawings would come later when time permitted.

By early March, 1925 the first Travel Air was taking shape and beginning to look like quite an airplane. Without cover on the fuselage, the seamless steel tubing stood out as the major departure from the New Swallow. From the designer's standpoint, the airplane was a three-place, open cockpit biplane, with the passenger seat up forward and the pilot seat behind it.

Diagonal steel tubing braced the passenger area from the seat forward to the engine mount, and No. 10 steel wire was used from the pilot's seat aft to the sternpost. The wires ran diagonally from bay to bay and were fitted with individual clevis and turnbuckle fittings to permit tension adjustment.

The steel tailskid was made up of three pieces of spring stock, bolted together at a bracket just forward of the sternpost. No shock absorption cords were used.

The outside of the fuselage was faired with light spruce strips, and the spruce turtledeck was carried back to the sternpost, giving a nicely rounded appearance to the upper fuselage.

Stearman designed the engine mount as a removeable part of the fuselage structure. Rubber pads were used to isolate the OX-5 engine, both above and below the square engine bearers. The 30 and 1/2 gallon fuel tank was mounted in the passenger compartment, behind the forward instrument board. Fuel was fed to the carburetor by gravity flow. A small baggage hold was available directly behind the pilot's seat. It wasn't big enough for more than maps and a change of clothes, but it was a convenient feature Travel Air would stick with. Both seats were upholstered and padded for maximum comfort.

Stearman designed the fuselage for ease of entry, with only a 19 inch step-up from the left wingwalk to the passenger compartment. Thus, entry to the passenger seat was easy and the large amount of leg room made the step into the seat area quite simple, a fact that Beech and Stearman both knew should help in the sales game.

Controls ran from the pilot's compartment forward along the right sidewall, with a fuel shutoff valve mounted below the fuel tank, and throttle connection running through the firewall to the carburetor. Walter Beech had his ideas expressed in another area of Travel Air #1; the control cables for the elevator. There were two identical steel cables from the pilot stick back to the sternpost, where they attached to dual elevator control horns.

Beech wanted redundancy for the elevator should one cable ever fail, providing the pilot with full elevator control for handling the airplane. Walter believed that some backup elevator capability should be standard equipment on Travel Air ships, and Stearman agreed to the feature. When the fuselage was covered, a small Pyrolene inspection panel was installed to permit viewing of the elevator cables and horns.

Streamlined steel vees were used for the landing gear, with a duralumin spreader bar fitted between vees. Bungee shock cords were stretched around the axle ends and vee bottoms to provide shock absorption. The vees were bolted to the lower longeron at the firewall and at the junction of the first and second bracing bays. Two No. 10 steel wires added stability between vees.

Steel was used for the rudder and elevators, with tubing at the leading and trailing edges. The horizontal stabilizer had a steel tube leading edge with spruce spar

Lower wing shows push/pull tube for aileron control, and 3/16 inch plywood wingwalk found on both lower wings. Bracing was #9 steel wire. Stearman modified the British Fage and Collins airfoil section to permit higher top speed, good landing speed. This section became known as Travel Air No. 1 airfoil. (Beech Aircraft Corporation)

Upper wing construction showing spruce spars, which were 1-1/4 inch thickness at front spar and 1-1/2 inch thickness at rear spar. This changed on serial numbers above 300 to 1-5/8 inch for front spar and 2 inch for rear spar. Lower wings had same thickness on spars and underwent same change. Ailerons were on top wing only. 3/16 inch cap strips were used on ribs, with reinforcing strips on solid compression ribs. Internal wing bracing came from #9 steel wire for drag/anti-drag reinforcement. (Beech Aircraft Corporation)

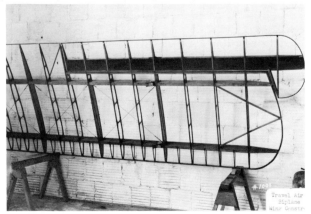

Lloyd C. Stearman (left) is congratulated by L.S. Seymour, president of the Wichita Chapter of the National Aeronautic Association. Event is trials on March 13, 1925 of Travel Air No. 1. Pilot is Irl Beach. He flew majority of tests that day. (Beech Aircraft Corporation)

and ribs. The pilot could trim the horizontal stabilizer from the cockpit to compensate for aerodynamic loads, and this feature would be used by Beech to sell Travel Air ships, stating that the airplane could be landed with the trim system alone. He was right, and it sold airplanes!

The vertical stabilizer was mostly spruce composition, with a small bolt and threaded fitting located at the very front of the stabilizer. This feature allowed the correction of engine torque by offsetting the stabilizer as required. Another selling point used by Walter. He would tell his prospect that right rudder was hardly needed in the Travel Air, because torque could be virtually eliminated by use of the bolt and fitting. Beech wanted to sell comfortable, safe, easy to fly machines, and these pilot-oriented design features went a long way toward doing just that.

Both the elevator and rudder used steel strap hinges, three on the elevator and two on the rudder. This arrangement was chosen because of simplicity and ease of repair/replacement. The hinges were also visible to the pilot during a pre-flight inspection.

Six steel wires braced the empennage, four from the horizontal stabilizer to the vertical stabilizer, two per side, and one per side underneath from the horizontal stabilizer to the lower longeron at the sternpost.

When it came to airfoils, Lloyd Stearman chose a Fage and Collins section, an airfoil of British origin, which he changed slightly to provide a lower landing speed while retaining its desired cruise speed characteristics.

One of the most noticeable features of the first Travel Air was the balanced ailerons on the upper wing. The overhanging portion of each aileron gave smooth, light and responsive aileron control. Stearman chose this remedy as it was the easiest and most common solution to heavy aileron control pressures.

Spruce was selected for the front and rear spars of both the upper and lower wing panels. Each spar was routed out between bolt holes, yielding a strong box section assembly.

Wing ribs were also spruce, with 3/16" cap strips. Compression ribs were solid, with four in the upper wing and five in the lower. All compression ribs were reinforced with spruce strips on both sides.

Nine false ribs were inserted between the leading edge and the spar on the lower wing while 12 were used on the upper panel. Trailing edges of each wing were 1/4" steel tubing and No. 9 steel wire made up the drag/anti-drag assemblies in the wings.

The control system for the ailerons was a different approach, but not novel. Instead of pulleys and cables, a "push-and-pull tube" was utilized. The tube was connected to the stick and ran through the lower wing to a box where the aileron bellcrank was housed. A streamlined steel tube ran from the bellcrank up to the aileron, where it attached at the number five rib of the aileron.

Both lower wings incorporated a 3/16" plywood wingwalk running from leading to trailing edge. Center section struts were also of streamline steel tubing and attached at the upper longeron.

By March 13, 1925 the first Travel Air was ready to fly. The wings were mounted on a flatbed truck and the fuselage was mounted so as to trail behind. After a slow-speed trip from West First Street to the California Section, east and south of downtown Wichita, the ship was assembled and readied for her maiden flight.

The ubiquitous Curtiss OX-5 engine of 90 hp. sat beneath a smooth, hand-formed metal cowl, very similar to the one Lloyd had designed on the New Swallow.

That fully enclosed cowling really made the biplane look good and it suggested finesse and dignity, too. The first flight was a complete success, and load carrying tests commenced the same day, with Irl Beach (no relation to Beech) at the controls.

L.S. Seymour, president of the local chapter of NAA (National Aeronautic Association) witnessed and certified the tests for the FAI (Federation Aeronautique Internationale).

Of three speed runs made, the ship did 96 MPH with pilot and one passenger, and climbed 1,000' with the same load in one minute six seconds.

Takeoff tests were made with a load of 1119 lbs. of bagged sand. The ship lifted off the ground in 451 feet and climbed to 500 feet in two minutes, three seconds.

The men of Travel air were satisfied with their airplane. It had met all design goals. The empty weight, with water aboard, was 1300 lbs., and the ship had been flown with 1119 lbs.; a weight nearly equal to its own empty weight!

Travel Air was already building a reputation. AVIATION reported that the Travel Air proved to be

Vern Brown of Perry, Oklahoma ordered this custom Travel Air with Aeromarine 6 inline engine. Airplane featured an electric starter and generator. Delivered in August, 1925, ship had top speed of 110 MPH, range of 400 miles. (Beech Aircraft Corp.)

Above — Another view of #1 showing metal latches on cowling, mass-balanced ailerons. Ship exceeded expectations of Lloyd Stearman. Top speed was 96.5 MPH, landing speed 38 MPH. Stearman initiated design of this airplane before leaving Swallow, with Beech and Cessna contributing their inputs later, after Travel Air had been formed. (Beech Aircraft Corporation)

Right — The first Travel Air, ready for flight at the California Section, March 13, 1925. Stearman's ability to design a clean, functional biplane is evident in this view. Note cockpit door, exhaust stacks and tail skid. (Beech Aircraft Corporation)

"a very efficient" model considering its 90 hp. engine. Efficiency usually comes from a good match of design talent and numbers. Here are the numbers that Lloyd Stearman designed into #1:

Span, upper wing	33 feet
Span, lower wing	29 feet
Chord, upper wing	5 feet 6 in.
Chord, lower wing	4 feet 8 in.
Total wing area, with ailerons	300 sq. feet
Weight, with water	1300 lbs.
Useful load	750 lbs.
Weight, loaded	2050 lbs.
Wing loading	6.8 lbs./sq. ft.
Power loading	22.8 lbs. per hp.
Height	8 feet 6 in.
Length	23 feet 6 in.
Maximum speed	96.5 mph.
Landing speed, full load	38 mph.
Fuel capacity	30½ gal.
Fuel reserve	4½ gal.

After the first test flights, wing loading was recalculated at 6.93 lbs./sq. foot and power loading at 22.77 lbs. per hp. Total wing area was stated as 296 sq. ft., still including ailerons.

With the success of the first flight and the initial tests, Travel Air, Inc. was ready to embark on volume production of its design.

There was much to do. More personnel were required to meet the expected orders for the new biplane, but nothing could be built without equipment and workspace. Demonstration flights would be arranged, and there was always those tailor-made outlets for getting a new ship before the public — air meets.

Walter Beech helped make the name Swallow a household word in the aviation community, and that expertise would be put to work in selling the Travel Air. One thing the company needed was money for expansion and customers! Beech knew that winning races would help sales. There were plenty of races to be won, and once again Walter would find himself the traveling representative.

There was no doubt that Walter Beech was building a reputation, even at this early stage of his career. People knew Beech was a daring young pilot, and they would pay to see this "aviator" display his skills. Walter always gave them a good show, too.

Stearman's name was also very well known among pilots and designers of the era. With the Travel Air design hot on the heels of Lloyd's New Swallow triumph, the time, product and men associated with the new aviation venture called Travel Air, Inc., assured success.

But a great deal of hard work lay ahead. As spring began to cloak Wichita in warm sunshine and prairie wind, the entire city emerged from winter's numbing grip. They had much to look forward to. The Air Capital had gained her second son.

CHAPTER THREE
Early Days

One of the best signs of a growing city is its traffic system. Wichita was growing, no doubt about that. But so was the population of automobiles.

About 25,000 versions of Henry Ford's contraption roamed the streets of Wichita by 1925, causing the usual traffic pileups and accidents. Traffic cops often got caught in the middle! The answer was "electric cops."

The new-fangled device was either hung on a cable over an intersection or placed atop a pole. Red, green and amber lights signaled the drivers to stop, go or prepare to stop.

First it was speed limits, people complained, now it was light signals! Driving was getting too difficult and the "fun" was going out of it.

Much of the public followed the feats of polar explorers like Byrd and Amundsen, daring exploits that could not have been accomplished without the airplane. That was another "contraption" that was beginning to make its presence felt in Wichita. But the "aviators" did have one advantage over the drivers; no "electric cops" to harass them! No police to write tickets! Maybe airplanes were new, but they sure did sound like fun!

Down at the Travel Air factory the "green light" was on. Lloyd Stearman had 1,000 pamphlets describing the new Travel Air printed and distributed to individuals and organizations across the country. The news was out, at last.

The advertised price of the Travel Air was $3,500.00 FOB Wichita. That was a sizeable sum in 1925! Beech would soon have #1 sold, but it wouldn't be easy to sell Travel Air airplanes at that price. War surplus Curtiss JN-4 and Standard J-1 ships were available for $500 in flyable condition, so why should a person invest seven times that amount?

Walter Beech, Clyde Cessna and Lloyd Stearman told them why. That was the big challenge: convince the prospect that he HAD to have the Travel Air because it was worth every cent and would outperform the "Jenny" and Standard.

By late March the company had employed 15 men, all skilled in their particular trade. Welding, woodworking, and metal forming were the three biggest talents one could possess if he wanted to build the Travel Air.

Beech, Stearman and Snook had worked at these trades and others while at Swallow. They talked to other men at Swallow, trying to get them to leave and work for Travel Air, Inc. They had some success, too.

Walter "Pop" Strobel left Swallow. So did Bob Phelps. These two men had perfected a method of building wings for the Swallow. Instead of requiring one week to build wings, Phelps developed a jig to build the

Travel Air "Special" at rest with the men who designed and flew her to victory. Walter Beech (left) congratulates Mac Short (center) and Lloyd Stearman after Beech's win in the 50-mile "Free for All" race at Tulsa, Oklahoma, August, 1925. Beech averaged nearly 100 MPH in the "Speed Ship" designed by Stearman and Short. Gleaming finish of gloss black fuselage and gold wings with nickel interplane/cabane struts was an eye-catching combination. Curtiss C6A inline engine exhausted out left cowling through 12 short stacks. Note airfoil landing gear and different empennage form. (Beech Aircraft Corporation)

"Special" was actually given designation of "Travel Air B6," but the local press at Tulsa and Wichita dubbed her the "Mystery Ship"... a name born in prophecy of another Travel Air speedster 4 years later. B6 upper wing span was 31 feet, lower span was 25 feet. Majority of fittings were internal. 160 HP Curtiss was enclosed in a beautifully hand-made cowling.

Underslung radiator could be raised or lowered mechanically, giving least drag. Top speed of B6 was about 125 MPH. Ship weighed nearly 150 pounds more than stock Model A. In September Beech flew "Special" in first Ford Reliability Tour, finishing with a perfect score, as did 11 other pilots. (Beech Aircraft Corporation)

ribs separately. Time was drastically reduced. Phelps and "Pop" Strobel could turn out a set of wings in one or two days without a hitch.

The tiny factory at 471 W. First Street was humming with activity. Six OX-5 ships were being built during the months of March and April, 1925.

The advertising was beginning to pay off. Travel Air received orders from Tulsa, Oklahoma, St. Louis, Missouri and Moline, Illinois. Inquiries arrived daily.

E.K. "Rusty" Campbell was a Moline pilot who ordered two ships. He was one of the first Travel Air dealers, and was an ardent supporter of the company from the beginning. The best type of support he could give was buying two Travel Air OX-5 biplanes!

Walter Beech flew #1 to St. Louis not long after the first flight. He demonstrated the ship to O.E. Scott. Scott was quite impressed with the Travel Air.

So much so that he bought her on the spot! Walter had made Travel Air history with its first sale.

The rush of orders coming in to Travel Air, Inc. was gratifying to its founders. Success was theirs, with more on the way.

But even airplane companies were not immune from that great thief of time and money — paperwork. As orders came in, the paperwork piled up. As sales increased so did the amount of paper. Telephone calls and telegrams were eating up more time, time that should be spent on production, not office work.

The solution? Get a secretary. Wichita was full of them, but Travel Air needed one that already "knew the ropes" of running an office.

The search for a secretary began in early 1925. Olive Ann Mellor, employed by Staley Electric Co. of Augusta, Kansas, was interested in the position at Travel Air. Clyde Cessna hired her and she went to work as the newest member of Travel Air's staff.

She was only 22, but had a good education at a Wichita business college, having taken secretarial and business administration courses.

Originally from Waverly, Kansas, Ms. Mellor liked the Wichita area, and although she knew little about the airplane business, she could learn. Her office area in the 471 W. First Street building was small, but she "set up shop" as Travel Air, Inc. secretary-bookkeeper.

All that paperwork now had someone to care for it, and the men could go about their business without having to tend to such tasks.

After O.E. Scott took delivery of #1 in late March, more Travel Air ships were being delivered. Three of the OX-5 models were delivered to customers in Tulsa, Oklahoma. Two were flown to Moline by E.K. Campbell and five more biplanes were ordered by O.E. Scott for use in St. Louis.

The original OX-5 powered Travel Air models were not called by any particular model name. The first Travel Air had not been placed on display as planned, and no names for the model were suggested.

The biplanes were simply called "Travel Air three place OX-5 powered commercial airplane" in literature and advertisements published in the first few months.

Travel Air, Inc. was also known as The Travel Air Manufacturing Company by April, 1925, and the two names were used interchangeably. The company also began construction of hangars at the East Central flying field, seven miles from downtown Wichita.

No facility existed near the factory, so each airplane had to be trucked out to the site on East Central Avenue. This was quite inconvenient, as each ship had to be assembled, rigged and test flown at the field instead of near the factory as would have been desired.

14

Still, the arrangement was not unworkable for Travel Air. The hangars would afford shelter from weather. Storage and repair facilities were included, too.

Travel Air was not the first to use the East Central location. The Winstead brothers already had a hangar erected at the site as far back as 1922. They operated a repair and modification business for local and transient pilots. Small hangars made of corrugated aluminum and wood also stood on the northeastern perimeter of its field, housing Swallows and other makes of airplanes.

Several customers from Florida wanted Travel Air to build them "speed ships" that could be raced. These were to be delivered in early 1925. By the end of the third month of existence, the company had orders for 11 airplanes, and had to temporarily refuse orders by early May when a total of 15 ships were on order and the factory workspace had been utilized to the limit. Long hours were the rule of the day. It was essential that Travel Air biplanes be delivered as close to the accepted time as possible. The customer was everybody's bread and butter.

Stearman announced that the company would expect to resume taking orders by August, if the existing backlog could be fulfilled.

Stearman still needed information about the specimens he had sent to the Agronomy department at Kansas State Agricultural College. By the end of March no word had yet been received.

In a second letter to C.O. Johnson, Stearman wanted to know the exact composition of the steel they were using. He wanted the specimens tested both for tensile strength and strength as a column. When he finally received the results, they proved the steel was more than adequate.

Lloyd had also sent Charles Enlow of Manhattan, Kansas, copies of the specimens and photos of structural details of the Travel Air. It is interesting to note that Stearman included the statement "If there is anyone there interested in airplanes let us know and we will get in touch with them." Even the chief engineer made a sales pitch when he could!

By May, Travel Air, Inc. was still going full throttle to catch up with the production backlog of 15 ships. The construction rate had settled down to about two biplanes per month.

Walter P. Innes, Jr., stepped down as president in May. He believed the company was stable enough to elect a president, and Clyde Cessna was so installed on May 22, 1925.

Cessna was a daily worker at the factory during the early months, and commuted back to Rago on weekends. Some of his time was also absorbed by the family farm business.

Mr. Cessna must be credited with helping Travel Air, Inc. succeed in the first year of its existence. He injected $25,000 of his own money into the company during that time, as no bank in Wichita or the nearby communities would loan Travel Air any money until a profit margin of 140% was confirmed. Thad Carver, a banker from Pratt, Kansas and friend of both Cessna and Beech, held to the same philosophy. It was very fortunate that Cessna's farm was successful enough to support the young company.

May was an important month. Not only did the company have 15 ships on order, and a new president elected but they also purchased 80 acres at the East Central flying field.

The men of Travel Air, Inc. felt this move was necessary to ensure their continued access to the field.

It would also prove to be providential later, should a factory be built on the site.

Lloyd Stearman was not an aeronautical engineer, but was more of one than many "designers" of the period. A friend of his by the name of Mac Short was studying at Massachusetts Institute of Technology to earn the title from a top-notch college.

Stearman and Short went back to the days prior to World War I when both attended Kansas State Agricultural College. When the war involved America, Stearman went with the Navy and Short with the Army. Both studied aeronautical courses while with the military. Short attended ground school at the University of Illinois, and then went to Houston, Texas, for flight training. Assigned to a bombing squadron, Mac didn't get "into the fray" because the Armistice got in the way. He returned to Kansas State and completed three years of study leading to a degree in mechanical engineering. Short did some barnstorming while in college, and was most fortunate to obtain a position as Junior Aeronautical Engineer at McCook Field, Dayton, Ohio.

McCook Field was the "in place" for things aeronautical in the 1920s. Many experiments with airfoils, drag reduction, engines, supercharging and turbocharging, lubricants, fuels, propellers and armament, were being conducted.

Although their primary end use was for the military, some of the spin-off benefits would be felt by commercial aviation. Mac Short got valuable training and experience while at McCook Field, and he left Dayton to attend MIT. He graduated with a Masters Degree in June of 1925.

Mac and Lloyd had been in touch throughout this time. Lloyd urged Mac to come to Wichita and hire on with Travel Air. Lloyd had an idea for a fast biplane, one that could win races and advance the state of the art in airplane design, too.

Short applied for a position and got it. He went to work June 25, 1925, and he and Lloyd immediately put their talents together on a "hot" racing ship. Lloyd also envisioned a commercial use for the biplane, but he wanted speed above all. (More about this project later.)

Travel Air, Inc. was getting a good reputation around Wichita. People were slowly seeing the airplane as a business venture and a mode of safe transportation. Beech was most adamant on this point. Nobody was going to buy an unsafe machine.

To get the public "up in the air" about Wichita aviation, Travel Air, Inc. and Swallow Airplane Manufacturing Co. sponsored weekend flights for $1.00 per person.

This price brought people in by droves, most to take their first airplane ride. Farmers from as far away as 50 miles or more came to town. Even those who weren't too sure about how safe "airships" were broke down and gave it a try for a buck.

Swallow flew their passengers from Swallow Field at 21st Street and Hillside Avenue. Travel Air, Inc. flew from the East Central field. 309 passengers were carried on the first Sunday, July 19, 1925. So many people stood in line that by nightfall some had still not been aloft. 156 flights were made by three OX-5 ships, and to please the patient customers, 3,000 candlepower lights were affixed to the wingtips of the Travel Air biplanes. They worked beautifully for the night flights. The people who took the night rides said it was "worth the wait." Wichita looked nice all lit up, and it must have been quite an experience to go up for the first time in an airplane, and at night to boot!

The East Central field also had regular lighting facilities by July. This made the limited night operations feasible. The Wichita Chamber of Commerce and the Booster Building Association had fenced the field and provided the lighting.

Their reasons for this were to have fortunate results for Travel Air, Inc. later on. Kansas had no law permitting a city to own property beyond its legal city limits. The East Central flying field was, and still is, outside city limits. A group of businessmen and interested people got together and, with the help of the Chamber of Commerce formed the Booster Building Association. This group could hold land outside city limits until it could be sold to the city. The association purchased 160 acres adjacent to Central Avenue, east of Wichita in the vicinity of the flying field. Cost was $200.00 per acre. Thus, the good ground in that area was safe from development for housing or other uses, to be held, hopefully, for full-scale development into a first-class airport for Wichita.

And Wichita would need a first-class airport if it wanted "in" on the air mail route then being discussed in Washington, D.C. National Air Transport, known as NAT, had won the contract bidding for a Chicago to Dallas route. Wichita was a natural stopover along the way. But NAT demanded a good facility and 30 pounds of air mail per day, or the city would be bypassed.

It didn't make sense to the Aviation Committee of the Chamber Commerce, or the Wichita Chapter of the National Aeronautic Association to have Wichita left out of the picture because of unsuitable facilities.

Wichita boasted two airplane companies, increasing aviation activity and a good, potential airport. It was settled. The East Central flying field was groomed and improved to meet NAT requirements.

By August the field was inspected by NAT for the final decision, and Wichita was included as a stop on the route.

E.P. Lott, Chief Pilot for NAT, said the field was fine and looked forward to a successful relationship between NAT and Wichita. Service was to begin in May, 1926.

Walter Beech decided to get a little "press" in August. He talked to Wichita Eagle reporters about steel vs. wood.

This was an old subject for aviators by now, but it still had good appeal to the non-flying public. Beech stated the case for steel, coming up with the safety phrase "the passenger's life preserver" when describing the Travel Air fuselage.

Although he admitted it cost more to use steel, Travel Air airplanes would be built using steel tubing because of its inherent safety advantages over wood. Walter had made his point and Wichitans read all about it.

As fall crept around to Wichita, an interesting order was received. The International Automotive Protection Association of Ponca City, Oklahoma was a detective agency with a special requirement: an airplane to track down criminals!

Travel Air responded by building the ship to order. When finished it looked like any other OX-5 Travel Air, except for a slightly larger fuselage for storage room, as special provision had been made in the fuselage for carrying a detective's tools of the trade — bloodhounds and shotguns! Their Travel Air was the first airplane ever ordered by a detective agency in the United States.

Back in the design department, Lloyd and Mac had made plans for the talked of "Speed Ship," and expected at least 120 MPH from the speedster.

However, they had to convince Walter Beech to let them build it! There were good arguments on both sides. Lloyd and Mac stated that the company would receive good publicity if the ship won races, and Walter would argue back that production couldn't be interrupted to build a special airplane. But in the end Walter couldn't resist a superior machine. With the ability Lloyd and Mac would design into the newest Travel Air, "Let's build it" was the last word from Beech.

The Tulsa Daily World newspaper planned an Air Meet to be held August 30 through September 6 at Tulsa's airfield. Like Wichita, Tulsa was aviation-minded and believed in the future of the airplane.

The air meet would not only show support for aviation both locally and nationwide, but it was the perfect place for introducing the Travel Air "Special."

And this Travel Air was special, indeed. Lloyd and

Fred Day Hoyt, (left) strikes a fitting pose beside the original "Special" he purchased for $8,000. Airplane was totally refurbished and a full-length exhaust stack fitted. Hoyt was Travel Air dealer for California. Model A was also purchased by Hoyt. Photo taken January, 1926. (Beech Aircraft Corporation)

Mac had honed her edges, cleaned up her drag as much as they safely could, and powered her with a Curtiss C-6A inline engine to complete the transformation.

Construction began about July 25, 1925, with the first flight not occurring until Sunday, August 30th. The "first flight" just happened to be the ferry flight of the ship down to Tulsa! Beech piloted the biplane while J.H. Turner flew as passenger. They arrived in Tulsa 90 minutes after departure from the East Central flying field.

Also along for the air meet was Clyde Cessna, Mac Short and Lloyd Stearman, all flying Travel Air ships. Cessna's OX-5 Travel Air had a slight modification to it, as did all the airplanes he flew at that time. The rudder cables were connected in a criss-cross manner instead of directly from rudder pedal to control horn.

This requirement stemmed from Cessna's early days of flying. He taught himself to fly, and he designed his rudder control system so that a turn to the left, for example, required pushing RIGHT rudder! This made good sense to Mr. Cessna because when one rides a bicycle and desires to turn left, the right side of the handlebar is pushed outward, not the left. So every time Clyde Cessna flew a Travel Air he had the rudder cables crossed. The cables were reconnected in standard fashion after Cessna no longer required the airplane.

Also present at the Tulsa Air Meet was one of the stiff competitors of Travel Air, Inc.; Waco. Clayton Bruckner and Sam Junkin, along with Buck Weaver in the early days of the company, were producing the Waco Model Nine biplane, also OX-5 powered. The Travel Air and Waco were very similar in every respect, and could be considered near equals as far as pilots were concerned.

Man and machine. Francis "Chief" Bowhan grins his approval of the Model A he flew in the 1925 Ford tour along with E. K. Campbell and Walter Beech. Bowhan, who was part Osage Indian, became wealthy after oil was discovered on his property. Travel Air retained Bowhan's services as pilot on many occasions. (Beech Aircraft Corporation)

The Travel Air had its coolant radiator mounted under the engine, but Waco placed theirs on the cabane struts.

Travel Air, Inc. "cleaned up" at the Tulsa Air Meet. Walter Beech started things off by winning the 30 mile air race in a stock Travel Air. He flew the race in 15:29 seconds, three minutes ahead of the second place Waco. But the "Special" was on the ground all day Sunday to build the publicity effect as much as possible. Pilots and laymen alike admired the black and gold speedster. Military pilots wondered how fast it was, as did everyone else. Monday they would find out.

Questions were fired at Beech, Cessna, Short and Stearman. Is she fast? What kind of motor? How much power? Will it do 100 MPH? Oh yes, it would do 100 MPH and more, but nobody from Travel Air was giving reply of any kind. The crowds would have to wait to get their answers.

What the people at Tulsa saw was a new Travel Air, not a "souped up" stock model. Basically, the "Special" retained many construction methods of typical Travel Air biplanes.

The fuselage was steel tube, with the empennage reduced in size and the fuselage shortened. A smooth, curving vertical stabilizer graced the tail, and absent was the characteristic overhang rudder found on the stock models. The rudder faired in nicely with the stabilizer lines.

Wing span was 31 feet, six inches for the upper span, while the lower wing had a span of 25 feet, two inches. Chord was five feet for upper panels, four feet for the lower wings. A strong positive stagger existed between the single bay wings, with push-pull tubes moving the ailerons. The landing gear was of vee type construction with bungee cord shock absorption. A different feature of the "Special" was a small airfoil placed between the gear vees. It was of sufficient span and chord to compensate for the landing gear's weight with lift.

The next departure from standard Travel Air design was the cockpit layout. The forward cockpit had room for two, but the rear cockpit did, too. The controls in the rear were arranged to permit lateral shifting of the pilot's position to accommodate one passenger, making the "Special" a four place biplane.

Stearman and Short had their eye on more than just winning races with the "Special." The front cockpit could be converted in a few minutes to a 22 cubic-foot cargo or mail hold. If dual controls were desired they could be installed very quickly.

The powerplant was a Curtiss C6A of 160 HP, completely cowled in for streamlining. Another technical feature of the "Special" concerned the coolant radiator.

To minimize drag the radiator could be mechanically raised or lowered depending upon temperature of the coolant. Controllable shutters gave good control of the temperature.

To finish the "Special" in standard Travel Air blue fuselage and silver wings was unthinkable! Instead, the ship was painted a high gloss black on the fuselage and gloss bright gold on the wings. To accent these colors the interplane and cabane struts, including aileron control tubes, were painted a nickel color. She was the best looking and fastest commercial airplane at Tulsa. Beech knew it, Cessna, Stearman and Short knew it, but on Monday the whole world would know it, too.

Probably the most effective drag reduction effort on the "Special" was the internal location of all fittings. Landing and flying wires were of streamlined section, connected to their respective fittings concealed inside the wing and fuselage structures. Even the coolant expansion tank, mounted between the center section and upper cowl was faired in, and the exhaust stacks of the C6A were stubby, all twelve of them. The C6A series engines utilized four valves per cylinder, necessitating two exhaust stacks per cylinder. There's no doubt that the "Special" really roared when given full throttle.

Beech did not know exactly how the ship would perform in Monday's race. But he was quite confident he had an excellent chance to win. His increasing skill as a pilot and the advanced design of the "Special" were on the line!

The air meet events finally got around to the much awaited 50 mile "Free For All" speed dash. With the contestants lined up, Walter Beech pulled one of his typical aerial tricks; he "asked" to takeoff last.

This competitive gesture could only mean one thing: Mr. Beech was feeling smug as he sat in the cockpit of the "Special," waiting to unleash the Special on an unsuspecting field of pilots.

Suddenly, the starter's flag is dropped and the race is on. One after another the pilots bend throttles and airplanes leap into the air. Crowds cheer for their favorite pilot and machine. Amidst the dust and roaring cacophony of engines, back at the starting line sits Walter Beech and the Travel Air.

As the last airplane climbs away toward the first turn of the course, Beech opens up the C6A and 160 hp thrusts the "Special" into the Oklahoma blue.

Most of the field has a big start on Walter, but that's what he wants. Already he's gaining, and the throttle isn't to the stop yet! No use in running the engine hard, so he throttles back just a little.

The black and gold machine slips past one then another of the competing ships. The race continues for 50 miles and for 50 miles the crowds see the "Special" easing to the front of the pack.

Beech watches ahead as the slipstream from the charging Travel Air whips against his cheeks. A little stick to the right, a little more power. There, safely around another competitor. Around and around flies the Travel Air.

Nobody thinks Beech would be this fast! Twice in the race he has gained five-mile laps on three competitors, attesting to the speed and design of the "Special."

As the final lap begins, the Travel Air is solidly ahead. Walter takes the flag after flying a race of 29:26 and 2/5 seconds and raising a lot of eyebrows! Crowds converge on the ship for another, closer look. They get answers to all their questions. Travel Air has a winner in the "Special." Even the military boys are impressed.

So were Lloyd and Mac. Their design had vindicated any doubts they had about it. They had produced an airplane like none other in commercial aviation, and they did it even though the "Special" weighed 150 pounds MORE than a stock Travel Air, mostly due to increased weight of the C6A engine.

The Tulsa Air Meet felt the presence of Travel Air six more times during the week of events. Lloyd Stearman won the On-To-Tulsa race for heaviest load carried and Mac Short won the On-To-Tulsa race for stock ships.

Altogether, Travel Air won five firsts and two seconds at the meet. The trophies were proudly displayed in the front window of the factory at 471 W. First Street, silent testimonials to the men and machines from Wichita.

The press loved a story like the one Walter Beech and the Travel Air boys gave them at Tulsa. The Wichita Eagle called the "Special" a "Mystery Ship" because Travel Air was still quite conservative in revealing data

about the biplane. That nickname would be heard again in the future when another Travel Air would be a race winner.

But Stearman and Beech saw a golden opportunity to make some good publicity, so they scheduled a demonstration of the ship for all of Wichita to witness. And for good measure they invited an Eagle reporter to ride along and record the event for the papers. On September 7th Beech and the "Special" were ready. Once the reporter was strapped in, Walter gave the biplane another chance to show her stuff. For 10 minutes the two riders of the wind climbed, dived and turned, their obedient mount responsive to every command, every wish of the man at the stick.

Wichita was impressed. Travel Air really had a good thing going with that ship. Of course, Beech and Stearman were quick to point out that all Wichitans could be proud of the ship because Travel Air was part of Wichita. The victories at Tulsa and the victories to come belonged to them all.

After the demonstration Walter was asked how fast the airplane could go. His reply was "between 100 and 200 miles per hour." Walter Beech knew how to give an answer without giving the answer away! Actually, he was right. The "Special" had hit nearly 200 MPH in some of the dives, but could only make about 125 MPH straight and level at full throttle.

Mac Short helped out in designing other Travel Air features, but his main contribution was the co-design effort on the "Special." He returned to MIT in the fall of 1925 to accept an assistant professor's position with Professor Edward P. Warner. Short later went to California to work with Lloyd Stearman after the Stearman company had started.

Edsel Ford was about to have an effect on the commercial airplane industry that would continue for seven years. He donated a trophy, four feet high and made of gold and silver, to the Detroit Board of Commerce. They planned a tour of airplanes to prove the reliability of aerial transportation. Known as the Ford Reliability Tour, each manufacturer desiring to enter the tour was required to certify that their airplanes were safe and structurally sound. Pilots were supposed to promise they did not take alcohol in any form and state they were in good health.

Wichita was well represented in the first Ford tour held from September 28 through October 4, 1925. Travel Air sent three ships to Dearborn, Michigan for the tour. Two were stock OX-5 and OXX-6 Travel Air models and the third was the "Special."

Walter Beech would fly the "Special" and two other pilots would handle the stock ships. One was E.K. "Rusty" Campbell and the other was Francis "Chief" Bowhan. Bowhan was part Osage Indian and became somewhat wealthy after oil was discovered under his alotted property. The government paid up and Bowhan got off to a spending start by learning to fly and doing a good enough job of it to please Walter Beech.

Campbell was assigned race number "O," Bowhan number "2" and Beech number "4." An interesting part of the tour was the fact that "Chief" Bowhan's wife, Charlotte, flew the entire tour with her husband in the Travel Air. She did not mind the flight, either. In fact, she enjoyed flying immensely.

Swallow sent Earl Rowland, Jake Moellendick, Hart Bowman, John W. Stauffer and Edgar Goff, Jr. in three of their ships. Moellendick flew with Rowland, who was a well-known pilot.

Weather was not cooperative for much of the first

Ford tour. Despite this problem, the airplanes made the event a success, although Anthony Fokker and his tri-motored monoplane helped turn the "tour" into a free-for-all race. Fokker was a flamboyant individual and believed in his products, but he pushed his pilot and his machine to be first into every stop along the tour route.

Walter Beech didn't care much for Mr. Fokker's tactics, so he devised a little scheme to upset the Flying Dutchman.

On one of the tour legs, Beech climbed the speedy little "Special" high above the other participants, singling out the Fokker in particular. As the group approached their destination, Walter dove the Special at full throttle in a race with Fokker for the finish line. It was very close, but Walter lost points because of his tactics. It didn't really matter, anyway. All each participant had to do was maintain a percentage of the 80 mph planned schedule and each would be declared a "winner."

No first prize was designated. When the first Ford Reliability Tour was finished, 11 pilots and machines had completed the tour with "perfect scores." All three Travel Air entrants were in this category, but only Earl Rowland finished with a perfect score for Swallow.

A cash award of $350.00 was given to each participant with a perfect score, and their name was engraved on the trophy. Subsequent Ford tours would be tougher competition, but Walter would be back in '26 with a new ship, an "avigator" to handle all navigation duties, and victory on his mind.

By November of 1925 Travel Air was still busy with back orders plus new ones. Daniel C. Sayre of Boston Airport Corporation went to Wichita to consult with Beech and Stearman about buying some Travel Air equipment.

Not only did he contract for three ships but he put some money into the company, too. Sayre flew back to Boston in one of the three airplanes he purchased. The other two were to be flown back east later by "Chief" Bowhan and B.F. Billings, another pilot for Travel Air. Sayre had decided on Travel Air airplanes because of a study completed by he and Professor Edward P. Warner of MIT into the relative merits of different airplanes on the market.

Their results favored the Travel Air, so that's what the Boston Airport Corporation bought. But Sayre had other ideas up his sleeve. He discussed designing an amphibious Travel Air to be put in service around the Boston and vicinity waters, presumably as a charter/air taxi service. Apparently Travel Air didn't think much of Mr. Sayre's idea, as nothing ever developed from it.

One other very important event took place the week of November 18th. J.H. "Jack" Turner, owner and operator of the J.H. Turner Coal and Building Materials Co. in Wichita, closed a five-year contract that would allow Travel Air to move into much larger quarters, something they needed desperately.

Turner's building at 537 West Douglas, just across the river from the original Travel Air facility, was made available. Its 50 foot x 120 foot size would allow much needed expansion room, and furnished offices were included. To top that off, Turner included an 800 x 1000 foot tract of ground adjacent to the building for a flying field. This was located on the north side of what was then called Payne's Pasture, and this field would allow Travel Air to do their flight testing at the factory. The flying field was literally "downtown" with buildings all around, but it was a workable site. However, Payne's Pasture was not used for the flying field, as the East

Central site was considered superior, and Travel Air continued to utilize it.

The move was made in the first weeks of December, 1925, bringing to a close an eventful year of success in both sales and recognition for Travel Air.

The company had produced 19 airplanes in its first year, and orders were in for more. By the end of 1925 Travel Air was solidly established as one of the leading manufacturers of light, commercial airplanes in America.

The officers of the company sent the Annual Report back to state offices in Topeka. The following men were named as shareholders of stock:

Daniel C. Sayre	200 shares	Value — $10,000
Clyde V. Cessna	124 shares	6,200
Walter H. Beech	114 shares	5,700
J.H. Engstrom	10 shares	500
W.R. Snook	6 shares	300
Lloyd C. Stearman	4 shares	200
C.G. Yankey	4 shares	200

By early 1926, Daniel C. Sayre would divest his interest in Travel Air, and Thad Carver and J.H. Turner would purchase his share to become major shareholders of the company.

1926 promised to be another banner year for Travel Air. New designs were in the works. National Air Transport needed new mail and passenger airplanes to meet the needs of their Chicago to Dallas run. And new developments in aircraft powerplants would begin to lead the way from OX-5 to Wright and Pratt & Whitney, Warner and Siemens-Halske, Challenger and Hispano-Suiza.

Travel Air, Inc. was ready for the future. Her leaders had met the challenges of the past year head-on and won every round.

Much had been accomplished, yet there was much to do. But that was the way of aviation back then. Everybody had a chance at the stars . . . only the stout-hearted and dedicated dared pursue them.

In August, 1925 the International Automotive Protection Agency of Ponca City, Oklahoma purchased this custom-built Model A. Special compartments for shotguns and bloodhounds were major changes. At left is Frank Wigton, pilot. G.E. Darland, general manager, is also shown. Later Model A's featured airfoil landing gear, revised tail skid. (Beech Aircraft Corporation)

CHAPTER FOUR
Down on Douglas

Jack Turner had made a fine gesture of support by obtaining a building big enough for increased production. The Travel Air Mfg. Co. could set up a serious construction schedule and meet their rising number of orders.

By late December, 1925 the company had moved into the West Douglas facilities and the production line was busy. Campaigning on the slogan "Our Policy: A Better Airplane For The Same Price" Travel Air biplanes were coming off the line at increasing rates.

The move from the Kansas Planing Mill didn't take too long as there wasn't much to move! Some woodworking equipment was the property of the mill, so that had to be left behind, leaving Travel Air with the Cessna-loaned woodworking equipment.

535-537 West Douglas had enough room for building airplanes, but not by much. Woodworking machines were at the front of the building with welding jigs at the rear. Near the welding area was a space large enough for detail assembly on instrument boards, engine controls, landing gear and fuselage.

Next to this assembly area was a window-equipped wall. It separated the main floor areas from the paint room. The fabric-covered surfaces were given coats of Travel Air blue and silver here, unless the customer desired a special paint scheme.

Although quite small, this painting area was sufficient for the present. However, it would not do if the production rate continued its upward climb, and, the way inquiries were being received by Ms. Mellor in the front office, that looked very likely, indeed.

All surfaces were spray painted. This process had been used by the automotive industry for years, but the old tried and true method of brushing on the taughtening dope and pigmented dope still persisted in many airplane workshops.

Walter and Lloyd had seen the spray process when the McKenzie Carriage Co. sprayed wings for Swallow.

They could spray two sets of wings in less time than it took to brush one set, and the finish was far superior to that of a brush. The entire airplane looked better and that made the customer happy, too.

With the benefits of spray painting known and proven, the Travel Air biplanes received their coats of glistening blue and silver from a spray gun, not a brush.

Beech, Stearman and Snook, who ran the assembly line, just picked up on the process and refined it as necessary to meet their needs. Only one man was employed to do the painting at that time, and he was surrounded by elevators, wings, fuselages and small detail parts in the spray "booth."

A handy set of wing racks allowed the painter to stand erect and spray with even, smooth rhythm and motion across the cotton-covered wings. The rack could be rotated to facilitate spraying both top and bottom surfaces and all edges. Small surfaces like elevators were "hung with care" from a horizontal tube. It was simple, but effective.

Furnished offices were a real boon, too. Walter had his office, Mr. Cessna his, and even the engineers, namely Stearman, had a place to work. Ms. Mellor also had more space to conduct her important work.

[Today the West Douglas factory still stands, now being used as a Honda motorcycle dealership. The Kansas Planing Mill Co. building was destroyed in the late 1920s.]

Employment of nearly 30 people by early 1926 was another sign to management that they were doing something right. But there was a problem — pilots. Walter and Lloyd could do some testing, but Walter was mainly concerned with the very important job of demonstrating Travel Air ships all over the country and setting up dealerships. Clyde Cessna helped, but his time was also limited.

In November of 1925 the situation was serious enough to warrant the hiring of a test pilot. His job would be to work with the rest of the factory men building airplanes, but had the additional responsibility

Factory on West Douglas gave Travel Air much needed room. Building houses motorcycle dealership today. (Beech Aircraft Corporation)

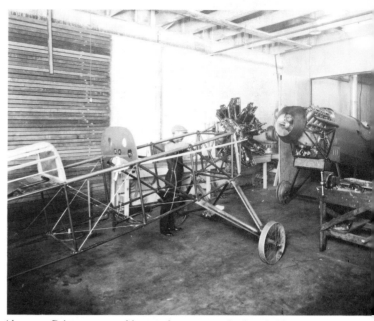

Above — Welding area inside Douglas facility. Early J-4 biplane at left, fuselage jigs in foreground. (Beech Aircraft Corporation)

Below — Spray painting was standard at Travel Air. Here the painter is applying the first finish coat to wing, which is mounted in moveable rack. Ailerons, vertical stabilizer, rudder and control stick assemblies dry on hangers. (Beech Aircraft Corporation)

Above — Primary assembly was done near paint booth. Note J-4 engine, booster coil, throttle and spark controls on right fuselage side. Travel Air would place engine controls on either side, based on customer desire. (Beech Aircraft Corporation)

Below — Clyde Cessna donated woodworking equipment to Travel Air until company could purchase its own. Planer, shaper and bandsaw are hard at work with employees, building another Travel Air. Note shop coveralls. (Beech Aircraft Corporation)

of assembling, rigging and flight testing each new machine.

Between advertisements and word of mouth the needs of Travel Air Mfg. Co. reached the peaceful Kansas town of Garnett, not far from Wichita.

A young pilot named Clarence E. Clark thought the prospect over and went to Wichita. He was interviewed by Walter Beech, who asked only a few brief questions of the applicant.

Chief among these inquiries was what kind of equipment Clarence had been flying. Clark got most of his dual instruction in a Curtiss JN-4 and the less ubiquitous Standard. He had been flying about three years when the Travel Air request came along and he decided to apply for the job.

Harry Kruetzen, a former Army pilot instructor in the war had taught Clarence how to fly in 1923. Beech was

suitably impressed with the pilot from Garnett, Kansas. Clarence seemed to have the background required, and Beech knew the Travel Air was easier to fly than the "Jenny" or Standard.

But flying, Walter stressed, was only part of the job. Clarence was reminded that he wuld have to assemble, rig and then test fly the airplanes.

With that came the rest of Walter's questions. What about technical and mechanical skills? Clarence replied that he had helped rebuild Swallows and "Jennies," and even got to work on barnstormer Billy Burke's little single-seat, 80 HP Le Rhone powered biplane. Burke's little ship was designed to break down and be transported from exhibition site or fairground to the next engagement.

Beech didn't even give Clarence Clark a check flight. If the young man said he could fly, that was good enough

Clarence E. Clark poses next to early Model BH with Wright-Hispano engine. Clark was chief test pilot for five years at Travel Air, and checked over 700 new ships from the production line! Small propeller on right lower wing powered fuel pump. Coolant radiator shutters show up well, as do brake actuator cables along landing gear struts. (Beech Aircraft Corporation)

for Beech. Time would tell, anyway, but Clarence made the grade.

He went to work soon after his interview. Clark learned how the Travel Air went together, how it was rigged and finally, how it flew. His first ship was serial #10. There would be hundreds of serial numbers to follow that first test flight.

Paperwork was required, too. Every item Clarence checked had to be recorded on a form. These were retained in a ship file.

After all was satisfactory Clark would "test hop" the biplane and check coordination of controls, stalls, glides, engine readouts and stability in straight and level flights, as well as turns and glides.

If any adjustments were required he would land and have the changes made. It was the start of a five-year association between Clarence Clark and Travel Air. He became one with every ship he ever flew, feeling for any possible flaw in handling, and knowing exactly what to expect from each model on the first flight.

Travel Air, Inc. had a test pilot and rigging expert, but other pilots were being added to the flying roster. Two of the pilots Walter Beech had flying for him by 1926 were Newman and Truman Wadlow. Being twins, many folks had a hard time discerning who was Newman and who was Truman. Apparently, so did the girls! Word has it that Newman and Truman used their twinship to advantage on dates, but they would never own up to such a thing!

Truman was only 18 when he was invited by Beech and Stearman to leave Swallow and come downtown with Travel Air, Inc. for the sum of $10.00 per week. However, Beech promised to see that Truman was taught to fly, free of charge, while he worked for the company.

Truman thought it over and decided to make the change. He had been working at Swallow part-time, mostly on weekends as he was still attending high school. He sold tickets for "joyrides" and did odd jobs around the factory. Good experience for a Kansas boy who wanted to be around airplanes.

Truman soloed in August of 1925 in the heat of the summer in an OX-5 model Travel Air. He was allowed by Beech to fly passengers only during the week, as the weekend volume was considered too great for the still inexperienced Wadlow. On a hot August day Truman found out what inexperience was all about.

Hopping a passenger, he took off from the East Central flying field and proceeded to climb out to the north. Just after crossing Central Avenue, the OX-5 decided to change its mind about this flight and quit cold.

Truman wanted to turn back to the airport, and he had 1500 feet altitude to work with, so why not? As he eased the Travel Air to the left it stalled. Having never been given much stall recovery dual, his natural reactions took command; left rudder was kicked in, and the stick hauled back!

The ground was coming up, so Truman pulled back on the stick, inducing a left spin. Truman had never had any spin training, so he didn't know what in the world was going on. The biplane rotated faster than it was descending, or so it seemed to Truman, but the next thing both he and his passenger knew there was a terrific WHUMP! followed by sounds of busting wood and hissing steam; then silence. The Travel Air rested in a hedgerow.

Truman got out, hauled his passenger out of the front seat, laid him a safe distance away from the indignant Travel Air and headed for somewhere Walter Beech wasn't!

Truman Wadlow, age 18, stands next to Travel Air Model BW with 200 HP Wright J-4 radial engine. He earned his basic airman license in this ship. (Truman Wadlow)

Later, Walter didn't press the young man too hard, but the company didn't build airplanes for spinning into hedgerows! The ship was rebuilt, but it did cost the company money they could ill afford to lose. Fortunately, the passenger was not seriously hurt.

Although Wadlow wasn't allowed to fly Travel Air ships for awhile, he did get some help from Clarence Clark who understood Wadlow's needs as a budding aviator. In exchange for helping Clark assemble and rig the biplanes for test flights Clarence gave Truman dual instruction in stalls. It really helped the young pilot. He didn't spin in anymore.

The West Douglas factory was a beehive of activity. News of the NAT air mail contract still had people talking. If they were going to use old surplus De Havillands how were they going to carry passengers? The Curtiss Carrier Pigeons did have the capability of carrying both passengers and mail, but they weren't the most accommodating arrangements for a paying customer.

With NAT winner of the Chicago to Dallas route, things were happening out at the flying field. Travel Air, Inc. obtained privileges to build a six-plane hangar on the site.

In preparation for the coming air mail business, the Derby Oil Co. began construction of a modern filling station to serve both airplanes and cars. Eating and drinking facilities were being considered for the convenience of passengers awaiting flights or resting between airplane departures.

Yes, it looked as though Wichita was really going to get on the map with the air mail coming through town. The 30 pounds of mail required each day had to be met by Wichitans. The Chamber of Commerce queried businesses and individuals to be sure they would promise participation. They did and Wichita was ready for NAT. It wouldn't be long, now. Spring was on the way, and that meant more work for Travel Air Mfg. Co.

With the advent of the Wright J-4 radial engine introduced in 1926, all of the airplane manufacturers had something different to offer their customers.

The J-4 radial was a re-engineered version of the Lawrence powerplant. Wright Aeronautical Corporation purchased the design and put George Mead to work on it. Mead was a talented engineer with a background of natural ability and potential.

By redesigning the Lawrence engine Wright had a compact, relatively lightweight engine of 200 hp ready to market without the huge costs of a totally new powerplant. It was designed to be an aircraft engine of high reliability and good sales potential.

The only drawback was the price. All that technology had to be paid for, and W.B. "Skipper" Howell, Wichita oil man, was willing to spend $5,700.00 to buy one of the new engines. Of course, he planned to hang it on a Travel Air. Howell had previously owned an OX-5 Travel Air, but wanted more speed and overall performance.

Travel Air received the order in January, 1926. Some changes had to be made in the basic Travel Air fuselage to accept the engine, but engineering could handle that easily.

Beech was happy to get this order. It would certainly help the bank balance, as the total cost would be $9,800.00. Snook put his best woodworkers, welders and metalworkers on the Howell ship. Lloyd calculated the weight and balance data with the Wright engine and the necessary changes to the fuselage were made in the shop.

By March the airplane was ready to fly. Bob Phelps was on hand to do the assembling and assist with the rigging. When finished, Bob reported to Lloyd Stearman that the ship was ready. "You forgot something, didn't you?" Stearman asked. "I don't think so," replied Phelps. Lloyd then stated that the coolant radiator was not installed and how did Phelps expect to cool the engine without a coolant radiator? Bob walked back out to the Travel Air and looked her over again.

Then it hit him. The Wright was air-cooled! He turned and looked at Lloyd who was having a good chuckle back in the hangar. Phelps just smiled.

Walter was called out to the flying field and inspected the biplane. The crank was inserted and the inertia starter whined away as Phelps "wound her up." The magnetos were turned to "hot" and the engine roared to life after two or three revolutions of the propeller.

W.B. "Skipper" Howell bought the first radial-powered Travel Air airplane in January, 1926. Ship cost $9,800, with 200 hp Wright J-4 costing $5,700 of that amount. (Beech Aircraft Corporation)

Howell used his biplane to fly to oil field locations, often with Clarence Clark at the controls. Howell owned Model A before ordering this ship. Production line change to shock cord-style landing gear was made in late 1925, with improved performance over straight-axle configuration. (Beech Aircraft Corporation)

Beech checked the engine. He let it run for a few minutes and then taxied out for takeoff. Not only was this the first Wright-powered Travel Air, but it had the new Curtiss-Reed steel propeller. This was fitted to Howell's ship to extract the power produced from the J-4.

After a good runup Beech took off. He climbed and flew around the field, but at a low altitude. As Lloyd and Bob watched, along with other Travel Air employees, Walter brought the ship around and flew past the onlookers.

A minute later he was on the ground and taxied back to the hangar. Climbing from the cockpit he explained that the ship was very noseheavy, and needed rerigging.

So Bob and Lloyd pondered the problem for a moment, then decided to change the stagger one inch. After this was done Beech took the ship up.

Again he flew past the crowd but this time he held both hands high in the air; the Travel Air was flying straight and level!

About the time Howell's ship flew, Clyde Cessna was having a good time designing and building an airplane, on his own time, at his own expense outside Travel Air's factory.

Ever the monoplane man, Cessna wanted his own design to fly using his design principles. He had built eight other monoplanes on his own since 1911, but this one was to be an all-out effort to enclose the cabin and the passengers, too.

He made his intentions known to Beech and Stearman, who had no argument with the proposal. They knew about Cessna's penchant for monoplanes.

Clyde went to work and had the fuselage welded up in two weeks with the help of Guy Winstead.

Cessna's plan was to market the design if the expected performance was attained. He wanted to get in on the competition for monoplane transports, as Fokker and Ford were doing with much success by 1926. If the airplane was all Cessna hoped it would be, he would consider installing three engines and entering the market against Fokker and Ford.

That was really something to think about! A pilot/farmer in Wichita contemplating competition against two of the biggest names in aviation. But Clyde knew he could succeed somehow with the monoplane he so strongly endorsed.

The five-place machine would be powered with a 110 hp Anzani engine, carry 1,000 pounds and land at only 45 mph. A 300 pound semi-cantilever wing was was mounted above the fuselage, with dual lift struts attached to fuselage and wing along the fore and aft spars.

The cabin was entered through a single door on the left fuselage side, and four wicker chairs were attached to the wooden floor. These could be removed in five minutes to convert the ship into ambulance configuration.

The pilot sat up front with good visibility in most directions. The landing gear was conventional for the time with shock cord in tension on a vertical strut assembly.

Cessna spent about $6,000 on this machine, and he flew it for the first time June 14, 1926. The test flight lasted only 20 minutes, but Clyde was very pleased with the ship's performance. The next day Cessna flew the 1,200 pound airplane again with two passengers aboard. Walter Beech flew it next and was favorably impressed. Being a biplane advocate, Mr. Beech now saw the advantages of the monoplane design and it changed his thinking as far as a Travel Air with one wing. Cessna flew the monoplane down to his Rago, Kansas farm as harvest time approached. He planned to sell the ship after harvest season was over and complete testing could be performed. It was very important to Clyde that the machine have no hidden faults or deficiencies prior to the sale.

Finally May arrived. Not only was the weather nice, but NAT opened the long awaited air mail service on the 10th. A big citywide celebration was held out at the East Central flying field.

Three types of Travel Air biplanes are shown in this view at the East Central flying field, March, 1926. Model BW at left with three Model B ships and one Model A at far right. Men standing with Model BW are, left to right: Walter Beech, "Chief"

Bowhan, unknown, Doyle Bradford, unknown, Clarence Clark. Two of the Model B biplanes were flown to Florida by Bowhan and Bradford a few days later. (Beech Aircraft Corporation)

Many speeches were made that day. With the big Curtiss Carrier Pigeons sitting in the grass at the flying field, ships in the air and hundreds of Wichitans walking about, it was quite an affair.

But best of all were the races held that afternoon. And right in the thick of it was Walter Beech, Clarence Clark and Fred Hoyt, flying Travel Air biplanes. Clark won the 100 hp class race, and "Chief" Bowhan took first place in the dead stick competition with Beech second.

When the time rolled around for the free-for-all race it was Beech in another J-4 Travel Air who took the winning flag. He "loafed" around the course for four laps, then hit the throttle and walked away from everyone for the win.

The big attraction that afternoon was Fred Hoyt doing his acrobatic routine, or "stunting" as they called it then.

Hoyt wrung out his ship in every way he could think of. Loops, rolls, spins, vertical dives and turns all served to thrill and excite the crowd. Later that day awards were given for the winners of the day's events. Hoyt was feted as the star of the show and received an attractive cup for his efforts.

Not a week after his performance in Wichita, Hoyt took off for home in his Travel Air. He set an unofficial speed record of 17 hours, 15 minutes between Wichita and Santa Monica, and he did it in a stock Travel Air.

It seemed like everyone should know about Travel Air dependability, speed and safety by now, but perhaps the folks up in Flint, Michigan should have a demonstration of those characteristics.

To accommodate the Flint population, Beech entered a C6 Travel Air in the Fly-To-Flint race held June 4th through 6th, 1926. Walter only placed second in the dead stick contest, but when the race for the Manufacturers Trophy was held, Beech was ready.

The course was not very large and was marked by the usual pylons. As the race started the crowd was aghast at how tight and close to the pylons the Travel Air was flown. Everyone else was giving them a little room in the turns, but whoever was flying that Wichita ship was daring! He rounded every pylon with precision and skill.

Walter loved every minute of this competition. It was in his blood.

At the end of the Flint meet, Walter and the C6 Travel Air flew home with the Manufacturers Trophy. It sat proudly in the window of the West Douglas factory, and still rests with pride, along with many other Swallow and Travel Air trophies, in the executive conference room at Beech Aircraft Corporation in Wichita.

With the latest victory still fresh in the minds of the

Clyde Cessna's Anzani-powered monoplane, June, 1926. Cessna built this airplane outside of Travel Air control in March, April and May. Cost was about $6,000. (Beech Aircraft Corporation)

aviation fraternity, it was back to work at Wichita and time to prepare for the second Ford Reliability Tour.

Travel Air Mfg. Co. sure wanted to win the Ford tour. They had made a good showing last year, but needed something new for the upcoming challenge. While Lloyd and Walter were thinking it over, they had another request come in for a biplane.

It seemed that a mining company down in Mexico was being robbed time and again. The bandits were taking the company payroll and the employees were getting a little upset.

The easiest way to solve their problem was with an airplane. They ordered the Travel Air to haul the payroll. Nobody had seen any bandits flying around, so the company's troubles would be over. C.V. Schlaet came to Wichita and piloted the plane down to Tampico.

There was much work to be done at the West Douglas factory if the company was to enter the second Ford Reliability Tour. To win that competition a special machine would have to be constructed, one capable of speed, endurance and navigational accuracy with the new instruments then available.

Walter and Lloyd had discussed the matter, along with Clyde and Bill Snook, too. It would cost them a bundle of bucks to make such a ship and have it ready by early August.

Not only that, but the production run would be interrupted. Customers wouldn't appreciate their airplane being held up so Walter would have his Travel Air for the Ford tour.

Meanwhile, the aviation-minded men of Wichita were up to something, too. They organized the Wichita Flying Club in July, 1926 with 100 members, the express purpose being that of making preparations to receive the tour planes when they stopped at Wichita. Nearly 40 planes were entered, so the club had their work cut out for them. They had to groom the city and the East Central flying field, make up posters and distribute circulars describing the event.

Jack Turner was president of the club. He was rapidly becoming Wichita's greatest aviation booster. He had helped Travel Air get a new factory location, arranged a flying field site, was deeply involved with civic affairs and now was ram-rodding the Wichita reception for the Ford tour.

Beech was still having trouble with the Board of Directors at Travel Air, Inc. concerning the funding for construction of the Ford tour airplane. He decided to go outside the company for the money needed to finance the airplane's construction, as he was meeting opposition from within his own ranks. The cost was over $10,000, and some key people in Travel Air such as Stearman and Cessna weren't happy about the company footing such a bill.

However, he soon realized that Wichita didn't have the money, either. There was only one thing left to do; call his friends in New York. Beech had connections back east that he could tap for funds. He knew they would at least listen to his plans, so he sent a wire to them describing his need for money and what it was for.

Within five minutes of sending the wire, Beech received his answer. New York interests would furnish the remainder of the funds required. Simple as that. The rest was up to Beech.

Walter went back to the factory with a fresh determination to win the Ford tour. He met no more opposition to the project financially, but what about the production line? Bill Snook was in charge of that. Beech approached him about the situation and asked "Well, what are we going to do about it?" Snook replied, "We'll build it!"

From that moment on the factory became just a little bit busier than it was before. Men were assigned to weld up another fuselage, but the specifications were changed to allow a slightly wider dimension in the cockpit area. Wings were standard Travel Air with balanced ailerons. A Wright J-4 would power the ship.

Lloyd went to work on the calculations required to build the different fuselage. Beech was busy making arrangements with the Pioneer Instrument Co., headed by Brice Goldsborough. The Pioneer company had ordered an OXX-6 Travel Air in 1925 and installed its new vertical scale flight and engine instruments. Also installed was the latest development in navigational accuracy — the earth inductor compass. Pioneer had developed this instrument to the point of reliability over long distances. The very latest version was scheduled to be installed in the Ford tour Travel Air.

Goldsborough had worked with Bendix before starting his own firm. He was an expert in navigation theory and practice, having prepared Admiral Richard Byrd's airplane with an earth inductor compass when the famed explorer went to the Arctic. Goldsborough also supplied the instruments for Captain Rene Fonck's ill-fated attempt to fly the Atlantic from New York to Paris in 1926.

Pioneer wanted a "flying showcase" of their vertical readout engine and flight instruments plus the installation of the earth inductor compass. Brice and Walter agreed to work together to win the Ford tour. If they could combine the Travel Air reputation with that of Pioneer Instrument Co., a hard-to-beat team would result.

Add to that the skill of Beech as pilot and the expertise of Goldsborough as navigator and they had a very good chance of winning the Ford tour in 1926.

After adding up all the figures, the Travel Air entrant would cost $12,000 to build and equip. But the glory of winning the Ford tour would likely bring many orders for new ships to Travel Air. It was a favorable wager, indeed.

Important as accurate navigation and reliability were

to winning the tour, the 1926 Ford tour would include some pre-tour contests for the entrants to compete in. One of these was the stick/unstick contest. This event tested the airplane's ability to take off in the shortest run and land to a stop in the shortest distance.

The airplane that did well in stick/unstick time would add many points to the score on the tour itself. The airports the tour would visit had runways of varied lengths. Judges were stationed along the runways to determine when the ship touched down and rolled to a stop. The length determined the score.

The airplanes equipped with brakes should do well in this category of stick/unstick. Five ships had wheel brakes in the 1926 Ford Reliability Tour. One of them was the Travel Air. The other four were a Stinson Detroiter, Mercury Biplane, Ford Tri-Motor and Buhl/Verville Airster.

Walter had brakes of Travel Air design and construction installed on the J-4 biplane. They were cable-actuated from the cockpit. Beech felt the incorporation of wheel brakes was a necessity for the tour, and he was correct, too!

The combination of Travel Air biplane, Wright J-4 engine, Pioneer instruments and wheel brakes gave Beech and Goldsborough a serious edge on the competition.

By the end of July the biplane was finished and made ready for the tour. Carrying tour number 2, the Travel Air looked ready for action. The hand-painted logo of Pioneer Instrument Co. appeared on each side of the fuselage, and across the top wing "PIONEER" appeared.

The equipment installed was impressive by 1926 standards. Two liquid compasses were positioned for each cockpit, one just forward of the rear cockpit windscreen and the other hanging from the center section underside for the front cockpit. The earth inductor compass was in the rear cockpit, with a circular, wind-driven vane for power located on the aft turtledeck. The vane turned a generator.

Vertical readout instruments in the rear cockpit only, included tachometer, airspeed, rate of climb/descent, a pitch indicator, engine oil pressure, oil temperature and fuel pressure. Circular versions of the airspeed indicator,

Model BH flown by Clarence Clark in 1926 Ford tour. In stick/unstick competition Beech placed first, Clark second. Both *airplanes had Travel Air-designed brakes. (Beech Aircraft Corporation)*

altimeter, tachometer and rate of climb/descent, along with engine instruments, were included on the front instrument board.

A venturi was mounted on the right cabane strut to drive the gyroscopic turn and bank indicator, found in both cockpits on the instrument panels.

The turn and bank instrument was one of the very first "blind flying" instruments, and enabled pilots who knew how to interpret its indications to keep the wings level while in clouds. Little was known on how to fly "instruments" in 1926, but the technology was advancing rapidly. Pioneer had done much to promote the reliability of gyroscopic flight instruments. The days of "seat of the pants" flying was beginning to end. True all-weather utility of the airplane was still many years away, but progress was being made.

The great advantage of the earth inductor compass was its enhanced stability and accuracy. It was much more accurate than a standard liquid compass whose characteristics of behavior had to be known by the pilot in order to navigate.

It might be said that the earth inductor compass made the long distance flights of the late 1920s possible. Lindbergh used it, as did many others. It was, indeed, a forerunner of things to come; a quantum jump in technology for aviation.

To compensate for wind drift, another device was mounted on the biplane. One indicator was mounted on the left side of the rear cockpit instrument board. It showed Goldsborough drift data to help him estimate the drift from intended course. As each leg of the tour was flown, deviation from course was displayed on the earth inductor compass controller.

To calculate the course correction required a special drift indicator device was used, mounted on the left cockpit cowling at the rear seat. It consisted of a simple vane with two sight wires on it, and an eye cup for sighting the ground. A scale was included for adjustment of the vane to match airplane altitude so that the ground viewed through the eye cup was always exactly one mile between sight wires.

Using his ground checkpoints as reference, Goldsborough would look through the eye cup and sight wires at the ground, start a special stopwatch when the checkpoint passed the front sight wire and stopped timing when it passed the rear wire.

The special stopwatch used was graduated in miles per hour instead of time. This feature obviated the need to calculate the airplane's forward speed.

By taking drift readings as the flight progressed and comparing the results with previous drift checks, any change in the winds aloft were identified and course corrections made.

Another instrument included in the Pioneer installation was the "Air Log" unit. This ingenious device calculated air miles flown. A small wind-driven unit was mounted on the right interplane strut. Using wind power and venturi suction the instrument would readout total miles flown and distance per leg. Goldsborough always knew distance flown and distance remaining on each leg.

Ten-mile increments were plotted on the maps used for the tour. Emphasis was placed on checkpoints along each leg. Goldsborough did much pre-flight planning as each day of the tour passed by. He wanted accuracy to perfection in navigating the Ford tour. Walter and Brice would have to work hard, but they were ready!

Louis Meister was first off in the 1926 Ford Reliability Tour. Eddie Rickenbacker dropped his flag and the Buhl/Verville Airster was aloft and flying the first leg from Ford airport to Kalamazoo, Michigan. The Travel Air was next.

The entire city of Wichita was rootin' for Walter and the Travel Air. As their turn came to depart, Beech and Goldsborough set their equipment. Beech would take up the compass course given him by Brice and, as checkpoints passed, Goldsborough would begin using all that technology to keep them on course.

Every leg counted. Each one had to be flown with precision and teamwork. Between August 7th and 21st the tour would visit Kalamazoo, Chicago, Milwaukee, St. Paul, Des Moines, Lincoln, Wichita, Kansas City, Moline, Indianapolis, Cincinnati, Cleveland, Fort Wayne and end up back at Ford Airport in Dearborn.

The Wichita Eagle had set up a special scoreboard on the east side of the Eagle building, at William and Market streets. Each day of the tour the public could see how well Travel Air was doing. They did pretty well! Beech and Goldsborough were first into Kalamazoo and Chicago. The teamwork was already paying off. Beech was informed at Chicago that he had won $1,000 given by the Chicago Ford dealers to the first airplane to land at Maywood airport in Chicago.

The wheel brakes had already proven their worth. Prior to the beginning of the tour, Walter and Clarence Clark had won first and second in the stick/unstick contest. Clarence was flying the new Hispano-Suiza powered Travel Air, bearing tour number 3, even though number 32 was painted on his ship.

The navigation equipment was working, the brakes were working and the J-4 just purred along. So far so good.

Louis Meister was tough competition. He was a hard-flying pilot who knew exactly what he had to do, and the Travel Air and Buhl Airster were in the thick of it from start to finish. The Buhl/Verville Airster was a good ship, the first airplane to be type certified in the United States, later in 1927.

By the time the tour reached St. Paul, Walter and Brice were leading Meister by only 44 points. The Travel Air made the Milwaukee to St. Paul leg at 137.4 MPH, and Walter felt they were doing good.

The J-4 ship required much in the way of preventive maintenance, however. Lloyd and Walter conferred on the phone about the condition of the biplane. Beech noted that no major problems were developing, but lots of work was required to keep the ship in tip-top running order.

Stearman also told Walter that "Skipper" Howell would be flying up to meet the the tour in Lincoln, and he and his pilot Ira N. McConaughey would fly with the tour to Wichita.

Lloyd was very busy with arrangements for the tour planes. He was in charge of servicing the ships when they arrived, and seeing that they and their pilots got what they needed.

Wichita was going all out to greet the Ford tour. Walter won the leg from Lincoln to Wichita, flying at 128 MPH to win another leg and the White Eagle Oil Co. silver loving cup. This award was given for winning the Wichita leg and was presented to Beech at a banquet given in honor of all the tour participants.

Miss Ruth Richardson, "Miss Wichita" for 1926, gave each pilot a rose and small key to the city. This went over very well with everyone on the tour.

Pioneer Instrument Company ordered OXX-6 Model B outfitted with their latest flight/navigation instruments. Delivered in spring, 1926, it was flown to the east coast to test function of new earth inductor compass system and vertical readout engine/flight instrumentation. (Beech Aircraft Corporation)

Right — Another view of winning J-4 Travel Air. Fuselage was slightly wider than standard ship to accommodate special equipment. Airplane was sold in September at the Philadelphia Sesqui Air Meet. Note fairings over wing/fuselage fittings. (Beech Aircraft Corporation)

Below right — Cockpit view of 1926 Ford Reliability Tour Model BW. Aft cockpit is equipped with Pioneer vertical readout instruments and earth inductor compass. Drift device is on left fuselage side, wind-driven power vane for inductor compass on turtledeck. (Beech Aircraft Corporation)

Below — Walter Beech in front and Brice Goldsborough in rear cockpit of Model BW. "Air Log" drive unit is mounted on right interplane strut. Venturi over Beech's head operated turn and bank instrument in front cockpit. Precise navigation and dead reckoning by Goldsborough enabled Beech and Travel Air to clinch victory. (Beech Aircraft Corporation)

Friendly people, a good airport and very pretty young ladies, too!

The tour would remain in Wichita for the weekend and depart Monday for Kansas City. During the weekend a tragedy occurred that marred the festivities. On the evening of August 13, Lloyd Stearman went up to perform "stunting" for the large crowds at the field.

As he taxied out from the hangar area, at the north end of the airport, no cars were parked along the roadway that doubled as a taxiway. Lloyd never gave it another thought.

Upon landing, Lloyd was taxiing back in, going very slowly as he didn't want to hit anything, and visibility over the nose of the Travel Air was restricted.

Unknown to Stearman, George Theis, president of the Arkansas Valley Interurban Co. had parked his Packard in the taxiway area. He and his family were observing the airplanes both on the ground and in the air.

Theis was resting one foot on the running board of his car, watching a ship performing overhead. His back was toward the approaching Travel Air. Lloyd had just maneuvered his ship to avoid a government airplane. Without warning he felt a shudder run through the biplane. He cut the switches as fast as he could.

But it was too late. Theis had not heard the airplane coming and was not warned by his wife, who pulled the two children from the car seconds before Theis was struck by the whirling propeller of Stearman's Travel Air. Theis was picked up twice by the propeller, throwing him around like a puppet, killing him.

Lloyd had no idea what had happened. Mrs. Theis collapsed in shock. People were everywhere, but still no one had seen the accident except one bystander. He ran up to the airplane yelling that he had seen the whole thing, that Lloyd just killed someone! Stearman slumped in shock. "Skipper" Howell had arrived at the scene. Slowly he helped Lloyd from the ship. He took Stearman home, and it was some time later before Stearman was told the full details of the accident.

No one blamed Lloyd. A formal inquiry was held into the matter, but nothing else was done.

It was a time of extreme remorse for both Lloyd and Ethyl Stearman.

(This event may have contributed to Stearman's departure in October, 1926, to start a company in Venice, California.)

The Ford tour was of great interest to the people of Wichita. The Aviation Committee and the Wichita Flying Club were able to arrange with the Coleman Co., also of Wichita, to furnish 100 kerosene lamps so that the public could inspect the tour ships at night. As many people were at the airport throughout the weekend, this idea of night lighting proved a good one, and everyone enjoyed seeing the huge, three-motored Ford monoplane shine bright in the lights.

The Travel Air and the Ford tour went on to Kansas City on Monday. Beech and Goldsborough were first to land at Richards Field after a flying time of 1:30. The score for Travel Air was getting bigger every leg, but they didn't win them all.

Not only Meister in his Airster provided competition, but Eddie Stinson was there with his Detroiter, Johnny Livingston was flying one of three Waco Model 9 ships entered in the tour, and he was always tough to beat. The popular C.S. "Casey" Jones was there, too, flying his beloved Curtiss Oriole biplane.

There were Woodson Express biplanes, Alexander Eaglerock ships from up in Denver, and a Super Swallow from the Swallow factory.

All were winners, but none of them could beat the Travel Air. By the end of the tour, 4,043.4 points were chalked up for Walter, Brice, Travel Air and Pioneer. The tour was theirs.

Throughout the tour Goldsborough was able to inform Beech within 45 minutes of their destination what time they would arrive. He was never off by more than two minutes for the entire tour. Impressive navigation and flying, by standards of then or now.

The tour netted $2,500 for Travel Air. Added to the $1000 he previously won plus other small amounts won during the tour, the total came to $3,850. The Edsel Ford Trophy was inscribed with the winner's names and shipped to Wichita on October 9, 1926. It sat proudly on Beech's desk for a short time after its arrival before it was displayed in a guarded case at the Chamber of Commerce.

The trophy cost Ford $7,000 to have made, so the care and protection of the prize was most essential. Travel Air would never win the trophy again, but they had let their name be heard and enshrined for all time during the month of August, 1926.

Of all the triumphs Walter Beech and Brice Goldsborough accomplished during the tour, they proved that the airplane could be flown from point to point with precise results. Beech gave Goldsborough much of the credit for the win, and how true that was! Without Brice in the aft cockpit it is doubtful Beech and the J-4 Travel Air would have won.

But win they did, and that victory was the last straw for Jack Turner and the Board of Directors of Travel Air Mfg. Co. The company MUST have new facilities. If not, the present factory space on West Douglas would surely be overwhelmed when orders came pouring in for Travel Air ships. They were right; the tour had just sold more people on the name Travel Air, and Turner had an idea to help out.

He also had some land. He proposed a $30,000 factory be built on two acres of ground located at Turner Avenue. The 50' x 200' facility would be sufficient to meet the expected demand for airplanes.

Turner estimated that the present production rate of 6 to 8 ships per month could be increased to 16 to 18 per month. The only drawback to the plan was the factory site itelf; it would still be located seven miles from the flying field. All the men on the board knew consolidation of factory and assembly/flight test was highly desirable, but could it be done now? And how could they find one site to do both functions easily?

Everyone knew the problem but it was agreed to go ahead with the Turner Avenue factory to meet demand. In late summer, 1926 there was a movement within the aviation fraternity to entice Travel Air Mfg. Co. away from Wichita. Overtures were being felt from Detroit, where hopes of turning out "aerial flivvers" like they turned out cars were riding high. All they needed was a good product. Hopefully one they wouldn't have to spend any money on to develop. Winning the Ford tour gave Detroit the product they were looking for in Travel Air.

But Jack Turner told the press Travel Air Mfg. Co. was staying in Wichita. That's where it started, and that's where it would remain. No serious offers were ever considered from any city.

Walter Beech flew the J-4 Travel Air up to New York after the tour. He wanted to thank his financial backers for their assistance, and he wanted them to see the ship, too. From New York Walter flew to Philadelphia for the Sesqui Air Meet, to be held from September 4 through 11. Lloyd Stearman was to join him there, with four Travel Air ships they would try to sweep the air meet and garner more glory for their company. But it was not to be. The flying field at Philadelphia was a quagmire at best, as rains plagued the event from start to finish. Walter managed third place in the Independence Hall trophy race, won by C.S. "Casey" Jones in his modified Curtiss Oriole.

One bright spot for Travel Air, Inc. was the On-To-Sesqui race held prior to the opening of the meet. Fred Day Hoyt, the Travel Air dealer from California, flew a stock Travel Air biplane from Cape Mendocino, California to Philadelphia in 31 hours to win $1200.

Lloyd had a little trouble just getting to Philadelphia,

let alone try to compete once he got there. With Walter P. Innes, Jr. as passenger, Stearman left Wichita September 1, but got forced down in weather near Wheeling, West Virginia. Unable to get the word they were safe to anyone at Wichita or Philadelphia, the next day brought plans for a large aerial search party to look for the aviators. Beech was organizing the search and intended to lead it personally when word came that Lloyd and Innes were safe. The search was called off, but Lloyd was forced down again at Pittsburgh the next day. He was too tired to compete when he finally got to Philadelphia!

All four of the Travel Air biplanes were sold at the Sesqui Air Meet, including the J-4 Ford tour machine. That was success enough for the men from Wichita. Now it was time to go back to the prairie city and experience the welcome of a proud and grateful public.

(Courtesy Aero Digest Magazine)

CHAPTER FIVE
Monoplane Fever

Walter Beech loved a good fight. It didn't always matter who was fighting whom, but Beech was a frequent visitor to the fights held in downtown Wichita.

So it was on the night of September 23, 1926. Walter wasn't at ringside but he was near his radio awaiting the start of a great prize fight. Jack Dempsey was meeting Gene Tunney in a highly publicized bout for the championship crown.

Radio station KFH in Wichita carried the fight. Tunney whipped Dempsey in the early rounds and the nation had a new boxing king.

That was great for boxing fans, but Travel Air didn't have a suitable factory in which to build airplanes and that wasn't great for their fans.

Like Jack Dempsey, if the company didn't throw some good punches it might go down in the early rounds of 1927! But just as expected, the orders kept coming in, although there was insufficient room at West Douglas to meet demand. Talk of a new factory again came up.

A meeting of the board of directors was called on September 25th to explore some action. Some of the men believed the East Central flying field was the place to build. Others favored Turner Avenue as the site. The only problems were money and utilities. The money could be raised, but if the board chose East Central,

Five-place cabin Travel Air was designed by Lloyd Stearman soon after company started. First example shown here was sold to Gerbracht Aeronautic Corporation, Travel Air dealer in Iowa. (Beech Aircraft Corporation)

Kansas Gas and Electric Company might not extend service that far east. Turner Avenue had utilities. More investigation and research were needed, so the board withheld further action.

New developments were occurring at Travel Air. Jack Turner announced that a transportation department was being added to Travel Air on October 5, 1926. Turner was president, and the department would engage in aerial charter service under the name Travel Air Transportation Co.

On October 8th, Travel Air lost its chief engineer. Lloyd and Mrs. Stearman headed west to join Fred Hoyt and begin their own airplane company. There was big money out west, and Hoyt had the prospective customers lined up. Lloyd thought it sounded promising . . . and he bid Travel Air farewell. Walter and Clyde carried on.

The second year of operation for Travel Air, Inc. was rapidly drawing to a close. It had been more successful than anyone had dreamed. 1927 held much promise, too, but still there was no new factory.

In early December the solution was found. The Booster Building Association, which had purchased 160 acres for $35,000 in 1925 at the East Central site, agreed to sell six acres to Travel Air, with the Booster organization planning to finance the whole arrangement.

Walter P. Innes, Sr., Jack Turner and C.L. Henderson put the financial package together. A stock issue of $30,000 was to be sold by Howard V. Wheeler and Harry A. Dillon, experienced stock brokers in Wichita.

Biplane's wing span was nearly 42 feet, with no center section. Wings butted in cabane area. Radiator shutters are clearly visible. Ship was delivered in early 1926. (Beech Aircraft Corporation)

The new factory would be located where Walter and Clyde wanted it, and Kansas Gas and Electric had agreed to provide service to the new facility.

Plans called for a building of stressed concrete and steel, with dimensions of 75' x 275'. The official site survey was conducted on December 2, 1926, with Walter Beech and Clyde Cessna in attendance.

By the middle of December the plans were being drawn up by architect Glen A. Thomas and the position of machinery and equipment was supervised by Beech and Cessna. It was to be a factory of efficiency in manufacturing airplanes, and both men knew where the best locations for dope and fabric rooms, wing assembly, final assembly, welding and woodworking ought to be to maximize production.

With the factory situation well in hand, Travel Air turned its attention to the air mail competition. Back in October NAT invited Travel Air to develop an airplane suitable for carrying mail and passengers.

The Curtiss Carrier Pigeons were getting old and they did not have the modern efficiency NAT desired. Although a good load hauler, the Curtiss design was on the way out.

Lloyd Stearman and Clyde Cessna had been working on a monoplane design. With Lloyd gone, Clyde and Walter, assisted by others, proceeded to build the first Travel Air monoplane. Cessna incorporated many of his monoplane's features in the new design. Construction began in early October and was completed by the middle of December. The new design was ready in only 69 days!

Whirlwind-powered, the new Travel Air could carry 1,100 pounds and cruise at 105 MPH. It seated four passengers in comfortable wicker seats inside a fully enclosed, heated cabin. Large side windows afforded good visibility.

The pilot was seated slightly above passenger level in a separate cockpit forward of the cabin. A removable cupola-style canopy, that could be jettisoned in flight, covered the cockpit.

The engine section was designed to swing away from the fuselage for maintenance, and the instrument panel was integral with the engine mount. When an engine change was needed, all the ground crew had to do was remove the bolts holding the engine to the firewall, disconnect fuel and oil hoses and remove the engine/instrument panel as a unit.

This feature was designed into the new monoplane as a competitive edge for the NAT contract. Travel Air engineers knew that quick engine changes would be required for an airplane doing air mail and passenger work. Should an engine need replacement, only 15 to 20 minutes were required to remove the old engine and install a new one, including all connections and function checks.

Spare engines and other essential parts would always be kept in stock at the stopover points along NAT's routes. This capability of quick-change engines was an innovative idea.

Walter Beech flew the new monoplane up to Kansas City on December 18th. Egbert P. Lott tested the ship for NAT and was very enthusiastic about it. If Travel Air won the competition, NAT would want larger versions of the prototype for service use.

During 1926 yet another Travel Air design was flying, a five-place biplane. The first ship, powered by a Wright-Hispano of 180 h.p., was sold to Gerbracht Air Service of Ames, Iowa. Two examples were sold in January 1927, one to the Travel Air dealer in Alaska, Jack Laass, the second to a Mr. Cope of Alaskan Airways Transportation Co., who planned to use the big biplane for hauling freight and chartered hunting parties. Travel Air was happy to furnish custom airplanes to fill a particular need. Alaska required special equipment, and Travel Air could build it.

On January 7, 1927, NAT awarded Travel Air a contract for eight monoplanes, to be delivered within 120 days, at a cost of $128,676. That was asking a great deal from a small company such as Travel Air.

It meant overtime and maybe weekends, too. The men were willing to work, and Travel Air believed they could deliver the eight airplanes on time . . . so work began at once.

Almost simultaneous with the NAT contract came a request from Colonial Air Transport of Boston. They wanted six Wright-powered biplanes as soon as possible, but Walter and Clyde had to turn them down. There was no way they could build six more ships on top of present orders and the NAT demand.

One company would be getting their airplanes, though. Pacific Air Transport in California received three biplanes from the Wichita factory in late January. The air mail and passenger line was planning to convert their entire fleet to Travel Air models in the near future. They

Alonzo Cope and Jack Laass pose with Walter Beech as they take delivery of their first of two Model CW cabin biplanes, destined for Alaskan service. J-4 of 200 hp is installed. Note sunken exhaust manifold, developed by Travel Air engineers. (Beech Aircraft Corporation)

were already operating six ships, and liked everything about them.

Up in Topeka a different kind of work was under way. It wasn't anything related to building airplanes, at least not directly, but it would have a major impact on Wichita aviation for decades to come.

Representative Bert Lindsley had introduced a bill in the Kansas legislature that would allow a city, such as Wichita, to own property more than one mile from its limits. The bill was designed for Wichita from the beginning, with the aim of allowing that city to buy the East Central flying field.

The bill was made law on January 27, 1927. The park board of Wichita could now buy the land from the Booster Building Association. The importance of the Booster Building Association cannot be overemphasized. The men who formed the association were provident in their decision to buy the 160 acres of land back in 1925. From that decision came a well-drained, modern airfield that was one of the best on the Chicago to Dallas mail route.

The wisdom of those men enabled Wichita to have, finally, an official aerodrome, and Travel Air had a place to grow.

It was good news about the new law, but Clyde Cessna had some bad news for Walter Beech. It came on January 29, 1927. Cessna sold his 179 shares of Travel Air stock for $90 per share, to three men — Richard M. Gray and John Rigby of Gray-Rigby Hotel Co., and J.A. Woods of the Bridgeport Machine Co.

Clyde had plans to build his own company, but nothing firm was scheduled. He thought about building a 'flivver' monoplane, but down inside he had the burning desire to build the ultimate monoplane — one with a full cantilever wing.

During the winter, Cessna obtained a workshop at 1520 West Douglas and began design and construction of his monoplane. He called it the "Comet" and it first flew in the summer of 1927. With this airplane Clyde

Clarence Clark prepares to fly the Travel Air monoplane at the East Central flying field. Cessna influence can be detected in design of this prototype, but Lloyd Stearman had much to do with getting the airplane built. (Beech Aircraft Corporation)

Cessna started the Cessna Aircraft Company. He was briefly associated with Victor H. Roos, who was with Bellanca-Roos Company of Omaha, Nebraska. The association did not last long, however. Cessna was solidly on his way to becoming a highly respected and sought-after designer/builder of rugged, dependable monoplanes.

Clyde Cessna, with his son Eldon, built a reputation and legacy that stands to this day, and forever.

Such was the climate of aviation in the 1920s. From the Swallow Aircraft Company sprang Travel Air, Inc. From it was born Stearman Aircraft Company, and then Cessna Aircraft Company. The fledgling aviation industry was "flexing its wings" and finding the environment ripe for development. It was better that way, for America, for men such as Lloyd Carlton Stearman and Clyde Vernon Cessna, and for the industry they labored to build.

Walter Beech found himself in temporary charge of the company. Until official elections could be held, he was acting president of Travel Air.

One of the first things he did was wire the Department of Commerce in Washington, D.C. He wanted them to send out an inspector to license Travel Air pilots at the factory and to certify Travel Air airplanes as airworthy according to the new government regulations. Everyone in aviation saw the days of regulation coming. There were more and more airplanes in the air every year, more new manufacturers springing up, too. Pilots were on the increase. Sooner or later Uncle Sam was bound to move in.

The regulations were the result of the Air Commerce Act of 1926, authorizing the government to set standards for both pilots and airplanes.

The request from Beech was answered. Department of Commerce director, Clarence M. Young, sent Inspector Hosch to Wichita. Hosch certified Beech, Clark, Laass and Charlie Landers as qualified pilots. The Travel Air models were given a thorough analysis and found airworthy. Soon it wouldn't be legal to sell an airplane to the public without an approved type certificate from the Department of Commerce. All designs had to be submitted for careful scrutiny, and factories

inspected to assure acceptable practices were being followed. Travel Air passed all tests and was looking forward to more business as a result.

Beech was elected president of the company on February 15, 1927. The meeting of the board of directors also yielded some other changes in personnel titles. Thad Carver and Jack Turner were elected vice presidents, C.J. Yankey was treasurer and Gray, Woods, and Jack Engstrom were now members of the board.

William "Bill" Snook was elected secretary, and continued his primary responsibility of managing the factory and production line.

This was the first real rearrangement of Travel Air as a corporate entity. Much had happened over the last two years. The first year of business had seen sales of $54,936 . . . with a net income of $11,056 after taxes. This increased to sales of $185,169 in 1926, with a profit of $25,003. From 19 airplanes sold in 1925, the number rose to 46 in 1926.

All this success and the winning of the Ford Reliability Tour meant good news for the company. And progress was under way on East Central with the new factory.

More room was desperately needed. In January, 1927, Beech had ordered 35 Wright Whirlwind engines to meet the expected demand for radial-powered airplanes. The engine from Wright Aeronautical Corporation was beginning to pick up great popularity, and it was selling despite its high initial cost of nearly $6,000.

Travel Air needed the engines for the NAT contract plus the orders being received for the J-4 biplane model. Travel Air reduced the price of the basic model biplane, now called the Model B, from $3,500 to $2,785 by January, 1927. The expanded volume of production, increased labor force and good management were primarily responsible for the lower price.

Other model names were changed, too. The Whirlwind Travel Air biplane was the Model BW, using the J-4B of 200 H.P., and the new five-place biplane cabin model was known as the CW, while the Hispano-Suiza-engined model was the BH.

The Hispano engine, like the OX-5 and OXX-6 had its roots back in the First World War, and was also of V-8 design and layout.

Designed by Marc Birkigt, the Hispano-Suiza was known as a fine piece of technology and a prized aero engine. But the price was so high that Travel Air didn't plan to contract for any of them. The engine was built in the United States by Wright Aeronautical Corporation under license from the French and Spanish govern-

ments. Wright recognized the potential of the engine and sought to develop it further. If the customer would furnish the Hispano-Suiza, or Wright Model E or A as it was called in America, then Travel Air would build a biplane to go with it. The first Model BH was flown by Clarence Clark in the 1926 Ford tour.

With the stock issue selling well, a contractor for the new factory was chosen by February, 1927. The Henrion Improvement Co. started work on the site in February and had the ground graded and prepared for the foundations by the second week. By the end of the month the 75' x 275' foundation was poured.

The company hoped to be in its new home by July, and the construction was progressing nicely toward that goal.

But the aviation world was progressively being taken over by race fever. Raymond Orteig of France had offered $25,000 to the first person/persons to fly the Atlantic in either direction between New York and Paris. There were many who would like to win the prize, including Walter Beech. Not that he wanted to do the flying, but he would like to build an airplane for the attempt.

Still, only one pilot approached the firm with just such a proposition. Charles A. Lindbergh was flying the mail for Robertson over in St. Louis, where Travel Air #1 still made its home. Travel Air received a proposal in the form of a telegram dated February 4, 1927. Here's what it said:

"New York-Paris flight under consideration. Requires Whirlwind plane capable of 45 hours flight with pilot only. If you can deliver, state price and earliest delivery date."

Walter Beech had to think about this one. He read the message and walked out into the shop. Bob Phelps and another worker were busy working on the monoplanes for NAT, but they stopped long enough to listen to Beech. "Read this and tell me what you think," Walter said. Phelps read it and replied, "I think we could build it." Walter paused, then retreated to the office.

He decided against the offer. There was just too much work to be done as it was, let alone produce a rush job for a flight to Paris. Beech sent his reply back to Lindbergh.

However, the fever was contagious. Travel Air got another request in March for an even greater project

Left—Interior of first monoplane, Model 5000. Seats were padded, cabin was heated. Side windows slid open and closed. Note control cables, curved shell of pilot cockpit. (Beech Aircraft Corporation)

Below—Monoplane could carry 1,100 pounds, cruise at 105 mph on Wright J-4 power. Beech and Cessna flew ship to Richards Field in Kansas City on December 20, 1926. E.P. Lott flew the airplane, liked performance and accommodations provided for passengers. Design earned Travel Air an NAT order for 8 machines on January 6, 1927. (Beech Aircraft Corporation)

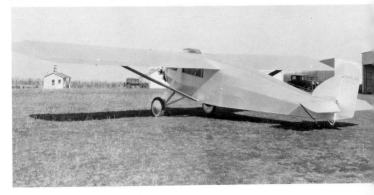

34

Cessna's first full cantilever monoplane, the "Comet," was ready to fly by spring, 1927. Cessna left Travel Air to build his own designs in January of 1927, selling his stock to three Wichita men. (Cessna Aircraft Company)

than Lindbergh's. A company asked Travel Air to build a "giant transatlantic ship" to be used for passenger service between New York and Paris. Walter had to turn down the same company not once, but three times!

Lindbergh flew off to Paris and glory in a Ryan, but what he accomplished for the entire aviation industry at that time is incalculable. The effects of that 33½ hour epic journey are still being felt today.

By March 18, 1927, the first NAT ship was ready to fly, but had not received its Whirlwind engine. It was assembled at the flying field and made ready for the Wright as soon as it arrived. Painted Travel Air blue and silver, the monoplane was the way of the future, not just in its wing configuration but, more importantly, in its enclosed cabin.

Travel Air would begin to experience a very gradual decline in orders for open cockpit ships in the next 24 months, as the cabin monoplanes became available. Airplanes were growing up. Helmets and goggles were not considered as necessary anymore. People wanted to fly in their dress clothes, not bundled up in a clumsy flying suit.

West Douglas factory, early 1927. One NAT monoplane in background is near completion. Fuselage for another being welded at right. J-5 radial engine hangs in center of crowded workshop. New factory on East Central was two months from completion when this photo was taken. (Beech Aircraft Corporation)

NAT certainly did its homework well. They knew that paying customers were after comfort and speed, and the enclosed cabin monoplane fit the requirement.

Travel Air was hearing from all parts of the world about its products, too. Letters were received from South Africa, Nicaragua and Canada. The inquiries wanted to know about all models produced and prices. The South African letter even asked about setting up a Travel Air dealership.

With the Whirlwind engine installed, the first NAT ship was flown by Beech, with E.P. Lott of NAT, Marcellus Murdock (owner of the Wichita Eagle), Mr. Gray, Mr. Woods, Jack Turner and Jack Engstrom flying in the monoplane and another biplane flown by Newman Wadlow. Both airplanes left Travel Air Field, as the site was becoming known, and headed for Ponca City, southeast of Wichita. The town was celebrating the opening of its airport and service by NAT.

The monoplane drew much attention. It was christened "Miss Ponca City" when a bottle of gasoline was broken over the propeller by a young lady. NAT was ready to go with their new airplane and seven more on the way.

Back at the factory, the second NAT machine was being built; however, NAT ran into a problem with the delivery schedule. They would not need the second ship as soon as they thought, so NAT released the ship for sale by Travel Air. Beech found another buyer in Pacific Air Transport in California.

The monoplane was accompanied by an OX-5 Model B purchased by Travel Air's newest dealer, D.C. Warren of San Francisco. He had been in Wichita to discuss business with Beech and test out the new Travel Air. "I want to take over the distribution of some real airplanes in the Pacific States. I want them to be the best ships I can find, with a high reputation, and priced fairly. There is only one kind for me to handle — Travel Air."

While in Wichita, Warren got more than he bargained for. He not only returned to San Francisco with a dealership and an airplane, but an employee, too!

Louise McPhetridge was her name. She didn't know much about aviation in 1927, but she was willing to learn and Walter Beech gave her a chance. Louise was in and out of college from 1925 to 1927, and had a job working for Jack Turner, selling coal, fuel oil and building materials, but she was often seen at the Travel Air factory. She was considered a "nuisance" by some of the workers, but she looked on anyway.

Deep down inside she felt the burning desire to fly. Airplanes were wonderful things, not just for men to fly but women, too. Back in December, 1926, on the day of the first flight of the Travel Air monoplane, Louise was at the field hoping to see some flying action. She also saw Jack Turner. Expecting to be scolded for watching airplanes instead of selling coal, Louise was met with a laugh, and Turner allowed her to stay on and watch the maiden flight.

The next day she was called in to talk to Jack Turner. She was expecting a reprimand from her boss; instead Louise was questioned about her true interests in aviation. Jack Turner said that something would be done about the young woman who wanted wings. Louise didn't know what to expect next, but she was excited.

A few days later she got a call from Beech. He wanted her to come over to his apartment and meet someone, so in a few minutes she was knocking on Walter's door.

She was introduced to D.C. Warren and told that Warren had agreed to take Louise out west and teach her the aviation business. And, Beech added, she would be taught to fly.

Louise couldn't believe her ears! Not only was she going to California, but she would be taught to fly. And in Travel Air airplanes at that.

On April 2, 1927, she left with Warren in the Model B. Louise McPhetridge would soon learn to fly and set records in Travel Air ships. One of her favorite planes was the Model BH. She would bring fame to the name Travel Air, and herself, in the next two years.

With the Pacific coast now equipped with an outlet for Travel Air airplanes, Walter Beech felt good. So did the stockholders. If business continued as it was, the company could expect even more production and profit.

NAT took delivery of its first monoplane on April 28th. E.P. Lott piloted the ship to Kansas City, where it was placed in service.

Walter Beech was a progressive thinker. He not only thought progressively, he acted upon his thoughts. There was no doubt in his mind that monoplanes were here to stay. If the public would accept them on the NAT line, then maybe some effort should be put forth for a production cabin ship.

The seeds of innovation were planted. The events of the time would delay Beech's plans. Way out in the Pacific, James Dole, the Pineapple King, had declared a $25,000 award to the first commercial airplane flown from Oakland, California to Wheeler Field, Honolulu, Hawaii. Could Travel Air enter a ship in that contest?

Beech and the directors of the company felt they could. It looked like transatlantic fever had turned into transpacific fever! Races were being planned in all directions to every place imaginable. 1927 was going to be the year of long distance flights.

By May, 1927, the factory work force had increased to 50 men working day, night and weekend shifts to complete the NAT contract and meet customer demand for standard ships. The West Douglas factory was severely handicapped for lack of room. The small factory was bursting at the seams, and move time to the new factory on East Central was still 40 days or more away.

The second NAT monoplane was almost finished by the middle of May, and two more were under construction. With all the frenzied activity that was now commonplace at Travel Air, the company didn't have a chief engineer with whom to confer, or to work on advanced designs, like monoplanes. Herb Rawdon, C.B. Bennett and Walter Burnham were three of the primary engineers at Travel Air, but a man of more experience was needed.

Stearman and Cessna were gone and Walter Beech was not an engineer. He knew the basics of construction and assembly, but he could not claim to possess any true engineering background. His forte was flying and selling the Travel Air, not designing and certifying it.

In addition to that, the government also required each aircraft company to retain engineering staff. Engineers were required not only for new designs, but to submit existing designs to the Department of Commerce for approval.

To fill the chief engineer's position, the company corresponded with Horace E. Weihmiller. Born in Baltimore, Maryland on February 8, 1902, Weihmiller attended Baltimore Polytechnic Institute in 1920, then went to Massachusetts Institute of Technology, where he graduated with a B.S. degree in general engineering, aeronautical, in 1925. From there he learned to fly at Brooks Field, Texas in 1926, while he was working for the Army Air Corps. He was assigned to McCook Field in Dayton, Ohio.

The experience he gained at McCook was extremely valuable. Some of the best thinkers and inventors, pilots and craftsmen were assembled there to unlock new secrets of flight.

Weihmiller was the kind of man Travel Air needed. Beech wrote to Weihmiller explaining the needs of the company and the general duties of chief engineer, and offered him the position.

Weihmiller accepted the offer of employment via letter on April 4, 1927, and Beech acknowledged his reply on April 6th. Weihmiller went to work in May.

As spring turned into summer, thoughts of the Third Ford Reliability Tour were surging through Beech's mind. He would like to see Travel Air design and build an airplane that could again win the coveted trophy, and if he could win it three times the company would have permanent possession of the prize.

Unfortunately, Walter (and others) thought the tour would begin in August, as it had in 1926. The tour took off in June instead, and the notices sent out were late in arriving at Travel Air. Walter wasn't happy. He was very disappointed in receiving the start date at a time considered too late for construction of an entry. He expressed sincere desire to fly the tour, but business pressures and obligations to customers were additional reasons for not participating.

Eddie Stinson won the tour in his Stinson SM-1 and collected the $2,500 for his efforts. No Travel Air airplanes were entered.

In addition to being a competitor, salesman and aviation booster, Walter Beech was always interested in helping somebody out of a jam, and one day in May he was presented with a real ear-opener! Clarence Clark had taken Mr. W.L. McVey up for a ride in a Travel Air in hopes that it would help McVey's hearing problem.

Louise McPhetridge Von Thaden . . . Travel Air pilot and saleswoman. Louise got her "break" in aviation from Walter Beech and D.C. Warren. She went to California in April, 1927 and learned the business. (Bill and Pat Thaden)

Monoplane engines could be changed in 15 minutes by experienced mechanics because of the powerplant package concept shown here. Controls, instruments and panel came off with engine. (Beech Aircraft Corporation)

Doctors had told him that there was nothing they could do to help medically. And the gentleman seemed to think that first ride had helped his hearing a little.

If one treatment of flying worked, why not another? This time Beech was asked to do the flying. Walter gladly accepted, and the two men were off in a Model BW. Beech decided to really pour it on this time around. He climbed the ship to 12,000 feet. With McVey instructed to scream as loudly as he could, Walter put the biplane into a power dive for Mother Earth.

All the way down the flying wires screamed. All the way down McVey screamed! All the way down Walter wondered if this procedure would help the poor chap!

Within 200 feet of the ground Beech leveled off the biplane and landed. Both men had nose pains, but McVey still had his ear pains to boot! One treatment was enough for Walter. No more power dives for him! His ears were fine and he wanted to keep them that way. Mr. McVey would have to seek some other method of treatment for his ear trouble.

Travel Air was treated to another interesting offer in late May, 1927. Harold Bixby, who co-purchased the first Travel Air and was still flying it, proposed that Travel Air move to St. Louis and build airplanes. Bixby even went so far as to cover expenses and was willing to set up financing and facilities for the company. It really sounded good, but once again the board of directors at Travel Air were not interested. They had started the concern in Wichita, and there the company would remain and grow.

It certainly was growing! The new factory was almost finished, though not yet available for occupancy. The NAT monoplanes took up a great amount of room, being so much larger than the biplanes, and the West Douglas site was really crowded! Workers were almost back to back. They banged into each other at times just trying to

work with the grinder or a welding jig. Hoses and tools, equipment and materials were everywhere one looked. However, the job got done despite difficulties and hardships in the shop. But there were events outside of Travel Air's walls that would soon have a lasting effect on the Wichita company.

Down at Bartlesville, Oklahoma, Frank Phillips was operating the Phillips Petroleum Co., and had a very aggressive research and development branch in operation. They were working on a new type of aviation fuel called "Nu-Aviation" gasoline. It was refined from a process that used casing head gas. The result was a fuel that weighed 5.68 pounds per gallon opposed to 7 for competing brands.

The fuel needed a nationwide tour and some good, hard use in an airplane engine. W.D. "Billy" Parker, head man of the Phillips aviation department, had a solution for that. He and Walter Beech were friends, and Parker knew what the Travel Air could do, so he ordered a J-5 biplane the first week of June and took delivery a few weeks later. Such a short wait time was due to the fact that Travel Air workers were producing almost one ship per day by June, 1927.

Once Parker received the airplane, he began tests with the new Phillips fuel. Full throttle runs, both static and in-flight, lean/rich characteristics, effects on cylinder head temperatures and many other experiments were carried out. The results were satisfying to Parker and Phillips.

They were ready to market the fuel and began to do so immediately. Parker might have had some desire to fly the Dole race to Hawaii, using "Nu-Aviation" fuel, but this was never acknowledged by either himself or Phillips. He didn't enter the race, but he did fly the Travel Air to many states, giving demonstrations of the new gasoline. Phillips would get into the Dole contest in a big way, though. He would sponsor two Travel Air monoplanes and provide the fuel. Only two months remained until the race was to start in August, 1927.

The officials at Travel Air were wondering what they would do if orders for Dole race ships materialized. Maybe they wouldn't, but the chances were too good for that possibility. Pilots would need special airplanes for such a race, and Travel Air expected some orders.

By June 12th the Henrion Improvement Co. advised Walter Beech that the new East Central factory would be ready for occupancy by the 15th of the month.

All the new and modern woodworking equipment was already in place. More new equipment would be added, and some would be moved from the West Douglas site. Total floor space was 21,650 square feet, at a cost of $32,000. Five offices were located at the west end of the building, including the main offices, offices for Beech and other officials, with engineering located directly above on a second level.

A decision was made to complete four of the NAT monoplanes at the West Douglas factory, while all other production was moved to East Central.

This proved a good idea because the larger monoplanes would have been difficult to move in their state of construction. Remaining biplanes under construction were finished and the monoplanes alone remained, with a workforce to complete them.

As scheduled, the factory was released by June 15, 1927. Production was immediately increased, and all the workers labored hard to meet the order book demands. Eleven monoplanes were under construction. Three already had been delivered to NAT, who had five more coming.

A check of the production records showed that by June, 1927, Travel Air had built and delivered 80 biplanes since it started business. They had come a long way from the Kansas Planing Mill, but nobody dreamed the company would experience the popularity of its product as it had in the last year. 1928 was not too far away, and that year would make the first three look poor!

Walter Beech received a nice surprise soon after Travel Air moved into the East Central facility. Charles A. Lindbergh sent Beech a thank you telegram for a special congratulatory note and floral tribute that greeted him in Paris. Beech was one of the first persons to receive a word of appreciation from Lindbergh. Apparently Beech was pretty sure of Lindbergh's abilities because he sent the note and flowers before Lindbergh arrived in Paris!

Travel Air learned in the middle of June that things were getting a little difficult for the Booster Building Association's plan for the city to acquire the flying field.

It seems the Kansas Supreme Court would have to give a legal and time-consuming interpretation of the recently passed state law. Beech wasn't worried about the matter, however. The men of the association had helped Travel Air get where it was, and there was no doubt in his mind they would arrange for the city of Wichita to buy the flying field sooner or later.

Late June found Travel Air in its new factory with the assembly line going full throttle. Some departments were in the process of building up to production speed, but overall the building was busy, busy, busy. June also found Travel Air with 17 orders for Dole race airplanes! They would not build 17 ships, just two for the men Travel Air officials believed had the money, knowledge and skill to make a good showing.

By summer of 1927 the whole nation, and indeed the world, was on fire for aviation and its possibilities. James Dole had offered big prize money to the first commercial airplanes to fly from California to Hawaii.

The Prize money would go to the first and second commercial planes reaching Wheeler Field in Hawaii. $25,000 would go to the first flight across, the second would get $10,000. The flights had to be nonstop and

Detailed view of engine and forward fuselage area on Travel Air Transport. Note sunken exhaust manifold. Pilot had toe brakes, vertically-adjustable seat, good visibility. Travel Air-designed landing lights were also controlled from the cockpit by a lever. Note fairings over magnetos behind spinner. (Beech Aircraft Corporation)

completed within one year after the starting date of August 12, 1927.

Dole's announcement came four days after Lindbergh landed in Paris. The race fever was still building, and there were plenty of willing entrants. People everywhere talked of the explosion of transoceanic flight.

Wichita, the "Peerless Princess of the Prairie," was talking about it, too. Would Travel Air get requests for an airplane to fly the Dole contest? Could Travel Air supply one, maybe more?

Big questions that needed big answers. Beech sat in his office, a lazy spiral of smoke ascending from his pipe. Puffing gently, he pondered such answers. It wasn't his decision alone, of course, who would get Travel Air ships for any race, but he was president and his opinion meant much.

Hawaii, he thought. A tiny speck out in the vast

One of the last NAT ships built ready for flight. Known as the Travel Air Transport, the airplane made travel between Chicago and Dallas fairly comfortable for 1927. (Beech Aircraft Corporation)

Another view of NAT transport. Landing light under left wing is extended. Magnetic compass at front of windscreen. Cupola canopy aft section was designed to separate in flight via release wire in cockpit in the event quick exit was necessary. (Beech Aircraft Corporation)

reaches of the Pacific. Not an easy mark to hit. "Lindy" had an entire continent in front of his Ryan, but whoever flew the Dole race had only a group of islands as their target.

Navigation would be the key element. An error of two or three degrees could spell disaster: the fliers would miss landfall and fly on to oblivion. Could be a risky situation for an airplane manufacturer, too, especially if the fliers flew on to oblivion in a Travel Air!

One man in Honolulu had money on the line for someone to win. Another man in Wichita sat behind his desk thinking about the whole affair. Would a monoplane be best? a biplane, perhaps? Biplanes were really too small to accommodate the necessary fuel tanks for the flight; however, the monoplanes were nearly "tailor-made" for such an endurance attempt.

Travel Air had its monoplane design to the point where it could be transformed from a mail carrier to a long-distance endurance flier. The primary change would be installation of fuel tanks.

Many airmen were planning to go after the Dole prize. However, it was the Army that made it to Hawaii first.

Pilots Maitland and Hegenberger left the mainland on June 28th and landed at Wheeler Field the next day. Attempting the same feat (but behind the Army ship by a short time) were two civilians flying the prototype Travel Air monoplane. The ship had been sold by Pacific Air Transport to Ernest Smith. Smith had financial backing for the Pacific flight from Anthony Parante, Edmund J. Moffett and others.

Smith had a man named Carter engaged as his navigator, and was ready to take off June 17th. Walter Beech knew all about this flight by Smith and Carter. He wrote Smith a letter offering to service the Travel Air properly for the long-distance flight, advising Smith that the monoplane was not designed for such an ordeal and should be suitably modified.

This gesture went unheeded. Smith and Carter departed Oakland's new airport shortly after the Army Atlantic C-2 monoplane. They only made the Golden Gate Bridge when trouble hit. The small wind deflector provided for the navigator separated from the airplane. Carter would have great difficulty in taking accurate celestial or sun sightings without the deflector in place. The sextant he used would be almost impossible to hold steady — a necessity for proper readings to be taken.

Smith was aware of the problem. He knew the deflector was gone and Carter would be in trouble without it. So was the success of the flight. He remembered the tiny error that could throw them way off course. Yet, he was sorely tempted to continue the

crossing, so badly did he want to succeed.

Carter, however, had other ideas. Attempts to get his pilot to turn around and return to Oakland were futile until he managed to strike Smith in the back of the head to get the point across!

Finally, Smith relented and reversed course. The Travel Air was very heavy with fuel. 370 gallons were carried, 300 in the fuselage and 70 in the wings.

There was no doubt in Smith's mind that the ship may not be able to withstand the landing load with such weight. Maybe he should have taken Beech up on that offer! The crowd at Oakland saw the monoplane approaching and their thoughts now allied with Smith. Could he land the airplane?

Gently, ever so gently, the little monoplane touched ground. The gear began to feel the full force of the airplane's weight. The tail was down, all lift gone from the wings. They had made it!

With one problem now behind him, Smith encountered a more serious situation on the ground — Carter quit.

Ernest Smith could not believe his ears. He pleaded with Carter, almost to the point of tears. Carter held fast to his belief that the flight was a total loss after the deflector broke. The Army ship was ahead of them, and by the time the airplane was repaired and reserviced, they would be hours behind and out of the "glory."

Again Smith tried to persuade Carter to remain with the Travel Air and try again. No, said Carter, he was through.

Smith left the airport a very distressed and dejected pilot. Without a navigator he couldn't make the flight. And now his three backers began to argue amongst themselves. The whole arrangement looked about to collapse.

But Smith managed to hold things together, and after a search he found another navigator named Emory Bronte. The two men took off, flying from Oakland's field on July 14th, for the second attempt to reach Hawaii.

The ship was equipped with a transmitter and receiving set. Bronte hoped to use it to broadcast their progress at intervals in the flight and "talk" with passing ships along the sealanes.

Five days of rations were aboard, a distilling machine for changing salt water into drinking water, a rubber boat and four carrier pigeons. Also aboard were smelling salts and spirits of ammonia to combat getting drowsy. Neither man had thought of this requirement, but the advice came from Maitland and Hegenberger, who used

"All aboard, please," somewhere along the Chicago-Dallas route. NAT No. 17 receives her cargo of baggage and passengers while ticket agent writes manifest in his fancy ticket office. (Smithsonian Institution Photo No. A44561A)

the drugs on their flight. It was fortunate for Smith and Bronte that the two Army fliers were back in Oakland to suggest this aid. A rider was dispatched to a drug store to obtain salts and ammonia.

The radio set quit shortly after the flight was out over the wide, blue Pacific. Bronte took his sightings with the aid of the new deflector and he dispatched two of the carrier pigeons with messages. The birds were not seen again. They may have made landfall off the coast, but made no attempt to return to their loft located in San Francisco.

Smith and Bronte made history as the first two civilian airmen to fly a commercial ship to Hawaii. They landed on Molokai island the day after their takeoff from Oakland. The Travel Air was badly damaged in a forced landing.

Ernest Smith was very fond of his airplane, and Walter Beech remembered Smith as being determined to rebuild the ship for a return flight to California. No such flight was ever attempted, however.

Smith and Bronte had been the first civilian "aeronauts" to make the crossing, but they were almost a month too early to win the Dole prize.

One Travel Air had made it to Hawaii, why not more? By early June the company had already received 17 requests to build monoplanes for the Dole race. The board of directors, along with Beech, Snook and others, would have to sift through all of the requests to decide who was to get a contract and an airplane.

One request came from Arthur C. Goebel, a California-based stunt pilot for National Pictures, Inc. He learned to fly in 1920 and operated a shop at Clover Field, Santa Monica. There he made his name as a good pilot and businessman.

Goebel had flown many airplanes in California to compare their performances prior to deciding what ship he wanted for the Dole race. He was very aware of the Travel Air monoplane and had probably seen, or even flown one out in California, where Pacific Air Transport was operating the second production ship.

Beech had Goebel's order in hand on June 17, 1927, when Goebel visited Travel Air and personally ordered the airplane. The tall, handsome airman was only 31, but Walter liked his attitude and style. There was no doubt about his flying capabilities.

For five days the Travel Air officials questioned, observed and sought judgments on flying from Goebel. There was much at stake in building a monoplane for this race, not the least of which was the pilot! He had to be the right man for Travel Air.

Walter Beech was satisfied, as was everyone else. So Art Goebel was shown where to sign the work order and plunk down his $5,000 deposit. Beech estimated the airplane would be done by early August. No firm date was given.

Goebel then returned to California to begin preparations for the race. Cal Chandler was selected as Goebel's flight manager. Financial support came from Goebel's friends in California and he invested his own money as well. To make the final payoff on the Travel Air, a sum of nearly $15,000, Art Goebel later obtained financial aid from Frank Phillips.

The Oklahoma oil magnate agreed to pay off the balance of the money owed Travel Air, stipulating the ship carry the name "Woolaroc" on both sides of the fuselage. "Woolaroc" meant woods, lakes and rocks, topography found at Phillips' ranch south of Bartlesville, Oklahoma.

Hot on the heels of Goebel were two other fliers who

Walter Beech (left) listens to D. C. Warren praise the Model B after it lifted over 1,000 pounds of bagged sand. Warren signed up as a Travel Air dealer in California and took delivery of this OX-5 ship and one employee, Louise Thaden. Model 5000 in background was destined for NAT as their second ship, but sale was made to PAT (Pacific Air Transport) of California instead. Both airplanes were flown west in April, 1927. (Robert Pickett Collection)

East end of new factory, summer, 1927. Final assembly area is busy with Model BH, NAT monoplane and wing work. Wood shop is at left, behind biplane's empennage, with dope room behind brick firewall and fireproof, rolling door at right. (Beech Aircraft Corporation)

wanted a Travel Air. Benny H. Griffin and Al Henley contracted for a monoplane for the Dole race late in June. They put down a $5,000 deposit and specified that the airplane be as light as possible.

Both ships would be identical in construction except that the Griffin-Henley machine would weigh somewhat less than the "Woolaroc." The excess weight was stripped from the ship at Griffin's insistence, leaving the airplane nothing more than a fuel tank with wings. Goebel's ship was built as a standard model, with only modifications for the tanks and the navigator's compartment included.

Art Goebel wanted to fly alone if possible. But the race required a navigator, so the position was planned for ahead of race time. Goebel hoped to obtain his navigator at a later date. The reasons for his wanting to fly alone were not hard to understand: it would allow Goebel to carry more fuel, fly the trip as he saw fit and it would mean more money for him when the race was won.

Benny Griffin would fly the "Oklahoma," as the second ship was named. His background included pilot training during the war, where he accumulated about 35 hours flying time before being shipped "over there" to

Above-Original Travel Air monoplane was flown to Hawaii by Ernest Smith and Emory Bronte on July 14-15, 1927. It was the first commercial airplane to make the crossing. (Smithsonian Institution Photo No. 81-2189)

Below—Model BW used by Billy Parker for tests of 'Nu-Aviation' fuel, developed by Phillips Petroleum. (Phillips Petroleum Company)

fly Nieuport bombers on the Italian front.

His navigator, Al Henley, had 10 years flying experience under his belt and had learned the navigation trade from the Army. He was good and Griffin felt fortunate to have him.

The two men had their financial backing from four Oklahoma businessmen; George Henshaw, Fred Copshaw, Bill Armstrong and Jimmy Wilson. Frank Phillips also sponsored their entry, hence the name "Oklahoma."

It is important to point out here that Phillips originally sponsored only Griffin and Henley; Goebel sought his aid after the other two men had already done so. With that act Frank Phillips was in the race with two entries, both using "Nu-Aviation" fuel.

The "Woolaroc" and "Oklahoma" were rush jobs in the factory. H.E. Weihmiller was responsible for much of the engineering to accommodate the fuel tanks into the monoplanes, and the tanks were manufactured locally in Wichita.

Monoplane numbers 10 and 11 were assigned to the racers, and a much larger full-vision canopy was installed on the "Oklahoma," whereas the "Woolaroc" sported the standard cupola arrangement.

The new factory on East Central afforded enough room to build the monoplanes comfortably. Travel Air was now billing all of its monoplanes under the "Type 5000" name. The shift was under way from the older model designations to a series of "thousand" numbers.

Despite the new factory space, construction was still continuing in the West Douglas facility. Four monoplanes were being built there, and NAT ship #19, the fourth to be built for them, was nearing completion. Long, hard hours were put in by Travel Air workmen to get the NAT ships completed so the final equipment and personnel could move to the east side factory.

The date of the Dole race was closing in on Travel Air. Additional time was put in to finish, test and deliver the two monoplanes.

The "Oklahoma" was completed first, on July 29, 1927, and the "Woolaroc" was ready to go by Tuesday, August 2. Both ships were test flown by Clarence Clark, and no problems were discovered, the airplanes behaving as expected.

Both machines were painted Travel Air blue on the fuselage, gold on the wings; but this color was probably Travel Air's yellow pigment that would closely resemble a gold-color appearance. The yellow looked very attractive against the deep blue on the fuselage.

The "Oklahoma" differed externally from the "Woolaroc" by having a different window arrangement below the cockpit and the Whirlwind engine didn't have the Travel Air-developed exhaust manifold, designed to set flush with the cowling and fuselage. It reduced drag and looked quite functional and neat.

A last minute customer for the Dole race was Harvey M. Lemke. He had been a naval aviator for 10 years and much of his flying time was over water. He contacted Travel Air on August 1 and ordered a biplane built for the race! He wanted a monoplane, but that was impossible at that late date. The idea of a biplane was not so bad except for the fuel tanks. Where would they fit and who would build them? Travel Air did not have the means or time to construct a special set of fuel tanks. However, Lemke contacted the Back Airplane Co. in Santa Monica, California, and they agreed to build the tanks.

Harvey Lemke took delivery of his biplane, but nothing more was heard from him. Apparently he was much too late to be a serious entrant in the contest.

By early August, Goebel and Griffin were off for California. Phillips Petroleum had sent 20 barrels of "Nu-Aviation" fuel ahead to the Oakland airport for their use in the race.

Griffin and Henley had flown from Travel Air Field down to Bartlesville so Frank Phillips could see what he was paying for. Goebel did the same. The "Oklahoma" took off August 4 and flew off to the west. 13 hours and 45 minutes later the ship landed at Needles, California, where it was fueled and flown on to Santa Monica. The "Oklahoma" arrived at Oakland airport on August 6th, having averaged less than 90 mph on the westward flight.

Art Goebel, flying solo, took off from Bartlesville on August 6th, and arrived in Oakland August 9, 1927. Goebel was to have his Pioneer earth inductor compass, drift sight and other navigation equipment installed at San Diego, and when he arrived at Oakland he was fitted out and ready to go. All he needed was a navigator.

Goebel's friend, Lieutenant D.W. Tomlinson, knew of a good man for the job: Lieutenant William V. Davis, Jr. The meeting of Goebel and Davis was not the first; they had met before while attending California air race events.

Lieutenant Davis was well qualified for his task. He was a graduate of Annapolis in 1924 and from Pensacola in 1926. He served aboard the U.S.S. Idaho and, the grandfather of all aircraft carriers, the Langley. Davis knew radio equipment and how to use it. He was also trained in both celestial and marine navigation techniques. Granted temporary leave to make the flight, Davis would be invaluable to the success of the "Woolaroc."

The same radio set used by Smith and Bronte was also used by Goebel and Davis. It was installed in the airplane and checked out along with the other equipment prior to the race.

Brice Goldsborough and J.D. Peace of the Pioneer Company were at the airport to help calibrate compasses and check Pioneer equipment. Goldsborough was well-received by the pilots; they knew he was an expert in his business and could calibrate their compasses accurately. Some of the Dole race entrants were poorly equipped for such an ordeal as ocean flying, with only one or two magnetic compasses, while the majority carried up-to-date earth inductor compasses and radio devices. The accuracy of such equipment was, therefore, of utmost importance. All knew very well the price extracted for poor navigation across the 2,500 miles of water.

August 8, 1927, found eight contestants huddled in the office of C.W. Saunders, NAA official for the race. James Dole had turned over all race affairs to the contest committee, and it was up to them to say who could compete and who could not.

Some pilots were not even licensed as yet, so oral tests and logbooks were used to certify these airmen and issue a transport license.

The race had 15 entrants, but some had withdrawn; three were wrecked and one was disqualified. Those eight remaining pilots drew lots for takeoff positions. Griffin held the number one slot and Goebel was seventh. All the pilots could do was wait.

But the navigators, or pilots who chose to fly alone, were busy. Ben Wyatt, a government employee of the Department of Commerce, served as navigation examiner. He asked questions about compass corrections to hold course, what were the compass deviation effects for their airplane, and questions about airspeed, time and distance calculations. A short flight was given each contestant to ascertain the pilot or navigator's basic competence.

When August 16th dawned, the typical coastal fog was there, shrouding the shoreline in a veil of white. By late morning it was gone. Throngs of people gathered for the upcoming departure. Everyone discussed whether or not all eight would get off safely, let alone reach Hawaii.

Griffin and Henley were in the "Oklahoma" and

"Oklahoma" ready for delivery to Al Henley and Benny Griffin, who flank Walter Beech in this July, 1927 photograph. Note cupola canopy extension, found only on this ship. "Oklahoma" and "Woolaroc" were the 10th and 11th Model 5000s built. (Mal Holcomb)

anxious to be off. The Travel Air was pushed up to the starting line at twelve noon, and the fuel-laden monoplane began its takeoff roll.

About 3,000 feet down the sandy runway she was airborne. The Dole race was under way. Slowly the "Oklahoma" climbed westward, the eyes of every pilot still watching to see if the ship would sustain the climb. The next airplane was wrecked on takeoff, ending all hopes for Norman Goddard and his "El Encanto" monoplane. Goddard lost control on takeoff and the airplane he designed lay on its left side, the right wing pointing upward in a farewell salute to those who would follow.

Goebel and Davis made their takeoff in the seventh spot without difficulty. At last they were on their way. Walter Beech was right there watching, too. He had flown a J-5 biplane to Oakland on August 7th to oversee and personally supervise every detail of the maintenance and servicing of both Travel Air ships.

At noon plus 40 minutes, things began to go wrong for a few of the racing airmen. The Buhl biplane "Miss Doran" was returning with engine trouble. Next came William Erwin flying the Swallow named "Dallas Spirit," a portion of the lower fuselage fabric trailing behind. He landed successfully with the heaviest fuel load of any entrant, but did not compete in the race after this incident.

Beech next saw one of the Travel Air monoplanes returning. It was the "Oklahoma" coming back after one hour of flying. After landing, Griffin reported that his engine was running hot, leading knowledgeable people to suspect the Phillips fuel as the cause.

Billy Parker was quick to deny this, stating that the fuel had been thoroughly tested and was being used all over the country. He went further. He blamed Al Henley. Henley was known to have run the Wright on the ground for long periods of time, at full throttle, without a thought about what it might do to the engine.

Regardless of the cause, the Travel Air factory and Phillips Petroleum Co. were down to one airplane and two men, flying somewhere over the Pacific.

The "Woolaroc" was doing fine. Davis was able to use his radio receiver to pick up signals from the Army's San Francisco-Maui radio range. This low frequency system had been installed for the Maitland-Hegenberger flight. It transmitted a continuous code, a dot-dash, then a dash-dot. When the fliers were far away from the San Francisco station and the signal began to fade, they hoped to receive the incoming Maui signal.

With a strong on-course signal coming through on the radio, Davis next took the first of his night celestial sightings to determine exact location. Davis was trained in the use of a celestial sextant. The navigator held the sextant in a level position, verified by a bubble level that

Frank Phillips (left) and his wife after inspecting the "Woolaroc" monoplane at Bartlesville airport. Art Goebel in suit and flying helmet flashes that famous smile for cameraman. 'Nu-Aviation' fuel logo is on aft fuselage, earth inductor compass drive unit atop fuselage. (Frank Phillips Museum)

was built in. A reading was taken on the reference star more than once, each time checking to be sure the bubble level was set on center. The average reading of the star's height and bearing from the airplane then gave position on the earth's surface.

Still, it wasn't easy when the air was rough or the slipstream was buffeting the observer, even when a deflector was installed. At night the bubble level had to be illuminated, requiring additional patience and skill. Too much illumination and the star was hidden — too little and the bubble couldn't be seen. Lieutenant Davis had experienced all these problems before, and had little trouble with his sightings.

Goebel flew Great Circle routes given to him by Davis. These courses were commonly used in long-distance flying. Davis laid them out one by one as the "Woolaroc" progressed westward. Goebel flew a course of 250 degrees initially, then changed to about 230 degrees to hit Hawaii.

Level at 4,000 feet, the Whirlwind singing its constant, reassuring song of power, the Travel Air was slowly swallowed up by the Pacific night.

Davis took sightings on the star Polaris, tuned the radio for the signal code, and transmitted Morse Code position reports.

By midnight they had climbed to 6,000 feet, just above a layer of stratus clouds. As dawn neared, Davis readied smoke bombs for a drift check. The Travel Air may have been blown off course during the night, and when the sun was high enough behind the ship, he

"Woolaroc" and company. Some of the men who made the Dole race a Travel Air victory. Left to right: Howard Baccus, Walter Burnham, Herbert Rawdon, William Hauselman, "Pinky" Grimes, Ted Cochran, Art Goebel, Ralph Morton, Harold Brooks, Horace Weihmiller and Clarence Clark. (Beech Aircraft Corporation)

dropped several bombs.

Drift lines had been painted on the horizontal stabilizer of the airplane to use in such situations as this. When the bomb hit the water, Davis would look out the window and estimate the smoke in relation to the lines. It was crude, but sufficient for him to correct course errors.

The predicted northeast winds aloft were there, and the ground speed of the "Woolaroc" was nearly 100 MPH. A nice benefit for fuel consumption.

Further drift checks verified that the wind was shifting to the east and southeast, so Davis sent a course correction up front to Goebel, telling him to steer to the south. Goebel didn't agree, but did as he was directed.

Hours later Goebel spotted a "cloud" that looked different from the rest. It didn't move as they got closer and he thought it might be land — Maui. It was Maui, and both men felt elated as they neared their goal. The aerial navigation of Davis and the steady piloting of Goebel was adding up to victory.

Soon the "Woolaroc" flew past Diamond Head and was met by a Boeing PW-9 pursuit ship from Wheeler Field. The pilot of the nimble fighter tucked in close to the Travel Air. Goebel and Davis both saw the pilot's smile and the signal that they were first — he was holding up one finger!

The "Woolaroc" flew inland and touched down on Wheeler Field 26 hours, 17 minutes and 33 seconds after takeoff. Two hours later the second, and last, entrant arrived, flown by Martin Jensen and navigated by Paul Schluter.

"Woolaroc" was disassembled and shipped back to the mainland aboard the steamship Monoa. Later Goebel flew the ship to various points in the country commemorating his victory. An interesting point of debate has existed about what fuel the "Woolaroc" actually used for the race. Goebel fed the Whirlwind 317 gallons of gasoline, and averaged 93 MPH. But some observers stated before the race that Goebel drained the "Woolaroc" tanks and filled them with Standard Red Crown aviation fuel.

Unfortunately, lives were lost in the Dole race. Despite bad press given the race because of the deaths, the Dole race was another step toward aviation progress. It was just as legitimate as the Atlantic crossings and showed a no worse track record for number killed.

Griffin and Henley were back at the Travel Air factory by early September. Griffin still complained about three bad cylinders on the Wright and wanted a new engine. Beech agreed, and the Wright was replaced.

Even though Travel Air had a brand new factory and work was moving along well, the factory stopped taking orders temporarily. This enabled the production line to catch up on outstanding orders.

There was no doubt another factory building was needed. Another contract was let to Henrion Improvement Co., which started work immediately in late September.

In October, Art Goebel returned to Travel Air Field flying the "Woolaroc" and was greeted by throngs of Wichitans. He laid the cornerstone for factory "B" as the new unit was called, and spent the rest of October 5, 1927, turning the first dirt for Clyde Cessna's new factory and dedicating Stearman's facility with a bottle of gasoline.

Walter Beech took time to recall Goebel's visit back in June. Beech was surprised at the young man who didn't even want to select the color or paint scheme for his new ship. He just left it all up to Travel Air!

TRAVEL AIR
MFG. CO. INC.

CHAPTER SIX
Bigger and Better

After the Dole race in August, the factory was still very busy trying to fill late orders. By September the production line was five months behind in construction. That same month saw yet another attempt to lure Travel Air away from Wichita. An Indiana group, who remained unnamed, offered to set up another "alternate" factory in that state to help the company meet its customer demands.

The board of directors at Travel Air had 30 days to consider this offer. They considered it out of the question. The problem could be solved within Wichita and with Wichita money. On September 22, 1927 the company authorized Henrion Improvement Co. to begin construction on a second factory building.

Four more acres were purchased through the help of men like Jack Turner, Walter Innes and others. The work would not take as long because this building was just like the first except there would be no offices. The structure was to be 75' x 275' and would be 100' to the east of the other building. A concrete apron would be poured between the two factories for use as an outdoor assembly/rigging area.

This second building would have fire-proofing built into the roof area near the center of the factory. This was done to reduce the fire hazard, as the new factory would house the paint and dope departments. The dope was very flammable, and special precautions had to be taken at all times.

Another important development in September was the trial installation of the new Caminez radial engine in a Model B airframe. The Caminez engine produced 135 hp, but turned only 1000 rpm. A ten-foot diameter propeller was installed, but the thrust line of the engine was quite high compared to the other Travel Air ships. This high mounting was required to give the propeller sufficient ground clearance in all normal attitudes, such as taxi, takeoff and landing.

Fuel consumption was attractive at 8 gallons per hour, but the Caminez was not fully perfected in 1927 and had its teething problems.

Other engines, too, were being considered for test installations. The Ryan-Siemens, or Siemens-Halske radial was of German origin. Designed around a nine-cylinder layout, the engine was popular and T.C. Ryan visited Travel Air in an effort to market the new powerplant. The combination of Travel Air airframe and Siemens-Halske engine was under design by the end of November, 1927. The first example was retained at the factory as a demonstrator, but two additional engines were ordered, and firm orders for this model were in hand as the year drew to a close.

Both the Caminez and the Siemens-Halske were examples of the new engines emerging to replace the OX-5. They were not inexpensive, but they were more reliable.

The monoplanes of NAT were brought back to Travel Air for modification to the cabins and to investigate a nagging report from pilots about lack of aileron control. Travel Air cooperated fully with E.P. Lott and NAT officials in conducting tests to find the problems.

While the fleet of monoplanes were down for tests, the factory made improvements in the cabin appointments, heating and chair comfort to enhance the appeal of the NAT ships. The passenger service was going well and NAT was very anxious to get the ships back into the

Above—Caminez radial engine of 135 hp installed on Model B airframe, 1927. Engine turned maximum of 1,000 rpm, but had vibration and reliability problems. Only three ships were built, with the prototype shown here. Type was called Model 8000. (Beech Aircraft Corporation)

Below—Model 9000 featured reliable Ryan-Siemens (Siemens-Halske) radial of 125 hp, and underwent testing at Travel Air, November, 1927. The prototype was retained by the factory for demonstrations. Two other ships were sold by early 1928. (Beech Aircraft Corporation)

44

Truman Wadlow (left) with friend at the St. Joseph, Missouri Travel Air dealership run by Wadlow. Model B was demonstrator. (Truman Wadlow)

air. The aileron situation was resolved by re-rigging controls and aileron travel to the satisfaction of NAT and service resumed by December.

Progress on the second factory building was good, and by early November the concrete had been poured and the outside structure was going up. The new building was to be available for production by early December, and Travel Air temporarily suspended orders during September and October to try and give the production boys some breathing room. Meanwhile, the Henrion Improvement Co. was exhorted to meet the deadline, as the company didn't want to refuse orders very long.

Wichita was feeling expansion of her aviation industry, too. Charles Laird and Lloyd Stearman were both back in town, and Stearman had set up shop in the Bridgeport Machine Co. facility.

The airplane they designed and built in California was a very attractive biplane, OX-5 powered, but they experienced tough times selling their product on the west coast.

Walter Innes again took control of the situation. He made enough contacts in one afternoon to raise $60,000 for Lloyd, Mac Short and Fred Hoyt. He wanted them to return to Wichita and build their airplanes.

They returned in 1927 and were well on their way toward a solid spot in the competition with Travel Air, Cessna and Swallow.

Charles Laird, brother of Matty Laird, was ready to build his own airplane by 1927. He started business in the same spot Travel Air did; the Kansas Planing Mill Co. C.B. Bennett, formerly with Travel Air as a production engineer, went with Laird to design and produce a four-place, Whirlwind-powered cabin biplane called the "Whippoorwill." Laird had worked for Swallow since his brother "Matty" Laird left in 1923, but wanted his own business and his own design. The first "Whippoorwill" was sold to Wallace Beery, famous actor and member of Lasky's Famous Players. The ship made its maiden flight in January, 1928, and had promising performance. Cruise was 105 mph with the Wright, and the accommodations were very plush in the cabin.

That added up to 7 airplane companies by the end of 1927; Travel Air, Cessna, Stearman, Swallow, Swift,

Lark and Laird. Swift and Lark were just getting started with good designs on the drawing boards.

The businessmen of Wichita were well acquainted with what aviation could do by now, and funds for new companies building airplanes wasn't as hard to get as it was for "Jake" Moellendick way back in '23.

The other manufacturing industries in the city were taking notice, too. Although building airplanes was different from producing lanterns, building houses and the like, the Manufacturers Club of Wichita recognized the unique industry they had within their prairie city.

Walter Beech hosted the club in November, 1927 and showed them the new factory building and the second unit under construction.

In late 1927, Beech had Horace Weihmiller impressed with an idea he had been carrying around in his head for months. The monoplane had proven itself on the NAT line, and now was the time to design and produce one aimed at the businessman who flew. Weihmiller set to the task along with other Travel Air engineers early in November. Beech made it clear what he wanted in the ship, and it was up to Weihmiller and company to make it alive. The result would be most successful and worthy of the Travel Air name.

Walter didn't tell the press much about it, though. He just said Travel Air was developing a "sedan model"

Prototype Model 6000 under construction. Walter Burnham is behind fuselage, at left. (Rawdon and Burnham Collection and Wichita State University)

that businessmen who needed fast, comfortable travel capability would want. The fact that Charles Laird had a good product in the "Whippoorwill" and the knowledge that Swift was building another four-place ship may also have prompted Beech to get the ball rolling over at Travel Air.

The businessman who flew was a new market for all airplane companies. O.G. Harned, who had been a dealer back east, worked sales and marketing and was the direct representative from the factory. He was kept very busy flying demonstrations for prospective customers and probing the market to see what they thought a monoplane ship should have to succeed.

The year of 1927 was ending on a very good note for Travel Air. The stock had a value of only $50 in 1925, but now it cost $100-150 per share and was difficult to buy as Travel Air was not a selling stock.

Capitalization was only $50,000 in 1925, but was a solid $200,000 now. Ms. Mellor was happy to report that, according to her records, Travel Air literally had an order for every day of 1928! Two hundred airplanes had been built since the company started. Sales had seen 162 Model B, 16 Model BW, 5 Model BH biplanes and 18 monoplanes built and delivered by December 31, 1927.

Walter Beech and Horace Weihmiller had those kinds of figures to chat about as they traveled eastward to attend a meeting in Washington, D.C. Manufacturers from across the nation had been called by the Department of Commerce to get together with the government and discuss changes to the present air regulations. After that event the two men went to Chicago for the big Aeronautical Exposition. Travel Air was there and the exposition afforded Beech and Weihmiller a good chance to talk with others in the industry and exchange views and ideas.

After returning home Beech was busy directing the move into the second factory building. He was just a supervisor, as his men knew what machines went where and how things should be, but Walter was always out in the factory for two reasons — he wanted his workers to know that he was interested in their work and well being,

Wingspan of 48 feet, 7 inches gave new monoplane good low-speed handling and landing control, a point of importance for pilots unfamiliar with monoplanes. (Beech Aircraft Corporation)

Model 6000 was billed as "Limousine of the Air" and featured comfortable cabin to prove it. The prototype, serial #230, stands ready for Clarence Clark. (Beech Aircraft Corporation)

and that the president of the company wasn't above getting his hands dirty. In fact, he often worked on the floor side by side with other workers. Beech also let the men know he wanted every ounce of effort they could put out. A day's wage for a day's work was Walter Beech's motto, and he meant it. Workmen still remember well the times Beech walked through the factory and observed each worker carefully. He wasn't beyond a verbal "kick in the tail" if anyone was caught slouching on the job. Get caught too many times and it was "out the door." Although a fair man, Walter Beech demanded 100% from everyone he was associated with.

With the second factory occupied by late December, 1927, the Travel Air work force was increased to 250 men with another 100 to be added. The order book overflow was beginning to get smaller now. The new factory was a blessing, and the work load was able to hold its own against the order book for the first time in nearly two years. Meanwhile, a new Travel Air was ready to fly.

Clarence Clark flew the Caminez Travel Air on December 14 and found it handled very well, although the engine took some getting used to. That propeller looked like it was windmilling out there it turned so slowly. Beech took the airplane up later in the day and wrung it out to his satisfaction. He was pleased with the ship, and a production run featuring this engine seemed likely. A young engineer by the name of Herbert Rawdon was responsible for the design details of the ship. He had been assigned by Beech and Weihmiller to

Horace E. Weihmiller, designer of the Model 6000, poses next to his creation. Weihmiller left Travel Air to design the Corman Tri-Motor transport, which eventually became the basis of Stinson's tri-motor airliner. (Mal Holcomb)

adapt the Caminez into the basic Model B airframe.

Fliers, Inc. of Albany, New York had purchased the Caminez-powered Travel Air. A representative was sent to take delivery as soon as Travel Air was through tests and certification with the Department of Commerce.

Travel Air ended 1927 with sales of $642,192 and a profit after taxes of $68,385. The future looked bright, and indeed it was. 1928 and 1929 would be banner years for Travel Air.

Business was good. About the only thing causing a

Interior of prototype Model 6000, licensed X4765. Wicker seats were later upholstered on most production ships. Crank windows were idea of Ted Cochran and worked well. Throttle is on left sidewall, crank for wing landing lights in headliner. (Beech Aircraft Corporation)

problem was spruce shipments. With seven airplane companies in one town it was hard to ship in enough good spruce to meet all the demand. Stockpiles were increased, but some of the factories were short. The spruce came from stocks in the northwest United States, and it took some months and urgings from Wichita until adequate supplies were coming in.

Early in January, 1928, Travel Air again heard from Benny Griffin. He wanted to set an endurance record with the "Oklahoma." Since he was not successful in the Dole race, perhaps he would be in staying aloft longer than anyone else.

The monoplane was brought in the shop and underwent modifications to the fuel tank system. It wasn't alone, though. The "Woolaroc" was there, too. Art Goebel had the same idea. He and Griffin even thought about making it a dual airplane record attempt — two Travel Air ships after the same record at the same time!

Goebel had flown the "Woolaroc" over 10,000 miles since August, and she needed overhaul and recover. Large sheets of fabric piled on the floor near the airplane as it was stripped of the original cotton cover.

Many of the workers cut patches and kept them for souvenirs. The Whirlwind had been looked at by Wright technicians earlier and pronounced in perfect shape, so little was required for the engine. The fuel tanks were increased to 525 gallons capacity for both the "Woolaroc" and the Griffin ship, renamed "Peerless Princess" after the city of Wichita.

Both airplanes had all navigation equipment removed to save weight. The air-minded men of Wichita were trying to raise a $7,500 purse to be offered for the endurance flight. Goebel and Griffin intended to make the flight at Wichita, but weren't sure if Travel Air Field would be long enough. At that time the main north-south grass runway was only 2,500 feet long — not long enough for two heavy, fuel-laden monoplanes to make a safe takeoff.

As a solution, preparations were made to use the California section to the southwest of Travel Air Field. A survey was made and grading work started on a mile-long runway. Neither pilot had chosen a co-pilot as yet, but Goebel was anxious to use Billy Parker if possible. Parker was still flying in the J-5 biplane demonstrating and advertising "Nu-Aviation" gasoline to prospective customers.

After modifications Griffin took the "Peerless Princess" down to Oklahoma City where a special set of fuel dump valves were installed. The valves would release fuel should an emergency arise, lowering the airplane's landing weight to a safe amount. Griffin was financially supported by the Southern Kansas Stage Line for his endurance attempt, but both he and Goebel began to have second thoughts about making the flight at Wichita. Perhaps it was the money — only $5,000 had been raised.

Goebel cited the field elevation of about 1,400 feet made it unlikely the "Woolaroc" could get airborne and climb sufficiently with the wings installed on the plane. A set of larger wings was required, but he did not have the money to procure them. Travel Air didn't really have the time to build them, either!

Both Goebel and Griffin knew cities in Texas were offering up to $15,000 for an endurance flight, and that temptation (coupled with the fact that one Texas city was almost at sea level elevation) probably swayed both pilots to seek either Texas or Florida as likely sites.

No endurance flights were attempted at Wichita. Art Goebel finally decided to retire the "Woolaroc," at least

Travel Air factory, summer, 1928. Boxing ring at left saw much action, had night lighting, too. X4765 is in foreground. Travel Air No. 1, with C241 on top wing is at far left near Factory "A." It was traded in by O.E. Scott for Model 4000 with J-5. Beech allowed $3,600 for C241, about what it cost when sold to O. E. Scott and Harold Bixby in April, 1925. (Madge and Dean Edwards)

for the time being, and Clarence Clark flew the ship down to a storage hangar at Arkansas City on February 5, 1928. But Goebel would be back for her in the near future with yet another flight on his mind.

The engineering offices at Travel Air were really busy. Horace Weihmiller was still working on the design of the "sedan" monoplane Beech had wanted to build. The company was running a first-ever market survey to determine the sales potential for such a ship, and the returns were very favorable.

Travel Air was busy getting more publicity down in St. Louis. Lindbergh had just flown his old air mail route, but in a new Travel Air biplane. Robertson ordered three of the modified Model BW's, with three 20-gallon fuel tanks located in the upper wings and center section. Mail and express was carried in the forward cockpit area.

Beech flew the first ship, the fuselage painted a deep maroon with silver wings, to St. Louis on February 19, 1928. Two days later "Lindy" flew it to Chicago.

Walter Beech got on the telephone and called Olive Ann Mellor back in Wichita. He told her of Lindbergh's satisfaction with the airplane and his flight on the air mail route. Ms. Mellor was to get that information over to the newspapers quick! It was good publicity, and Walter knew how to make it work.

The factory was on double shift with nearly 300 men working day and night to catch up production deficits. Another section of the company opened its doors for business in March. Travel Air Transportation, Inc. was available for charter, sightseeing rides or long-distance flights. Three ships were kept ready at all times. The department was run by Walter Beech's old friend and associate from the early days, W.H. "Pete" Hill. Pete and Walter flew together at Arkansas City in 1920, where Beech got some of his early flying experience with the Williams-Hill Co. Hill had helped Walter get hired on part-time at Swallow in 1921.

April 15, 1928 was another banner day for Travel Air. The prototype enclosed monoplane, much discussed in

aviation circles, was rolled out for its first flight.

Billed as the "Limousine of the Air" the new Travel Air was another innovation that would put the company ahead of the competition.

Painted overall Travel Air blue and carrying registration number X4765, Clarence Clark was first to take the monoplane up.

It handled beautifully. Travel Air expected to go into quantity production of the ship, christened the Model 6000, as soon as possible. Jigs were being readied for the fuselage tubing, wings and empennage. The production line was also making room.

The prototype 6000 was powered with the Wright Whirlwind J-5C of 200 hp. Six seats were provided in the cabin. The ship had a novel arrangement of side-by-side or "DEP" controls. Two doors on the right side of the fuselage gave entry, one at the rear for the cabin passengers and one up front for the "relief pilot" or another passenger.

Wing span was 48 feet, 7 inches using a Gottingen 398 airfoil section employed by Weihmiller. Overall length was 30 feet, 10-1/2 inches and height was 8 feet, 8-1/2 inches.

Empty weight was 2,200 lbs. with a gross weight of 3,800 lbs. Payload was 506 lbs. Top speed in early test flights hit 128 mph, with a cruise of 105 mph.

Axelson used Travel Air biplane, designated Model A-4000, for demonstration and service test use with their 150 hp radial. (Beech Aircraft Corporation)

Olive Ann Mellor (right) accepts letter for Detroit Women's Aeronautical Association from June Harrison Meyer. Olive Ann and Mildred Park flew in William Emery's custom-built Model 4000 to Detroit in July, 1928 and personally delivered the letter. (Roger Tengwall)

Landing speed was 50 mph and rate of climb 700 fpm (feet per minute) with a service ceiling of 12,000 feet. Clark was able to get the ship off the ground fully loaded in a no wind condition in 720 feet, and land in 300 feet with brakes. The cabin was heated and the wicker-style chairs were quickly removeable, permitting conversion to hauling express or bulky loads.

One feature that was added on late in the design stage was roll-down, automobile-type windows. Ted Cochran, a master woodworker for years and one of the foremen at Travel Air, designed this system.

The idea went over great with Beech and Weihmiller. By using this system the passengers would be able to lower their windows for ventilation on the ground and in flight. Only the cabin windows carried this feature, and were of plate glass construction.

Walter Beech took the new ship on the Kansas Air Tour in June of 1928, and nearly 100,000 people saw the airplane. Many demonstration rides were given and some sales resulted.

In September, Sales Manager O.G. Harned flew the 6000 on a good-will tour to the middle west and eastern states. He knew how to sell as well as anybody. Harned covered over 3,200 miles, giving 700 people demonstration flights. The figures at the end of the tour showed average speed to be over 100 mph, with the Whirlwind using 11 gallons per hour.

Beech had preceeded Harned by flying the ship out east in June, where he got 14 firm orders. Not bad for a few days hard work and flying.

That kind of work was pleasant for Beech, and he was glad to keep the factory rolling along producing Travel Air monoplanes. He expected great things from this design and it was becoming apparent he and the company would not go unrewarded.

The board of directors, Beech, Snook and other company officers had to fight off another "buy" attempt in June, 1928. The trio of Lindbergh-Robertson-Knight offered $275 per share of Travel Air stock, and enticed the company to move to St. Louis where more money and expansion funds were readily available. They were turned down, like all the others who had tried in vain to lure Travel Air away from the "Peerless Princess."

There was no reason for the Travel Air organization to move anywhere, any time. The racing events and the new Model 6000 were sparking sales. Sales figures showed that Travel Air was averaging almost $12,000 per day.

With all that success and still more on the way, other financial concerns were bound to look at Travel Air as a desirable possession. A group of men in Chicago were interested in talking with Travel Air officials about acquiring an interest in the company.

They offered a 2-1/2 for one stock issue, but an interesting twist of events had a large influence in the final decision by the men of Travel Air.

Thad Carver, from Pratt, Kansas had been associated with Travel Air since 1925. He was one of the board members who listened with interest to the Chicago offer. He and his wife were traveling through Chicago when Mrs. Carver took sick and was recovering well enough to return home.

Carver met one of his banking friends while in the windy city, and the two men were close enough friends that Carver told him about the Chicago deal.

Carver's friend was not very impressed with what he heard. He told Carver that Travel Air had worked too hard to get where it was. The company was worth more than a 2-1/2 for 1 offer, and he knew some people back east who would agree with him.

After returning to Wichita, Carver expressed his friend's view to the board of directors. Based on that information and their own hesitancy to sell any of the company, Travel Air refused any further negotiations with the Chicago organization. They would wait and see what Carver's friend could do back east. After all, they were obligated to do what was best for the company, the stockholders and themselves.

Meanwhile, the first Model 6000 monoplanes were slowly reaching the point of production. Tooling was still in the works, and the factory was making ready every department to ensure a smooth, uninterrupted production flow. The new cabin monoplane was expected to grow in such popularity that biplane sales would begin to shrink, but no one expected the good old biplane models to disappear.

Beech, looking at his marketing analysis, concluded that the ratio of open ships to enclosed ones would run about 60/40 — 60% of production would be biplanes with open cockpits, the other 40% being closed cabin jobs. The analysis was not far off initially, but the cabin monoplanes would eventually consume more than 40% of the production quota.

Just as monoplanes were gaining in popularity in 1928, the popularity of the Wright Whirlwind engine had spurred Wright Aeronautical to develop more powerful versions. The result was the Wright "Cyclone" of 525 hp at 1,900 rpm.

Over at the Stearman factory, Lloyd Stearman got one of the early Cyclones for his large air mail job, known as "Speedmail." Varney contracted for the ship, but there wasn't enough room in the Stearman factory to store the

William Emery's special DW-4000 with Warner "Scarab" of 110 hp, tight nose fairing. Note cuffs around landing gear shock cord and wing root. New "speed wings" are installed. Serial #708, licensed C6269. (Beech Aircraft Corporation)

The new "Woolaroc" as it appeared in November, 1928. Goebel had cockpit moved aft, "Wasp" engine installed and minor drag cleanup done. Top speed was 160 mph, but not fast enough for a transcontinental speed record attempt. Visibility from pilot position was very restricted. (Beech Aircraft Corporation)

engine, and it was put on display in the front window of the Innes Dry Goods store.

Ladies who were "window shopping" must have got quite a surprise to see the big engine sitting in the same window with fabrics and lace!

Travel Air had ordered 35 Whirlwind engines back in January of 1927 — a supply that was quickly dwindled as the J-5 Model BW gained popularity. It was the largest single J-5 order Wright had received up to that time, and by late 1928 Travel Air was ordering more Wright engines than ever before. Wright was also coming out with other static radials, too.

The Whirlwind's basic design was used to produce the J-5 of 220 hp, and J-6 of 165, 225 and 300 hp. These engines were five, seven and nine cylinder respectively. They were not too expensive either, with the J-6, R-540 model of 165 hp costing $3,000, the 225 hp J-6, R-760 was $3,900 and the J-6, R-975 model of 300 hp cost $4,800.

Guy Vaughan, vice president of Wright Aeronautical, voiced the impact his company's engine was having on the burgeoning aviation industry. He noted that before Lindbergh flew the Atlantic, Wright produced about 35 engines per month — after Lindbergh's epic flight the factory was hard pressed to deliver the 160 units per month that were needed.

Everybody having any connection with aviation was doing good business by 1928. Travel Air was no exception to this rule. Orders were obtained from almost every one of the 70 nationwide dealers.

With the introduction of the enclosed cabin monoplane, Travel Air decided to change the numbering system of all remaining models. This "thousand" series system was put into effect early in 1928. The production models were now known by these designations: Model B became Model 2000, the Hispano-Suiza (Wright Model A or E) Model BH became the Model 3000, the Model BW with the famous Whirlwind now became the Model 4000.

Three other models came into existence. The Caminez engine installation on a Model 4000 airframe was called the Model 8000. Installation of the Ryan-Siemens engine was known as the Model 9000. The Model 5000 and 6000 monoplanes continued with their same designations.

The cabin biplane Model CW of 1926-27 was built in very limited numbers after the appearance of the monoplanes. Known as the Model 7000, only one additional example was ordered in 1928.

Some "hot projects" were going on upstairs at factory "A" in the summer of 1928. The engineering section was developing a new wing to replace the standard airfoil on some ships, and would be offered as an option on others.

The old Travel Air No. 1 airfoil was great for low speed handling, but restricted top speed as a result. The Fage and Collins section had done a good job for Travel Air, and would continue to be offered. But something better was needed.

Pilots wanted not only good looks in an airplane, but more power and speed, too. Higher horsepower engines were not the best way to attain such goals. Aerodynamic improvements were needed.

A new airfoil, called the "Speed Wing," was thinner in cross-section than the Fage and Collins and offered better performance.

Ted Wells went to Wichita to take delivery of a J-5 Model 4000 in the spring of 1928. When he arrived, his ship was being used to test an early production set of speed wings. He accepted the airplane in that configuration. The speed wing airfoil section allowed im-

Travel Air workers enlarged side windows after initial flights. Full instrument panel and compass installation show up clearly. Goebel gave up idea of speed dashes with this airplane and returned it to factory in December, 1928. Winstead Brothers reconfigured ship to Dole race appearance and it was placed in special museum building at the Phillips Ranch, where it rests today. (Beech Aircraft Corporation)

Early in 1928, design changes were incorporated in the Model 6000 series. Cabin photo shows one example—throttle, mixture and spark controls were placed in quadrant on instrument panel. (Beech Aircraft Corporation)

proved top speed and cruise performance for some sacrifice in stall speed and takeoff/landing speed.

Wells flew the ship out to the Colorado Springs air meet in August, 1928, where he won speed and climb events.

Travel Air had put a set of experimental speed wings on a J-5 Model 4000 that was used in the Atlanta air races in July, 1928.

Travel Air really cleaned up the winnings at Atlanta. The factory team won every event, yielding only one second place to another make. The engineers had succeeded in creating a faster, more attractive Travel Air without great cost and disruption of production.

But Beech kept the speed wings quiet, even after the Atlanta victory. Not until the Colorado Springs air meet did Travel Air go public with the speed wing development.

Art Goebel came back for the "Woolaroc" in August. The ship had been sitting idle for nearly seven months, and when Goebel and Pete Hill flew to Arkansas City they could not get the Whirlwind started.

Hill concluded the magnetos were dead, so they returned to Wichita, got a good set, and soon had the "Woolaroc" flying again.

Goebel flew the airplane to Los Angeles where he

Popular 6000-B had Wright J-6 of 300 hp. This is serial #987, originally sold to Hobi Airways of Oregon. (Beech Aircraft Corporation)

arranged to put the ship on exhibition while he was flying in the New York-Los Angeles air derby. A nice bit of publicity and notoriety work, too! The famous Travel Air would be on display while its intrepid pilot was winging his way across the nation to set another record!

On August 20, 1928, Goebel's Lockheed Vega streaked from Los Angeles to New York nonstop in 18 hours, 58 minutes.

While Art Goebel was busy flying across the country, business at the Travel Air factory was increasing. The new Warner radial engine of 110 hp was fitted to a Model 4000 airframe and the Curtiss "Challenger" radial was also installed, resulting in two more prototype models.

Since the numbering system had progressed from 2000 through 9000, Travel Air decided to use the engine letter, such as "W" for Warner and "C" for Challenger as a prefix for each Model 4000 variant. The Warner "Scarab" became the W-4000 and the Challenger the C-4000.

There would be other engines to mate with the Travel Air airframe, too. One was the Axelson radial.

Formerly the FLOCO, which stood for Frank L. Odenbreit CO., the engine design rights were bought by J.C. Axelson in 1928. Axelson was a supplier of oil field equipment and decided to get into the aircraft engine business. When he purchased the FLOCO design, it had already cost its developers nearly 1 million dollars and nine years of work.

The engine sold for $3,500 and developed 150 hp at 1,800 rpm. A Model 4000 was purchased by Axelson to test the engine/airframe combination under the designation of A-4000.

What Travel Air was experiencing was the same trend all the airplane manufacturers were — that of new engines coming on the market that enabled better performance without high cost of purchase or maintenance.

The competition between airframe builders now spread to engine builders, too, creating a market and keeping prices in line.

By August, 1928, it was very apparent that the Model 6000 was going to be a good product for Travel Air. All the market research was paying off, and the last week of August witnessed a landmark in production: 52% of the license applications for Department of Commerce approval were Travel Air airplanes!

One of those ships that was licensed was William Emery's custom-built DW-4000. It was outfitted for the air derby from New York to Los Angeles, where he placed third in the Class A competition.

Early in October, 1928, Walter Beech and Earl Hutton went to New York to discuss business with eastern financiers, namely Hayden, Stone and Co., who had connections with the Wright Aeronautical Group. Upon return to Wichita, Beech and Hutton had nothing to disclose to the press about their visit except that a basic agreement had been discussed whereby Hayden Stone and Co. would purchase 50% of Travel Air and would admit Travel Air into the Wright Aeronautical Group.

Soon after his eastern trip, Beech flew to the Los Angeles Aeronautical Exposition in a Model 6000 along with Harned, Ira McConaughey, and Marcellus Murdock, owner of the Wichita Eagle newspaper. The monoplane flew many times while there, and several firm sales were acquired. Two of the customers were Wilbur D. May and Wallace Beery. Beery had been flying his J-4 Model BW and although he liked the ship, he really liked the comfort and performance of the Model 6000. He sat down with Beech and told him what he wanted installed in his airplane. Mr. May did the same. Selling to both men was quite an accomplishment, and Beech returned home all smiles.

O.G. Harned had more work to do, though. He was preparing to go east and set up a permanent sales base for the eastern half of the nation. He would be in charge of eight sales agencies. Travel Air was experimenting with a new system of selling that it hoped would yield more orders.

The publicity Travel Air was gathering throughout the last year was really having an impact on the order books. The Dole race, Atlanta, Colorado Springs air meets, the New York to Los Angeles air derby and more had brought the customers in, ready to buy.

Sales hit an all-time high of $93,485 in one week! People were beginning to wonder if this was really happening. How much longer could aviation and Travel Air sales keep getting better and better?

It seemed like Travel Air could never get racing out of its system — one reason being it helped get the product before the public and it advanced aviation technology.

A special two-place, clipped wing biplane known around the factory as the "bug" was built in September, 1928. Although powered with an OX-5, the fuselage was five inches narrower than standard and the biplane was streamlined. It was also fast — for an OX-5 ship. The airplane could do over 120 mph, and that fact made her a new menace to the 90 hp class events at races. With speed like that the "bug" shouldn't have any trouble beating the competition.

Wallace Beery ordered custom-built A-6000-A with 420 hp "Wasp" and special interior furnishings. Beery's airplane is shown in fuselage assembly area. Note window cranks and workmanship on wood. Heywood pneumatic starter is barely visible at rear of engine. (Beech Aircraft Corporation)

Ira McConaughey flew the "bug" to victory at Newton, Kansas in early October. Plans were to install a Warner "Scarab" in the near future to boost performance even more. The record is unclear as to whether this was ever done.

Art Goebel flew the "bug" to Jackson, Mississippi for air racing in early November. He liked the nimble little ship and named it "The Chaparral." But he had other things on his mind beside racing around pylons.

Frank Phillips wanted to get more publicity out of the "Woolaroc" and Goebel had been entertaining ideas about another transcontinental speed dash, planned for November.

Goebel talked to Beech about his plans, which called for the mild-mannered "Woolaroc" to be transformed into a Wasp-powered, slicked-up speedster. Walter Beech and the engineering staff had some doubts about this idea. They knew the monoplane only had the potential for so much speed, but if Art wanted a fast Model 5000, then Travel Air would do their best to meet the challenge.

Goebel flew the ship back to Wichita from Los Angeles and it disappeared into the workshop. The factory was shooting for a deadline of November 20, as Goebel wanted to fly that night as a full moon was available to help him navigate the route.

Art Goebel admitted he liked to fly with a full moon in the night sky, as did other pilots, because it helped by not having to fly on instruments all the time. If the ground was bathed in a soft moonlight, visual references were much more pronounced.

Workmen started modifications on the "Woolaroc" by dismantling the cockpit entirely. The pilot seat, rudder pedals, instrument board, and all controls were removed.

More fuel tanks were installed in that position, bringing the total fuel available to 600 gallons.

Goebel would sit where Bill Davis sat in the Dole race:

Beery's airplane, serial #816, licensed NC9015. Famous actor took delivery on December 14, 1928. Wings had 60 square feet of extra area, were strengthened for 420 hp radial and carried 130 gallons of fuel, a necessity for the thirsty Pratt & Whitney powerplant. Beery paid $20,000 for the ship, making it the most expensive Travel Air ever built. (Beech Aircraft Corporation)

in the aft compartment. A new instrument panel was built that held all flight and engine instruments, including a complete set of "blind" flying equipment.

A special seat arrangement was designed. A hole was built into the fuselage top above the pilot seat, and this would be open when Goebel needed to raise the seat. This was done by a "tripper" device, as Travel Air called it, that allowed the seat to elevate enough for Goebel to be in the open slip-stream. This would be helpful for takeoff and landing, as the ship would be very difficult to see out of from the aft position. That big wing just blocked out all visibility forward (This fact was mentioned to Goebel by Travel Air engineers, but Goebel insisted the aft cockpit would suffice.)

After takeoff Goebel could lower the seat and remain in the cabin enclosure during flight. Windows were provided on each side of the compartment, with the original door remaining for entry/exit on the right side.

The cockpit cupola was removed and the forward, upper fuselage completely faired over with fabric sheet. It looked good, and did help the drag reduction efforts.

A 400 hp Pratt & Whitney "Wasp" engine was installed, with individual exhaust stacks referred to as "bayonet" designs because of their appearance.

Despite hard work, Travel Air wasn't able to meet Goebel's deadline of November 20, but they did have the reborn "Woolaroc" ready by November 24, 1928.

Goebel inspected the ship and liked what had been done. Every drag reducing detail that was feasible had been accomplished. Even the landing gear was modified to present a smaller profile.

It was time to fly it. Goebel got in, posed for a few pictures and then fired up the big Wasp. The Pratt & Whitney settled into an idling lope, the exhaust stacks barking loudly.

Preflight checks were good. Art pushed the throttle forward. Acceleration was rapid, but visibility was almost non-existent! He was trying the takeoff from inside the compartment, without seeing through the opening above him by raising the seat. He looked out the windows and judged the situation as best he could.

Once airborne there was no problem. Walter Beech took off in a J-5 Model 4000 to check the speed performance of the monoplane and quickly found he couldn't keep up!

Full throttle yielded 160 MPH on the "Woolaroc's" airspeed indicator. Not bad, but not good enough. Cruise at 1,900 rpm was a disappointing 135 mph, as 160 mph was needed to break a transcontinental record. Goebel was discouraged, but hoped the ship would be fast enough to clinch another victory.

Art Goebel hadn't bargained for what happened next. He had trouble on the takeoff, but he really had his hands full of wandering, wild "Woolaroc" on landing.

The ship hit, bounced, hit again and bounced, Goebel feeding in bursts of power to keep her flying. He finally got the airplane on the ground and rolled to a stop, cut the switches and found Walter Beech.

Goebel told Walter what it was like to fly the ship, and asked if a quick fix couldn't be worked up so he could take off for New York.

Beech put men on the problem immediately. They lowered the seat further, cut the windows to a larger size and that was all they could do. Goebel made a test hop, found the visibility forward had improved and landed easily. He took off for New York.

It was dark when he arrived over St. Louis. He searched for Scott field, but could not locate it. Apparently the lights had not been turned on or there was some other problem, as Goebel knew where the airport was.

Searching for any airport he could find, one was spotted and he let down for his landing attempt. He had only landed the "new Woolaroc" a few times, and he was now trying it in the dark of night, without landing lights. Although the hurry-up modification to the windows helped, the airplane was not easy to land.

The "Woolaroc" touched down safely but hit a ditch that Goebel could not have seen. The ship lurched to a stop, her main landing gear damaged on one side.

That was it for Goebel. The next few days were spent repairing the airplane. When he took off he was headed for Travel Air Field. But Goebel got one more scare on the way.

Flying in a foggy mist on the west side of St. Louis, a water tower flashed past the side window, narrowly missing the wing. All Art Goebel could do was keep flying, and keep wondering why he had modified a perfectly good airplane into one that almost killed him. He landed at Wichita on December 1, 1928 and told Walter Beech and Frank Phillips he could not safely fly the ship.

Goebel remembered the water tower incident. He also remembered how Harry Tucker and his pilot, flying the same Vega he flew to a transcontinental victory earlier, were killed when the airplane hit a mountain ridge in the dark.

Phillips and Beech agreed with Goebel. The airplane was historically important and would be returned to its original configuration by Carl and Guy Winstead.

Frank Phillips then retired the ship. After it was reconfigured it was placed in a special museum built expressly for the purpose of preserving the "Woolaroc."

Back at Travel Air, market success with the Model 6000 was good, but her chief designer, Horace Weihmiller, left Travel Air to design the Corman Tri-Motor, a very attractive, three-engine monoplane.

One unfortunate incident with the prototype Model 6000 occurred before Horace Weihmiller left Travel Air. Weihmiller designed the fairing strips either side of the upper and lower main longerons to present a pleasing, semi-curved appearance when the covering was installed. He used 1/4" x 1-1/8" strips for this purpose.

Following fairing installation, the fuselage was rolled into the dope room and covered. Two coats of dope were then sprayed on and the fuselage left to sit overnight. The next morning found the fuselage strips scalloped and deformed from the tightening of the fabric. Beech was not pleased at all, and neither was Weihmiller. Ted

Cochran redesigned the fairing with a tapered edge and installed them in slightly different positions to correct the problem the next day.

Horace Weihmiller stayed with Corman until 1930, went with Ford as an engineer in their aeronautic division from 1930 to 1932, from there he went to Consolidated and finally to Republic Aviation Corporation. He had a long and very distinguished career in aviation and must be ranked as one of the best aeronautical engineers of his time.

Herb Rawdon assumed duties as lead engineer along with Walter Burnham, Cecil Barlow, and Howard Bacchus, who were working hard at improving the 6000 in the spring of 1928. The prototype Model 6000 had drawbacks — it was just a bit undersized and the cabin, while roomy, needed expansion.

The engineering staff worked out the solutions. The fuselage structure and wings were restressed to take any engine up to 300 hp. The forward cabin was widened 4 inches and lengthened 5 inches. The fuselage immediately forward of the horizontal stabilizer was also widened 4 inches.

The throttle was relocated to the center of the cabin and attached to the instrument panel. It had been on the left side in the prototype ship. Three levers on the control quadrant were for throttle, mixture and spark.

The forward door was eliminated, although some production ships did have it installed if the customer desired.

The crank mechanism in the cabin side windows was improved and the dimensions of the windows changed to 32 x 15 inches for greater visibility.

Another departure from the prototype was the use of a tailwheel instead of a skid, and it featured an Aerol shock strut assembly. Bendix wheel brakes were standard equipment with 36 x 8 tires.

A special DuPont fabric was used for the production interior cloth, but more plush and expensive fabrics could be selected by the customer.

The chairs were of wicker construction, retained to the floor by a socket-to-chair leg arrangement, and were quickly removeable for cargo purposes. The front right seat also could be removed. This was done when items of long length were carried.

The first production Model 6000, serial number 790, registered NC6469, was delivered to Wilbur D. May. Wallace Beery came to Wichita to take delivery of his ship, serial number 816, registered NC9015, on December 14, 1928.

Pete Hill drove up to Newton and picked Beery up in one of Travel Air's company cars. With Beery was his pilot, "Slim" Maves. Beery had flown many hours since he had his J-4 Model BW, and he earned his transport pilot license.

The famous actor was sick with influenza, but maintained his cheery disposition. He was brought to the factory and introduced to the women in the front office.

They enjoyed Beery immensely, being fans of his, as were most other people, too!

Besides shaking hands and exchanging smiles, Beery was carrying out some business in the office, too. He had to pay the balance remaining on the airplane. As he was talking to Olive Ann, he produced a wad of money in the amount of $10,000! Mr. Beery paid in cash.

The girls of the office got a real treat after Beery left. Olive Ann let them feel $10,000 in their hands for a few moments each.

Beery was very proud of his new Travel Air. The interior was plush. All seats were upholstered in velMur,

Serial #6B-2028, licensed NC449N had special divan installed along with full toilet/washroom facilities. (Beech Aircraft Corporation)

Toilet/washroom compartment was frequently found on ships used for airline service. A vomit tube was also included in the cabin floor for airsick passengers. (Beech Aircraft Corporation)

A-6000-A, serial #963 was used by Central Air Lines of Wichita. Landing lights are cranked down. The A-6000-A answered the need of buyers who wanted more power than standard Model 6000-B. (Beech Aircraft Corporation)

and the couch Beery had ordered was upholstered in a special mauve velour material. He intended to nap in flight and wanted a nice, comfortable place to do so. He got it.

The airplane also had hot and cold running water and a toilet. Holding tanks housed the water and a heating element provided the hot water. A folding card table in the cabin completed the special order items. The interior options cost Beery $1,000.

All these luxuries were inside the cabin where everyone could see them, but Travel Air engineers had also put some changes deep within the monoplane's frame.

To handle the 420 hp Wasp's power the wings were braced with additional steel tubing and the wings area increased by 60 sq. ft., allowing for increased fuel capacity from 80 gallons to 130 gallons. Total wing area was 340 sq. ft.

The big Wasp would need the extra fuel, as it burned much more than the standard Wright J-5 of 200 hp. Total cost of the airplane was $20,000. It was the most expensive Travel Air ever built. The Dole racers came close, but Beery topped their cost.

Walter Beech and Beery finished inspecting the airplane and Walter suggested they all go out to the Crown Uptown theater that night. A flying movie was showing and it was also "Travel Air night."

Clarence Clark had finished test hopping the ship a few days earlier, when the upper fuselage fabric came loose because of high airspeed. A better method of attachment cured the problem and all "Wasp" powered 6000's retained this improvement. Pete Hill and Wallace Beery were very enthusiastic about every detail of how the airplane flew and felt in the air. Beery was pleased and flew the ship himself later in the day and then flew about two hours with Maves in the late afternoon.

It had been two months since Travel Air and the eastern financiers had worked out an agreeable arrangement to allow Hayden, Stone and Company to buy 50% of Travel Air. The rumors were no more, and Travel Air was no longer a possession of Wichita alone. Beech travelled east once again to finalize the deal.

The agreement dissolved the original Travel Air Mfg. Co., Inc., and reorganized it under Delaware law as the Travel Air Co. One hundred thousand shares of new stock were issued, shares going to original Travel Air stockholders of record on a 20 to 1 basis. Shares were also issued to the Hayden, Stone and Company officials, along with Jackson and Curtiss, a partner firm.

The 4,000 shares of Travel Air stock before the agreement were held in escrow by L.C. Kelly, the appointed trustee. Each share of the new stock was worth $18.75. One of the central figures in the deal was Richard F. Hoyt, official of the Wright Aeronautical Corporation, Keystone and Loening. Travel Air now became another cog in the wheel of fortune.

Walter Beech and the board of directors felt they had made a very good business decision for the company and the stockholders.

The eastern group was happy, too. They had been able to do what no one else could — buy into one of the largest commercial airplane factories in the United States. Hoyt also was quick to point out that they wanted to see Travel Air grow, and plans were being made to expand the factory now that the needed funds were readily available. He was also firm during the discussions with Travel Air that Walter Beech remain with the company as part of the agreement. They wanted his leadership capabilities within their ranks.

The board of directors at Travel Air included some new faces and names. As established by January 1, 1929 the members were: Richard F. Hoyt, Chairman of the Board, Walter H. Beech, President. Captain F.T. Courtney, Harold Fowler, S.R. Reed and Chandler Hovey were also members. Members of the board who retained their status were Thad Carver, Jack Turner, C.G. Yankey and G.A. "Bo" Stearns.

Travel Air was buying the entire East Central flying field as soon as the city's lease expired. Wichita had paid the Booster Building Association $17,000 for the field in 1928, but plans were concentrating on developing the California section as the municipal airport.

Glen A. Thomas was once again selected as architect for the newest unit addition, factory "C." The board of directors authorized construction of the building in early December, 1928, and the bids were let by K.K. Shaul, comptroller for Travel Air, with assistance from

Jack Turner and Mr. Engstrom.

The Underhill Construction Co. won the bidding and the ground directly south of factory "A" was the site for the third unit. A smaller building, 40'x 50' in size would be added between "A" and "C" to serve as a parts room and experimental shop. The actual factory "C" would be another duplicate of the first two units, being 75'x 275'.

Travel Air detailed some of its own workers to start leveling the ground so Underhill could get right to work. The factory was needed as soon as possible and the finish date was estimated as early March, 1929.

Travel Air Co. spent the remainder of 1928 doing the high volume business they had done all through the year.

Louise McPhetridge, now Mrs. Louise McPhetridge Von Thaden, who was running the Oakland branch office for D.C. Warren, made Travel Air proud in December, 1928. She prepared for an assault on the altitude record, using a Model 3000 with the high-compression Hispano-Suiza engine of 180 hp.

Her Travel Air was ready, tuned to perfection by mechanics. She departed Oakland and climbed slowly, the Hisso purring under the cowling.

By 15,000 feet the temperature had dropped to near zero and Louise donned her improvised oxygen mask. Using a pair of pliers she opened the valve on the oxygen cylinder and breathed normally.

Passing through 20,000 feet she opened the valve a little more. Cold, wet moisture collected on her chin from within the mask. She concentrated on climbing the Travel Air with precision — every bit of airspeed had to be held — every touch of the stick made with care.

In one hour the topography of the Oakland area shrank to a strange, new world from her perch of 27,000 feet.

Now the Travel Air became rebellious. She mushed instead of climbed; quivered in the sharp, cold stillness of high altitude flight. The wings could no longer give Louise the lift for climb, and the Hisso was gasping for air, its power spent. Louise was feeling quite tired.

The ringing in her ears was strange to Louise — something to do with the oxygen, maybe? Next thing she knew the biplane was hurling earthward in wide circles, the engine running at high power. She had passed out, the intern at the hospital being right about oxygen — Louise didn't use enough or ran out of the precious

Louise Thaden flew this Model 3000 to altitude record. Using crude oxygen equipment, she forced the Travel Air up to 20,200 feet. Note speed wing-type struts but retention of mass balance ailerons on wings. Some early speed wings may have had this arrangement, but Frize-type ailerons were most common on production speed wings. (Bill and Pat Thaden)

gas. Fresh air at the lower altitudes revived her.

Louise and the Travel Air were soon back on solid ground. 20,200 feet was the official barograph reading. Louise and the Model 3000 had made history, and they had soared to new heights that no woman had ever touched.

Travel Air, its airplanes and people aimed for accomplishment every day. They were glad to be winners.

Checking the sealed barograph from Model 3000 used for altitude attempt. A revived but somewhat disappointed Louise Thaden looks on. She had hoped for a higher altitude, but made a good showing for herself, Travel Air and D.C. Warren. (Bill and Pat Thaden)

TRAVELAIR
MFG. CO. INC.
WICHITA KANSAS

CHAPTER SEVEN
The Scarlet Marvel

Clarence Clark carefully hooked up his flight-test parachute. He wanted it to fit just right. It could get pretty uncomfortable in the tiny cockpit he was about to enter.

There, all cinched up and tight, but a little awkward to walk in. It was hot. The August sun burned down on Travel Air Field with renewed determination.

The sun was also shining down on Clark's flight test ship. He was anxious to get her in the air, because just about the whole factory wanted to see Travel Air's newest design, dubbed the Model "R," fly.

The mechanic made ready with the propeller, and Clarence was strapped in the slim fuselage, going through his checks prior to engine start.

He was ready. The engine was not equipped with an inertia starter, so the Wright was hand-cranked. Everyone was anxious. Contact! The propeller was pulled around and the R-975 burst into life, the short stacks bellowing a new song — one of power, speed and sheer sensation!

Oil pressure was good. Better taxi quick, Clarence said to himself. Keep those cylinder head temperatures down before takeoff.

R-2001 (R614K) in foreground, with R-2002 (R613K) in background, under construction. Experimental department had frosted windows, tight security against unauthorized persons. (Rawdon and Burnham Collection and Wichita State University)

The little monoplane glistened in the Kansas sun as she trundled across Travel Air Field into takeoff position. Magnetos checked, controls free — not much visibility over the nose. No problem, the tail should come up quickly. That's what Rawdon and Burnham said, anyway. Clarence rechecked everything. The runway was clear. Slowly he fed in the throttle and 420 hp pressed him back with force he had never felt before. What acceleration! A little forward stick and the tail was up immediately, just like those engineers predicted.

Seconds later the "R" had reached liftoff speed, and Clark could feel she was ready to fly. A touch of back stick and they were airborne.

Walter Beech, Herb Rawdon, Walter Burnham and other members of Travel Air watched as Clarence climbed the bright red and black ship into the sky, disappearing to the east for a 20-minute flight.

Soon Clark was back in the landing circuit. Ninety mph felt nice on final as he slipped the ship in, wishing all his test ships flew this well. With power back, he glided in nicely to the waiting grass.

A smooth transition was made from the slip to flare for landing. Gently Clarence set the Model "R" down, ending the first flight of the best-known product of Travel Air Co.

It had gone well, too. Only a few minor adjustments were needed and the ship would be ready for the Cleveland air races — starting on August 24, 1929.

Herbert Rawdon as an early employee of Travel Air, working on the Dole racers and other projects. He initiated the Model "R" concept in 1928. (Beech Aircraft Corporation)

Clarence Clark piloting the original "R." Cowling was not installed for initial flights, but ship hit 185 mph without it. (Beech Aircraft Corporation)

Herbert Rawdon and Walter Burnham had created a craft that would catch the imagination and admiration of the entire aviation world. It would be remembered long after other ships were forgotten. The Travel Air Model "R" was pure speed, grace and the epitome of performance. She was truly a scarlet marvel.

Back in the spring and summer of 1928, Herb Rawdon had been working on the Model 6000 monoplane and a few other aeronautical projects requiring his attention.

A great amount of experience had been gained by Rawdon in his association with Travel Air. He hired on with the company as a young engineer, and was brought up through the ranks under the tutelage of men like Horace Weihmiller.

Rawdon also got to know Walter Beech. He knew him well enough to know without a doubt that Beech was always out to be number 1 — whether it was in selling airplanes or winning air races.

Both Rawdon and Walter Burnham worked on projects like the Dole racers, the OX-5 "bug" and experimental ideas, too. But Rawdon often wondered what it would take to build a real racing airplane, one that could defeat any military ship then flying.

His attitude was understandable. The United States military was a little cocky when it came to air racing. They would enter a souped-up biplane and breeze by everyone on the course. They did it so regularly that it was almost a forgone conclusion who would win.

Yet men like Rawdon and Burnham knew better. The government was spending as little as possible on the air service in the 1920s and early '30s. It was peacetime and the Congress was hardly in a mood to spend millions of dollars on new aircraft. America had slipped to a low point in military power compared with some of her allies and potential enemies. About all the military flyboys could do was work with what they had.

When the racing season rolled around, usually in the fall of each year, the Army and Navy would take a standard pursuit ship and work minor miracles with it to squeeze every sliver of speed out of an obsolete design. Of course, horsepower helped, too. At their disposal were Pratt & Whitney Wasp's, Wright Cyclones, Packards and the Curtiss Conqueror. That Curtiss engine could put out over 600 hp and was glycol cooled,

too! It could be streamlined inside a beautiful cowling. And equipped with 24 very short exhaust stubs it made a terrific, but wonderful, racket.

Through streamlining and higher horsepower the pride of Uncle Sam went out to the pylons and blew the civilian boys back to the drawing board.

Herb Rawdon knew there was a way to reverse that situation. It didn't require 600 hp and glycol cooling, either. All it did require was careful, deliberate design engineering. The plight of American air strength and the sometimes contemptuous attitude of the military could both be cured if someone would take the time and effort to administer a remedy, someone like Herb Rawdon.

The young engineer began to think it over. But two heads were often better than one, so he approached a fellow engineer and friend, Walt Burnham.

Rawdon described his idea to Burnham and recalled the meeting he had quietly attended in President Beech's office, not long after the 1928 National Air Races were over. Beech was proud of Travel Air's consistent winning ways, but he also knew the hottest thing on the Travel Air flight line was a J-5 Model 4000 with speed wings. Good, but not good enough.

The little OX-5 "bug" was not really a purebred racer, and it seemed to Beech that Travel Air could come up with a real winner if they tried to.

The answer to the dilemma was clear to Walter — a special ship designed to fly fast and hard. An airplane bred from the gear up to be a winner. Then, shaking his head and holding his pipe, Beech would say it was too bad nothing like that existed.

The production line was too busy turning out cabin monoplanes and standard biplanes to be interrupted with such a project. It would cost too much. And the board of directors would have their say about the matter, too. Looked like Travel Air would have to be content with its past laurels. Beech grimaced — that just wasn't his style. He was a winner, not content to merely observe from the sideline.

Burnham listened intently as Rawdon continued his talk. The way Herb saw it, a special machine would have to be designed, built and flown without company funding, and whoever did all the work wouldn't get a dime for their efforts, just some deep satisfaction for a job well done.

But could it be done? Yes, said Rawdon. And he wanted Walt Burnham to help him make his idea a reality. From this coalition the Model "R" would emerge. It was the remedy for Walter Beech's discouragement, too. But both Rawdon and Burnham decided to keep the project quiet and work on it when time was available.

The 1929 National Air Races were one year away. The task had to be started now, not two months before the event took place. This procedure would leave enough time, hopefully, to order the materials, construct and fly the airplane.

There was one other thing Herb Rawdon was counting on with little doubt—interesting Walter Beech in the ship. If Rawdon planned it just right he would hit Walter with the plans for a racer about May or June of 1929. Beech would be turning his attention to the race season again, as he always did. He was more occupied now than ever before with running the company, but Walter was always ready to race.

Rawdon's choice of Walter Burnham was a good one. Burnham was one of the most versatile and talented engineers to work for Travel Air.

Preliminary drawings and basic layout were made. The designation for the racer was R-100, but often shortened to just "R."

Herb Rawdon had a great admiration for the sleek, low-wing monoplanes that competed for the Schneider cup from 1925 to 1928. The Schneider race was always flown from water and there was little of the ordinary found in these hybrid airplanes. Their engines were

Walter Burnham teamed with Rawdon on the R-100 and contributed his ideas to the design. (Dorothea Burnham)

both of static radial and V-bank inline design. The British Napier Lion, Bristol Mercury and the Rolls-Royce H or Buzzard engine with 12 cylinders developing about 825 hp, were powerful, indeed.

Such high-strung engines operated on very potent fuels with ingredients like benzol, methanol and tetra ethyl lead, brewed up by one of the great experts of fuels in modern times, F.R. "Rod" Banks of Great Britain.

America was in the race for the Schneider Trophy, too. Lieutenant David Rittenhouse of the Navy won in 1923 flying a Curtiss R-3 racer. The race was held at Bay Shore Park, near Baltimore, Maryland, in 1925. The British were there with a pair of Gloster-Napier biplanes and the real eye-opener—Reginald Mitchell's new super-sleek Supermarine S-4. Jimmy Doolittle won the race for the Army in a Curtiss R3C-2 seaplane.

From such machines as the Schneider Trophy racers Herb Rawdon collected his basic design. The airplane should be a low-wing monoplane, wire-braced with fixed landing gear. (This feature of fixed gear was almost automatic, as retractable assemblies were few in 1928. Also, the complexity of the gear retraction system was not tolerable from a weight standpoint, and Rawdon had no experience with retractable systems.)

Only room for a pilot would be provided. The biggest problem was a suitable powerplant. None were available in the fall of 1928 when serious design work started. At least there were no engines that satisfied Rawdon.

He seemed to be thinking about an inline engine. It would be easy to cowl, provided less drag and added to the overall appearance of the ship. Perhaps he remembered the Travel Air B6 "Special" of 1925 — he knew about the performance that "mystery ship" turned in.

The inline engine configuration was used as a basis for fuselage/powerplant mating, but all weight and balance computations were based on the Wright J-4 of 220 hp so at least some figures could be arrived at. The estimated gross weight fell at 1700 pounds.

One thing neither designer wanted was a costly mistake in calculations that would affect the project later. In view of this all stress analysis was computed using a gross weight of 1750 pounds. A flight load factor of 9.0 (9 times the design gross weight of 1750 pounds) with a safety factor of 33% was considered mandatory.

Landing gear load factor was set at 7.0. The 33% safety factor gave the "R" an ultimate load factor of 12.0, which was the standard design target for all military pursuit ships of that day. By using the safety factor Rawdon would not have to worry much if the gross weight exceeded 1,750 pounds.

By early 1929 the "R" was moving along nicely through its stress analysis and performance calculations. This stage of the project was one of the most time consuming and mentally laborious for the two Travel Air engineers. It was done on weekends and weeknights at the Rawdon house or over at the Burnham place. It was a good thing they got along together. Wives and children didn't see them much, either.

By May, Walter Beech was busy tending to a growing company that faced another eastern proposition, this time from the Wright Aeronautical group. Wright and the Curtiss company were beginning to talk of merging, and this would involve Travel Air as they were now a part of the Wright Aeronautical combine.

In May, Travel Air management was shown plans for an inline engine said to produce 275 to 300 hp. The same month Rawdon introduced Walter Beech to his basic plans for a racing ship and Beech took it from there. He was ready to go full throttle and build Herb Rawdon's racer.

A setback occurred when the proposed engine was found to be in a very underdeveloped state.

It didn't really matter to Walter Beech. That ship of Rawdon's was a winner, and Walter sustained his enthusiasm for the project.

A search was started for a powerplant that would fit the needs of the "R." One of the obvious choices that Herb and Walt knew of was the Wright R-975 of 300 hp. It was a recent development but they had much respect for Wright engines and Wright engineering. Pratt & Whitney also had a static radial in the 300 hp class and this, too, was under consideration.

But one must remember that Travel Air was a member of Wright Aeronautical, not Pratt & Whitney. Yes, it was a political situation, but Walter Beech gave Guy Vaughan, vice president of Wright Aeronautical, a chance at providing an engine. A little intercombine cooperation was expected, but Beech was met with reluctance and skepticism instead. Vaughan agreed only to investigate any possibilities, but later told Beech that Wright would work with them on the project.

Herb Rawdon was sent to the Wright factory where he spend many hours discussing performance requirements with Wright engineers. A rating of 400 hp was desired, but Wright had an experimental engine in test and evaluation with a higher supercharger ratio, yielding 420 hp at 2350 rpm.

It was all the power Rawdon hoped for, but it came in a bulky, heavy package—the radial engine. Here was another problem that had to be overcome. Dry weight of the engine was 580 pounds.

The R-975 had a special supercharger setup of 10:15 to 1, and a bore of 5 inches and a stroke of 5.5 inches. There was plenty of power available—all Rawdon and Burnham had to do was figure out a way to mate the engine to the "R."

After Herb returned to Travel Air he gave a full, detailed report to Beech. Based on the sound of things, Walter gave the "go-ahead" for the "R" to be built. But he wanted to know how the engine could be fitted without unacceptable drag penalties, due to its large frontal area.

Rawdon explained that the NACA cowl should do the trick. Beech was quite familiar with this device. Ted Wells had fitted one on his 1928 J-5 Model 4000, and it was the first ship built by Travel Air to carry the cowling. This NACA unit completely covered the engine in an attractive, round metal cowl that reduced drag, and, more importantly, it "pulled" cooling air through the cowling for good cylinder head temperature control.

But Ted Wells had found out that it also had one drawback—it wouldn't stay put! One of the early flights he made with his Travel Air uncovered the problem. He was diving on a small town enroute to an air meet when the cowl pulled forward and contacted the propeller. He realized something was wrong and landed. Very little damage was done to the cowl but the propeller was not so fortunate! He realized a better retention setup for the cowl was necessary.

The cause of the forward motion was strictly aerodynamic; the lower pressure around the cowling resulted in a movement forward at certain airspeeds.

This lesson was learned by others, but Rawdon and Burnham would encounter the same thing on the "R"

but for a somewhat different reason: the "R" was nearly 100 mph faster than the good old J-5 Travel Air!

Very soon after Herb Rawdon returned from Wright the offer of another engine was made. Arthur Chevrolet contacted Travel Air with news that a six-cylinder, air-cooled, inverted inline engine was available for installation in a racing airplane. It would develop 250 hp and had the potential of 300 hp. It was marketed as the Chevrolair D-6 and caused both Beech and Rawdon to have great interest in its possibilities. The "R" had been designed around an inline powerplant, and even though the D-6 produced less power than the Wright engine, the benefit of less drag was very appealing.

Herb and Walt knew, however, that even with a lower drag effect the lack of 300 hp would not help performance. Beech decided to solve all problems with one stroke, after all, he was president. He authorized construction of two more ships in addition to the Wright powered machine.

One was to be a sister ship to the "R" but would be powered with the Chevrolair, and the other would be a biplane with modifications for speed and a Wright Whirlwind of 240 hp.

All of this decision making occurred in early June, 1929.

Both engineers really burned the midnight oil to get performance estimates together so that propellers could be ordered.

Only 10 weeks remained until the National Air Races. Not much time to build three airplanes. Materials had to be ordered and personnel selected from within the factory to work on the ships.

Not just anyone could do the work required. The men would have to be skilled, able to work without supervision and have the ability to complete the job correctly the first time, and fast!

Simple but effective landing gear unit of Model "R." (Beech Aircraft Corporation)

A group of about 25 workers were carefully picked from the departments within Travel Air. Every one of them was informed about the project and urged to keep it quiet, even in the factory. That's one job they all did exceedingly well, as the Travel Air house organ "Currents" noted in the August, 1929 issue: "Funny business is going on around the engineering and experimental departments. Mysterious packages and boxes are being delivered at odd hours. Groups of engineers and workmen can be seen huddled here and there holding "skull practice," immediately dispersing upon the approach of an outsider."

"We have put the question fairly and squarely up to Herb Rawdon — asked him what was going on so we might pass the "low down" on to you. And from him we got no answer except that perhaps in the next issue of "Currents" he would give us a peep. Have any idea what it is? Well, so do we — but we're not telling."

Such was the aura of secrecy that shrouded the "R" project.

Ted Cochran was one of the foremen assigned to the "R" workforce. Working behind closed doors in the experimental shop was remembered by Cochran as an amusing experience in one regard.

Beech ordered all the glass windows in the shop frosted so no one could see in. It wasn't long before this odd procedure was noticed around the factory and questions started popping up. The newspapers got wind of this and headed for Travel Air Field, camera at the ready.

Cameramen climbed ladders, stood on boxes and tried every trick in the book to get a photograph of what was going on inside that room. They never succeeded. Very few reporters got any information. Eventually the

R614K sits outside Factory "D" prior to Cleveland races. Careful design for aerodynamic efficiency is evident in this view. (Beech Aircraft Corporation)

Eagle and Beacon began referring to whatever was in the experimental room as a "mystery ship" and the name stuck forever.

Woodworkers were Earl Hyatt, C. Buse, Pearl Breitweiser and a Mr. Heffley. Howard Baccus was in charge of the welding crew, consisting of Ed Libby, Ervin Krueger and Andy Bland. Al Cunningham was the man on the lathe and Carl Burnham, Walt's brother, had Dennis Pitts and Bill Pitts with him working on the sheet metal parts. Ed Libby welded the landing gear assemblies, Andy Bland welded the tail surfaces and Ervin Krueger did all the welding on the fuselages.

Under direction from Rawdon and Burnham, Al Cunningham made the fittings and many detail metal parts required for the airplanes.

Ted took spruce former strips and laid them out along the fuselage, carefully clamping them in place one by one. He then sighted down the strips and readjusted them all until a smooth contour was achieved. Inside dimensions were next measured, giving the men measurements needed to make former bulkheads to which the former strips were attached. The fuselage was covered with 1/16 inch plywood and taped between pieces to form a very smooth surface.

One big challenge for the workmen was the many compound curves found in the sides and upper fuselage area.

A plan was utilized to soak the thin plywood with very hot water. After giving each piece several dunks in the pan, it was placed on the fuselage and strapped down with shock cord. When the desired shape was obtained the piece was clamped in place and later attached permanently.

The wings were another challenge. The airfoil section was the R.A.F. 34, of constant thickness from the butt rib outboard to the flying/landing wire attach points.

From there it gradually tapered to the wingtip. The wing planform was a combination straight-elliptical shape with the ellipse occurring in the outboard section. Ribs were built up truss and were spaced at 12-inch intervals along the spars, which were made of two spruce beams glued together but not routed out.

Compression ribs were built up with spruce truss and boxed with plywood webs. Reinforcing was required at the point where the flying/landing wires attached to the internal wing fittings. Three-fourths inch maple blocks featuring a taper and feather on all sides were made and installed for this requirement.

Wing chord was 60 inches at the maximum point with a total area of 120 sq. feet. The wings were covered with Haskelite 1/16-inch plywood. Wingspan was 29 feet 2 inches with the incidence set at 2.25 degrees with a 4 degree dihedral.

Wing tip bows were laminated carefully and feathered at the tip.

Baccus' welding crew set up shop and started to weld the fuselages. The construction was very straightforward and work progressed rapidly. Seamless chrome-molybdenum steel tubing was used for all three fuselages.

Howard Baccus and his crew laid out the steel fuselage tubing on the floor of the experimental shop, where dimension lines had been drawn for this purpose.

The tubing was then welded without the diagonal bracing tubes, and each fuselage set up on saw horses. Remaining diagonal brace tubes were added across the top and bottom. Longerons were sighted for alignment with a straight edge.

Each fuselage bay was welded one tube at a time. A tram device was used for squaring with clamps for holding the tubing in place. Baccus and "Dutch" Krueger continued this procedure until both "R" fuselages and the biplane fuselage were completed.

The elevator, rudder and stabilizers were SAE 1010 steel pressed into desired rib shape and welded to the spars of the stabilizers, forming a strong, integral unit.

The elevator and rudder rotated within simple strap hinges. Lightening holes were punched out along each rib of the stabilizers.

Ailerons were of the Frise type, actuated by a differential control system giving more travel to the up aileron. Push-pull tubes ran from the cockpit stick to the aileron.

Elevator and rudder were operated by standard control cables. A special, integral fairing was added to the lower rudder that faired nicely with the fuselage. This piece also turned with the rudder.

Landing gear was simple but unique. Four steel tubes with coil springs were used for shock absorption, the tubes having two oil cylinders per gear assembly. These tubes were welded to other tubing giving the assembly its basic form and strength. The whole unit was welded to "N" strut assemblies and attached to the fuselage stub wing, which was an integral, steel tube extension of the fuselage. Wheels and tires were suspended between the welded tube formations of each gear and were free to move vertically for shock absorption. No brakes were fitted. Bendix 24 inch by 4 inch wheels and tires were used.

A tail skid using a small hydraulic shock strut was streamlined and faired neatly into the aft fuselage. The entire main landing gear assemblies were braced by streamlined wires and when the wings were assembled the gear became an anchor point for the landing/flying wires.

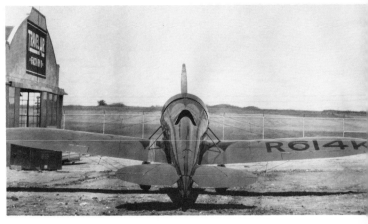

Fuselage was carefully shaped to accommodate Wright R-975 of 420 hp. Finish is very smooth on all surfaces. (Beech Aircraft Corporation)

Carl Burnham and his crew made up the two fuel tanks. The tanks were directly on the center of gravity of the ship, as the fuel load was the only variable factor of weight. The 42-gallon main tank was located at the 24% mean aerodynamic chord of the wing. A five-gallon reserve tank was fitted behind the main tank, but reserve fuel had to be hand-pumped into the main tank. Both fuel tanks were .040-inch aluminum, as was the firewall.

.040 inch aluminum alloy was used for the streamlined landing gear fairings. Called "pants" by some of the workers on the project, these hand-formed units gave the "R" a sleek, fast appearance. They helped to clean up a bulky assembly like the gear to a point that it was hardly noticeable or offensive to the observer. Carl Burnham spent many hours working out the contours of each fairing until it fit correctly. The two halves of each fairing were fitted together and welded along the center seam. Access was provided for inflation of the tire.

The first "R" was assembled to check fit and compatibility of assemblies. Everything went together correctly! That was a huge step in the right direction. The only other major job was building the NACA cowling. Dimensions were taken off the forward fuselage and the engine mount ring, which was .083 x 1-1/4 inch steel tube. It was known where the engine would sit in relation to the cowl and firewall, so it was just a matter of building the cowling to fit the engine.

Forms were made up and a Pettengill power hammer used to work out the two halves of the unit. The cowl hugged the engine as close as possible. No internal pressure baffling was used.

The cowl arrangement for the Chevrolair installation

Front view shows oil cooler under left wing root, faired gear and wire bracing for rigidity. R614K hit 225 mph with cowling, was 1929's most heralded aeronautical achievement. (Beech Aircraft Corporation)

R613K is run up by Clarence Clark. D-6 Chevrolair of 250 hp had oil temperature, pressure problems, other minor difficulties that hampered potential performance. (Beech Aircraft Corporation)

on the second "R" was completed a few days after the NACA job. The third airplane, known as the B11D was built along standard lines. It was a biplane powered with the Wright J-6-7 engine of 240 hp, but differed in having speed wings 4-1/2 feet shorter than production units. The fuselage was extremely narrow with only the pilot provided for.

Construction on this ship went very fast and it was ready to fly by early August, 1929. The little biplane was even smaller than the "bug" of 1928, and was the smallest Travel Air ever built.

August 18, 1929 was the big day everyone had waited for. The press was there at Travel Air Field, too. The secrecy surrounding the project had been tight, with the newspaper reporters expecting something big. A few people outside the factory knew what was going on — it was just too hard to keep a lid on something as hot as the "R" project.

The biplane racer was pulled out on the field first. It still required a few engine adjustments before flight so these were being carried out by mechanics. Throttle movements were made to check response of the Wright J-6-7. During one of these checks the engine backfired with quite a force and the wings caught fire.

The nitrate dopes really burned fast, so the man in the cockpit cut the switches and parted company with the Travel Air in record time! The flames were extinguished, but not before two wing panels had been seriously damaged.

Other wings were being built for this ship, and work commenced that day on getting the airplane repaired for the races. There was no guarantee that the work could be done by August 29, when the three Travel Air entries were to depart for Cleveland, Ohio, site of the 1929 National Air Races. The ship was not finished by that date and W.H. Emery flew it in the Portland to Cleveland race, finishing in fourth place for his class.

The Wright-powered "R" was first flown by Clarence Clark Saturday, August 18. The NACA cowl was not installed, as Carl Burnham was still completing it.

The experimental crew worked all through the previous night to finish the sleek speedster. No one really knew if it was a "speedster" as yet — it hadn't flown. But Herb and Walt had calculated a top speed of 205 mph once the cowling was in place.

The field was populated with a group of observers. Three of these were Beech, Rawdon and Burnham.

Clark got the ship off the runway, held her nose in level flight at an altitude of about 100 feet, letting the speed build. Then, to everyone's absolute fright, he nosed the "R" down in a semi-steep pitch manuever. Nerves went wild for a few seconds — he was going to crash!

But Clarence was just dipping low to "get the feel" for the ship. Quickly recovering from the dive, Clark checked full throttle and climbed out.

Leveling off, he flew away from the field and spent the next 20 minutes checking slow flight, stalls and speeds. The indicated airspeed at full throttle was 185 mph. Pretty fast for 1929, and the fastest ship Clark had ever flown.

She handled beautifully. Very little was amiss, and Clarence brought the airplane back to the field, landed, taxied up to the factory and shut down the Wright.

Rawdon, Burnham and Beech were right there to ask the usual post-flight questions. Clarence had a big smile on his face and that's all the three men needed. Walter Beech was so happy about the flight that he could hardly contain his enthusiasm.

No doubt he was already thinking about the name this vehicle of speed was going to make for Travel Air.

Twelve to 14 test flights were put on the first model "R." Clarence Clark flew them all, too. The NACA cowl was done, and when installed Rawdon expected the indicated airspeed to increase at least 20 mph.

He arrived at this figure because of experience gained with a J-5 Model 4000 with speed wings and another version of the NACA cowl. Ted Wells' airplane had exhibited nearly this much increase in airspeed, from around 130 to 145 mph.

There was good reason, then, to expect the same results with the racer. When Clark flew the airplane with the cowl in place he found indicated airspeed had increased to 225 mph—the cowling was the "icing on the cake" for the "R."

There were problems, though. The full throttle speed check pulled the cowling into the propeller. All but four of the special fasteners broke on the cowling, leaving it loose, so Clarence had to ease back to the field.

A fix was accommodated by increasing the strength of the cowling fasteners.

Departure day for Cleveland was only five days off, and the first "R" was ready to go. William Hauselman was the genius behind the paint design. The scheme for serial number R-2001, the first "R," was a bright red overall, with the wings, horizontal stabilizer and vertical stabilizer given a gloss black scallop treatment, as was the forward fuselage.

This scallop design was carried back in the form of gloss black stripes outlined in green border all the way to the empennage.

The wheel pants got the red and black paint job, too. Gloss black was applied to the "N" gear struts, cowling and forward cabane strut.

Department of Commerce number R614K was sprayed in gloss black on the upper surface of the right wing and lower surface of the left wing.

Some observers at Travel Air Field thought the "R" was something revolutionary. It wasn't, really. No part of its construction was novel or innovative, but the airplane did prove what could be done with good design techniques.

One day three men watched in wonder as Clark streaked by on one of his test flights. "Golly," said one of the trio, "it's so fast it takes three men to see it!"

The second "R," given Department of Commerce number R613K and serial number R-2002, was painted without the fancy scallops. It made its first trip into the sky on August 24, 1929. Clarence Clark again officiated in the cockpit.

Right away the air-cooled Chevrolet powerplant ran hot. Too hot. The ship flew fine, but was much slower than her sister.

After landing and reporting the problem to Rawdon, Clark added that maybe the engine wasn't giving full power and the cowl job was too restrictive for good air flow.

The Chevrolair D-6 engine was serial number 1. Arthur Chevrolet and his new company had designed a series of engines, all air-cooled and of inline configuration. These designs featured an emergency oil flow control that trapped oil in the engine in case of a leak in the oil line. But the high oil temperatures persisted.

The original exhaust stacks were aluminum. After a few test flights these stacks were melting and some had separated from the engine. Steel stacks were fashioned by Travel Air workmen and these gave no trouble.

Mr. Chevrolet said his engine was good for 300 hp, but the power just wasn't there. Top speed was around 150 mph—not too hot for a racer.

Clarence Clark experienced some other troubles with the D-6. For example, the engine seemed to have more power at 2/3 throttle than at full throttle itself. It used lots of oil, partly because of leaks and the oil temperature that consistently hit the 100 degree Celsius mark. The engine lost oil pressure when the oil level fell in the sump, making it a guessing game about how reliable the engine really was.

Later, enroute to the races, Clarence had to stop at Ottawa, Kansas City, Moline, Chicago, South Bend, Toledo and finally Cleveland. Each stop was for oil. Clark didn't like to fly the ship too much, but along with the Model 6000 that accompanied him all the way to

Doug Davis poses with the Thompson Trophy after winning Event No., 26 at Cleveland. (Beech Aircraft Corporation)

Dan Doyle (left) and Roy Edwards hold polished metal replica of Model "R." (Dean Edwards)

Cleveland, including stops, he made out satisfactorily.

The Chevrolair had potential for being a good power-plant, but the time available to Travel Air workmen perhaps precluded exposing its full capabilities.

The Travel Air racing team was off for Cleveland on August 25, 1929. Flying with the two "mystery ships" was Herb Rawdon and Walter Beech in a Model 6000. Ted Cochran was flying in the new Model 10 four-place monoplane, piloted by Newman Wadlow. The Model 10 had not been on the market long, and Walter wanted both monoplanes to be featured in the downtown Cleveland aircraft exposition, held concurrently with the air races.

R614K was piloted by Doug Davis, Travel Air dealer from Atlanta, Georgia. Davis was a friend of Beech and Walter trusted him with the fastest ship in the skies. Clarence Clark had hoped to fly the "R," but Davis' experience in closed course pylon racing and his lighter body weight suggested his selection. Clark gave Davis all the help he could and then Doug got in three flights before the group left Wichita.

Davis learned to fly in 1917, and by 1919 had set up shop in Griffin Georgia, offering aerial charter with a JN-4.

He later flew with the Cody Flying Circus and was quite successful there. He bought a Waco 9 biplane and started his second aviation business in Atlanta. Davis was an agent for the Advance Aircraft Co. (Waco) and later Travel Air.

Doug sold a good number of Travel Air products, and that Sunday morning in 1929 he was the privileged airman at the stick of a winner.

Making a low, high speed pass over Travel Air Field, Davis unintentionally contacted the ground with the gear. The impact was slight, but it occurred at high

Walter Hunter in R614K at St. Louis, September 4, 1931. Color is black fuselage with orange wings and trim stripes. Cockpit enclosure is opened up. Note larger NACA cowl for 600 hp R-975. (Courtesy The Hunter Family)

velocity. One tire blew, but he didn't know it until he landed at Kansas City enroute to Cleveland.

Once the two "R's" arrived at Cleveland they were placed in a hangar and roped off to discourage the curious. They were occasionally visible to onlookers, but little information was released to the press or anyone else.

Ted Cochran got up every morning during the races and checked the downtown display. When the salesmen arrived he left and went to the airport.

There he serviced the two Model "R" ships and tended to any repairs needed.

The public really got their first view of the "R" on August 30. Herb Rawdon's desire to show the military what a commercial ship could achieve was about to start.

Actually, it had already started with the arrival of the Travel Air team. The Army had to be content with only some of the press attention — Walter Beech and the story of the two speedsters from Wichita had already paved the way for some really good publicity.

But the Army was there, and with a hot ship, too. A Curtiss "Hawk" pursuit, serial number 28-189, had been modified for the main event of the races — the Thompson Products Free For All speed race, event number 26.

The Hawk was sporting a NACA cowling, tapered wings of typical Curtiss design, a smooth, rounded fairing tub that ran from the cowling back to the cockpit and nine short stacks on its Pratt & Whitney radial engine.

It was half of the expected competition for first place, the other half being a Navy Curtiss Hawk, also modified for speed and agility.

Captain R.G. Breene was piloting the Army ship, while Lieutenant Commander J.J. Clark would fly the Navy entry. It was shaping up just like it often did at the NAR—the Army vs. the Navy, or some commercial ship that was soon eliminated.

The "Goliaths" of speed didn't know it, but little "David" had traded his slingshot for a monoplane wing, and his five smooth stones for 420 hp.

The week of racing was underway. Davis won the experimental race in the Chevrolair "R," earning $400 for his efforts. It was Clarence's turn to compete next in the same airplane.

The oil temperature problem persisted when Davis was flying the ship, and Walter Beech decided the airplane should be quietly withdrawn from further competition. But fees were paid up for the 510 cubic inch displacement race, Event number 9. Beech told Clark to take it around the course just once and then land. That way the money would not be a total waste.

Once airborne, Clarence decided to go the distance. He throttled back the Chevrolair and made third place at the finish — and $200. That's one time when he was right in not following the boss's orders!

Finally, time for the big event of the National Air Races arrived — Event No. 26, the free-for-all contest everyone had been waiting for. It was a 50-mile race due to start at 2 P.M. Labor Day afternoon. The seven competitors were lined up, ready to go.

The Wichita racer, R614K, was resplendent in her scarlet scheme, the Wright idling nervously, waiting for the starter's flag. Captain Breene and Commander Clark were close by, their eager mounts quivering with power.

Then the start! All eyes focused on the Army ship. Breene jumped into the lead. Behind him was Clark and Doug Davis. Around the scattering pylon, every pilot seeking a position best suited for his race plan. Everyone in the grandstands was up and cheering.

Breene was still ahead, but the little red Travel Air was closing the gap! Then it passed the Army ship!

Doug Davis sat snug in his seat. The Wright was giving every ounce of her power to thrust the "R" ahead. Polished wings were keeping the Georgian and his mount flying as the ship banked hard around the pylons, the flying wires straining under tons of stress.

One lap, then two. Still the ship from Wichita retained the lead. Breene was pushing the Curtiss for all he could get. Five more laps quickly passed.

Model B11D racer undergoing ground runs in August, 1929. Wright J-6-7 of 240 hp was fitted to smallest biplane Travel Air built. (Beech Aircraft Corporation)

"Only three more laps to go," thought Davis as he leveled the mystery ship's wings and she streaked down the back-stretch. Doug was flying hard. "Here comes the next pylon — aileron and rudder in, back stick to hold altitude. Boy, this ship turns tight!" Davis *had* turned tight, too tight.

Davis thought he had cut that last pylon. He wasn't going to wait around and find out by being disqualified.

Doug yanked the "R" around and went back to circle the pylon again. Time was getting critical, and Breene now had a chance to gain on R614K.

Now Davis really laid the Travel Air over in a vertical bank so tight that he lost vision momentarily, but quickly recovered. Did he circle it that time? Maybe not, he couldn't remember for sure. Once again he hauled the ship around in another crushing, high-G turn. But Doug Davis wasn't slowing up for a second. "Full throttle!" he thought to himself—"Give it all she's got!"

B11D had speed wings 4½ feet shorter than standard arrangements and special interplane/cabane struts. Fire destroyed two wings before Cleveland departure, but single-seater was flown to fourth place in Portland to Cleveland contest by William Emery. (Beech Aircraft Corporation)

D-4000, serial #626, licensed NR6128 was flown to victory by Ted Wells in Portland to Cleveland race. "D" prefix indicates speed wing installation. (Beech Aircraft Corporation)

In fall of 1929 Truman Wadlow flew Louise Thaden's D-4000 back east to new owner. Carburetor ice caused engine failure, the ship flipping over during forced landing. Note bent interplane struts. (Truman Wadlow).

Louise Thaden talks with other pilots next to her specially-built D-4000, serial #1266, licensed NR671H during the first Women's Air Derby, August, 1929. (Beech Aircraft Corporation)

Response was immediate. Davis was speeding around the course so fast he lapped Roscoe Turner in his Lockheed Vega.

Seeing the aerial display of pylon circling nearly caused Walter Beech to bite his pipe stem in two! What ever Davis was doing he better be right. He was.

The commercial boys had done it! Herb Rawdon's prophecy had come true — the military had fallen at last. Washington would take notice of Event No. 26, and would start thinking about the sad state of America's airpower in 1929.

Doug Davis and his Travel Air had completed the race in just over 14 minutes and averaged 194.96 mph. That speed was the fastest ever recorded for any commercial airplane.

By the time Captain Breene had landed his defeated Curtiss, Doug was taxiing up to the winner's area. Still dressed in the shirt and tie he frequently wore when flying, Davis was introduced to Charles E. Thompson and presented with the Thompson Trophy.

And so it ended. Walter Beech went about collecting some bets he had made before the race. Stopping by the Army area on the airport, Beech had a twinkle in his eye as he collected from his disappointed debtors.

People crowded in close for a look at the "R." Small streaks of oil film tainted the fuselage — evidence of the struggle just over.

The R-975 crackled as the cylinders cooled. Time now to rest for awhile. History had been made today. Travel Air was proud, Wright Aeronautical was proud and so was Herb Rawdon. The aviation world belonged to the scarlet marvel.

After returning to Travel Air Field, R614K was polished to a high sheen and refurbished for more flying. Clarence Clark took her racing at Sioux Falls, South Dakota, and won the race there.

A racing license had been issued to expire March 1, 1930, with the owner being registered as Doug H. Davis, Candler Field, Atlanta, Georgia.

It was sold back to the Travel Air Co. on October 9, 1929, with the racing license still valid. Clarence next flew the "R" to victory at the Tulsa Oil Show held in October.

Davis had obtained permission from Travel Air to take the airplane from New York to Atlanta for promotion and demonstration work. He flew the ship 750 miles in 4 hours and 30 minutes flying time — another record for Travel Air.

Curtiss-Wright bought the racer in January, 1930 for exhibition purposes, and was issued a racing license until September. An accident in Des Moines on August 28, 1930, caused wing and landing gear damage. Curtiss-Wright halted further flying until a decision was made about repairs.

Walter Hunter now entered the life of R614K. He bought the Travel Air in June of 1931 and was granted a racing license to expire September 1, 1932.

Curtiss-Wright had been storing the ship at Lambert Field, and Hunter moved it to Parks Air College for repairs and modifications. Parks added two more fuel tanks, installed a full-vision canopy and they faired the cabane struts. Color was changed to black with orange wings. Another engine from the endurance Stinson used by the Hunter brothers was installed. Travel Air furnished a new NACA cowl after the Park's modifications, but a new 600 hp Wright later installed in Teterboro, New Jersey, barely fit inside it.

Hunter entered R-2001 in the 1931 Bendix race but was forced down south of Terra Haute, Indiana. The engine caught fire, but the flames were extinguished without serious damage. After repairs the "R" was flown to Cleveland for the National Air Races, where Hunter hoped to win the Thompson Trophy race.

On September 6, after making some minor adjustments to the racer, Hunter went up to fly the course and get familiar with pylon locations. It was early in the morning, and the grandstands were empty, but some witnesses recalled hearing the engine falter. Hunter switched fuel tanks, searching for one that would revive the Wright.

Suddenly flames were in the cockpit and Hunter had to get out, fast! Altitude was less than 400 feet, but Hunter managed to exit the airplane as it went nose down for the ground. He landed immediately after the parachute opened, and was unhurt except for the neck, face and hand burns suffered in the cockpit.

The Travel Air didn't burn on impact, but it was severely damaged. Hunter actually landed about 30 feet from his ship, and gazed at the wreckage while waiting for an ambulance.

In the same location where the "R" had burst upon the aviation scene in 1929, she now rested in silence, her graceful form would never again slice through the air.

The empennage now rests in the Staggerwing Museum Foundation facility in Tullahoma, Tennessee.

Another time of importance to Travel Air in August, 1929, was the Women's Air Derby. Louise Thaden (a shortened version of her full name and the one most often used) was going to be in it, flying a special biplane. Louise had recently married Herbert Von Thaden, an aircraft designer.

Not long before their marriage, Louise had set another record. She made 156 mph in a speed wing Travel Air—the first ever equipped with the new airfoil on the west coast.

When the truck pulled up to the Oakland airport that day in 1929 the wings were carefully unloaded. A letter was included with the wings. It read, "We believe the wings to be sufficiently strong, but since they are a new development we do not want you to take any unnecessary risks or chances." It was signed by Walter Beech.

The day of the speed record attempt, Louise waited for late afternoon before going up. Her airplane was ready.

She made two runs across a measured course of one mile, laid out at the Oakland field. Diving down, Louise aimed her machine at the tiny standard marking the west end of the course. At full throttle, the Travel Air came screaming downward.

Leveling off at less than 300 feet, the course was behind Louise in a few moments. Those speed wings were something else! Three more times the young woman pilot and the ship flew the course.

The officials gave Louise the record at 156 mph—not very fast, she thought, but a new mark nonetheless.

Soon after the speed record attempt, Louise reached her goal of becoming a transport pilot. Two hundred hours were required to attain it, plus a flight test with a Department of Commerce examiner.

She studied for months, learning airframe and powerplant construction, operation and maintenance. Navigation, weather and regulations were also on her list of subjects.

At the time of her examination only three women held a transport license. She passed the written test but the flight portion was yet to come.

She flew the Travel Air like never before — spins, vertical eights, dead-stick landings. Then it was time to land. She passed with ease.

Louise traveled to Wichita in late summer 1929 to give Walter Beech her sales pitch for the Women's Air Derby. Now, giving a sales talk to Walter Beech was like giving God instructions on creation.

Beech was one of the best salesmen anywhere. But he listened to the attractive lady pilot. He had been responsible for her learning to fly, so now he was paying the price. About all Louise got from Walter was "I'll think about it." But Louise wasn't just going to talk to Beech. She next went to see her old employer, Jack Turner. He listened, too. And it paid off. Louise would have her Travel Air for the derby. The cross-country race would be flown from Santa Monica to Cleveland, preceding the National Air Races.

But the competition would be very tough. Mary Von Mack, Maude Miller, Gladys O'Donnell, Thea Rasche, Florence "Pancho" Barnes. Phoebe Omlie, Amelia Earhart, Blanche Noyes, Ruth Elder and Vera Dawn Walker were in it, too. All these ladies were good pilots, and every one of them had the potential for victory.

Five Travel Air ships were being built for the derby. All were equipped with speed wings and Wright engines.

Clarence Clark tested Louise's airplane and pronounced it fit. She never doubted Clark. If he said it was

R613K was shipped back to Wichita via rail after the Cleveland races. Wright J-6-7 of 225 hp replaced ailing Chevrolair. Airplane was purchased by Florence "Pancho" Barnes in May, 1930 for $12,500. (Beech Aircraft Corporation)

R-2003, also written as R-103, licensed NR482N was delivered to Shell in March, 1930. Jimmy Doolittle and Jimmy Haizlip flew it in races, experimental work. (Beech Aircraft Corporation)

300 hp Wright R-975 was fitted to Shell racer. Overall color of NR482N was yellow with red scallop trim. New four-section NACA cowl was first installed on this ship, being easier to fabricate than original two-piece unit used on R-2001, R614K. (Beech Aircraft Corporation)

good, it was.

Beech had to rig up a four-inch tube that brought fresh air into the cockpit of Louise's airplane. Enroute to Santa Monica Louise had been overcome with exhaust fumes and barely made it into Fort Worth, Texas, from the Travel Air factory. Beech was waiting for her, having flown down in a Model 6000.

Not knowing her condition, Walter asked "Where the hell have you been?" a note of concern mixed in with his anger. "I don't know," said Louise. Then it was obvious what had happened. "My God, this is awful," said Beech. He soon fixed the problem with the tube, and Louise used it from that time on! She didn't mind breathing fresh air from a tube.

After the derby began, the press didn't handle the race very well, at least one newspaper didn't. It stated that "Women have conclusively proven they cannot fly." Another one said "Women have been dependent on man for guidance for so long that when they are put on their own resources they are handicapped."

None of the women agreed with such statements. The papers were critical of the derby, and when Marvel Crosson was killed in a Travel Air, things didn't improve. Miss Crosson crashed with her ship in the Gila River country south of Phoenix, Arizona. She was found dead, next to her airplane — her parachute unused. The cause was never determined for certain, but maybe carbon monoxide poisoning could top the list.

Louise, shaken by this tragedy, flew on. So did the other women. Crosson's death now became a symbol of courage and determination for them all. They had to keep going.

Florence Barnes wrecked her airplane in a landing accident at Pecos, Texas, and Blanche Noyes was out of the derby after an in-flight fire and subsequent forced landing. Noyes was particularly valiant in her efforts to salvage the ship. Once she noticed the fire (directly behind her shoulders in the small baggage compartment) she tried in vain to get the fire extinguisher free of its bracket.

She landed among thick mesquite, quickly dousing the flames with sand. Then she got the Travel Air back in the air, somehow avoiding any more damage than a blown tire and slightly wrenched landing gear.

Blanche was burned on the hands, and had flown the ship all the way to Pecos in terrible pain. She then landed gently on the right tire and the Travel Air slowly and very majestically groundlooped to a stop. Women can't fly? When left to their own resources they're handicapped! Blanche Noyes certainly proved both statements wrong.

Louise won the Women's Air Derby after 2,500 miles of very hard flying. The Travel Air Model 4000 never missed a beat the whole time.

After her victory in the first Powder Puff Derby, as it was later called, Louise went on to even greater achievements in aviation.

One of those laurels was winning the 1936 Bendix Trophy Race. With co-pilot Blanche Noyes she flew a

James H. Doolittle poses next to the rebuilt NR482N. Parks Air College modified the fuselage, wings and powerplant installation according to Doolittle's directions. On July 18, 1931, Jimmy bailed out of ship when aileron flutter occurred. He made one of the lowest, successful jumps in history, being less than 500 feet high when failure struck. (Beech Aircraft Corporation)

C17R Beechcraft Staggerwing to victory, becoming the first woman pilot to accomplish that feat. And the two ladies did it in a stock airplane with only extra fuel and oil tanks installed. It looked like female pilots were here to stay!

The Travel Air sweep of the 1929 Women's Air Derby and the National Air Races did much to keep the orders pouring in.

The two Model "R s" were still the talk of aviation publications months after the races were over. Wichita was very proud of what the factory team had accomplished, and the newspapers weren't afraid to say so, either.

R-2002 competed in only a few races at Cleveland. Beech withdrew R613K from competition after the 510 cubic inch event and the airplane remained in the hangar at Cleveland. Ted Cochran was instructed to disassemble the ship and have it shipped back to Travel Air.

The racer was dismantled, trucked to the Cleveland railhead and carefully placed in a boxcar. It arrived at Wichita a few days later.

The Chevrolair was removed and a Wright J-6-7 of 225 hp installed. Florence "Pancho" Barnes learned that the ship could be purchased, and bought R613K through a dealer in Los Angeles.

It was repainted yellow and red, with a scallop design similar to the one on R614K. Barnes installed a Townend ring on the Wright, but it seems to have been more for appearance than performance. With the J-6-7 powerplant, a distinctive break in the clean lines of the "R" fuselage was very prominent. The Chevrolair inline engine mated smoothly with the fuselage, but the Wright did not.

It is most likely that the Townend ring was there to help the cosmetic appearance of the ship. It was often flown with the ring removed.

Barnes paid $12,500 for the Travel Air on May 29, 1930.

A license was granted for racing with the J-6-7 on October 7, with expiration dates of January 15, 1930, March 15 and May 1, 1930.

After Travel Air sold the ship to Barnes in late May she received a license to race the airplane until September 1, 1930. Another Wright engine, this time a J-6-9 of 300 hp was installed in February, 1931. License to race this

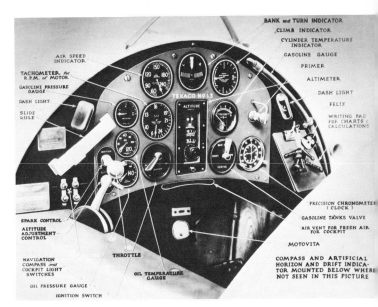

Cockpit of NR1313. Last three Model "R" ships had similar instrument layout, but Hawks had compass, artificial horizon and drift indicator on floor. (Smithsonian Institution Photo No. 81-3250)

version of the "R" was granted until March 1, 1932.

"Pancho" set a number of women's speed marks with the little ship, and it was one of the fastest machines on the west coast.

One interesting note about this airplane was its movie career. Howard Hughes' film epic "Hell's Angels" was made without sound at first, but when the film producer learned about the "talkies" he decided to remake the entire picture. Filming was redone and the engine sounds used for many of the scenes came from the Wright of R613K.

Paul Mantz bought the "R" from Barnes in September, 1938 and used it for aerobatic demonstrations and

R-2004, or R-104, licensed NR1313 was sold to The Texas Company for the exclusive use of Frank Hawks. Ship is in original configuration here, as delivered to Hawks on July 5, 1930. 300 hp Wright powered the airplane to over 215 mph on early flights. (Beech Aircraft Corporation)

Hawks had forced landing on July 11, 1930, at Travel Air factory. During test flight the engine failed, and Hawks tried to glide safely to the runway. He almost made it, but ship snagged telephone wires at north edge of field. Crash caused minor damage to "R", knocked Hawks unconscious. By July 23 the airplane looked like this, with new paint scheme, special 465 hp R-975 and a happy Frank Hawks. (Carl Burnham)

movie work. It was fitted with fake machine guns on the upper fuselage for work in one motion picture.

Mantz installed yet another engine, this time of higher horsepower. A Wright J-6-9 radial of 330 hp now graced the front of R613K by June, 1939.

Paul Mantz flew the ship for many hours and kept it in good flying order. He had to — his life was on the line in every one of his airplanes, so all were maintained with care. After all, even though the Travel Air wasn't crashed for any spectacular movie stunt it was often Mantz' personal mount for a good time in the air. He undoubtedly recognized its historical significance, too.

Frank Tallman and Paul Mantz operated TallMantz Aviation in Santa Ana, California, and Tallman came into possession of the ship on March 14, 1966, after Mantz was killed following the filming of "The Flight of the Phoenix."

In 1972 William Barnes, the son of Florence Barnes, bought the racer and planned an extensive and complete restoration. He was well along with the project when he died in a crash in 1980.

R613K is the only true Model "R" remaining.

Once the Model "R" had made its name, other pilots were interested in owning one. Model "R" serial number R-2003 went to the Shell Aviation Corporation in St. Louis, Missouri.

Travel Air received the order from Shell in early 1930, after Jimmy Doolittle and the Shell company had

time to evaluate the design.

Doolittle was working for Shell at this time, along with Jimmy Haizlip, another well known and respected flier of the era.

Shell ordered their "R" with changes to the standard design. A complete set of blind flying instruments were installed, the control surfaces were just slightly larger and a center section fuel tank was added.

The Wright R-975 produced 300 hp and was fitted with a ground adjustable Hamilton Standard steel propeller. A red and yellow scallop paint scheme, modified to suit Shell, was applied and the cockpit area had a semi-canopy that slid forward on two tracks, enabling the pilot to get in and out with relative ease. A curved, hinged entry door on the left fuselage side also aided this procedure.

With the center section fuel tank, Shell's airplane took on a slightly wider bulge around the fuselage-to-wing area.

The airplane was delivered on March 22, 1930, and was licensed NR482N. It cost Shell $16,900. A newly designed, four-piece cowling was installed on this ship. The original NACA unit on R614K was two-piece, and the halves mated along the horizontal axis. This was a cumbersome unit to construct, and Carl Burnham, along with his brother and Herb Rawdon, decided to make up any future cowlings in four separate panels. The four panels were then bolted together and fairing strips ran along each seam, 90 degrees apart.

Jimmy Doolittle came to Travel Air to take delivery for Shell. Clarence Clark had flown the airplane through the necessary test hops prior to delivery.

Haizlip flew the Shell ship to second place behind Charles "Speed" Holman in the 1930 Thompson Trophy Race. Holman was flying the Laird "Solution," the name supposedly arising from the need to beat Travel Air's Model "R," winner of the event the previous year.

The Laird was a very small biplane powered with the second prototype Pratt & Whitney "Wasp" Junior of 300 hp. Charles Holman was a crack pilot from St. Paul, Minnesota. He was very well known across the country and was instrumental in forming Northwest Airways, Inc.—later to be called Northwest Orient Airlines.

Holman was associated with Laird products for most of his career. He flew against many a Travel Air in competitive events around his own local area and on a national scale. "Speed" was his nickname because he loved to go fast.

After the lesson of 1929, the military went to work on an airplane that could beat the civilian competition.

In the summer of 1930 a Curtiss F6C-3 was in the Curtiss shops undergoing a complete transformation. It became a parasol-type monoplane powered with a Conqueror engine, and featured cantilever landing gear and wing skin coolant radiators.

The Laird workmen had just finished the tiny LC-DW 300 biplane literally minutes before the race. Number 77 was hastily applied below the cockpit and "Speed" took her up for a short test flight. On landing he suggested a few corrections to the wing rigging. These were done and he took off for Curtiss-Reynolds airport, site of the races. Lee Schoenhair had intended to pilot the craft and had ordered it built only three weeks before the race. He had already flown in two events that day and let Holman take the "Solution" up before the race. Since the ship was still officially owned by Laird, it was Holman that Laird chose to pilot the "Solution" in the main event.

In 1931 NR1313 had slight modifications to landing gear and paint scheme. Hawks set over 200 records with his racer from 1930 to 1932, in both America and Europe. (Beech Aircraft Corporation)

Up against Holman were Page in the Curtiss, Haizlip and Frank Hawks in Travel Air Model "Rs," a Travel Air with speed wings flown by Paul Adams, Benny Howard in "Pete" and Errett Williams flying the Wedell-Williams racer.

Page's Curtiss jumped into the lead and remained there for five laps. Holman and Haizlip were locked in combat for second place. Hawks was out by lap 3 with fuel starvation from a taped-over vent. Williams fell out of the race on the eighth lap and then Captain Page was seen to pull up and then bank to the left as he rounded the home pylon.

The Curtiss ship decended in a left turn and impacted the infield area. Page died the next day — another victim of carbon monoxide poisoning.

Page was fast. His airplane was about to lap the two civilians when he could no longer cope with the fumes. It was a most unfortunate and unnecessary loss, but Holman almost became the second statistic for the grim reaper.

The Laird was gassing him, too. Haizlip and Holman were in a battle for the win, and "Speed" held on just long enough to beat the "R" by a mere two seconds.

He landed the "Solution" after winning the Thompson Trophy race in the only biplane to ever be victorious. Holman was so sick he had to be helped to the sidelines.

So the military almost got revenge for their loss in 1929. But the Curtiss was a flying engine — over 600 hp was available. Herb Rawdon was still right — the Army and Navy continued to hang big horsepower engines on their airplanes, but they did go to a monoplane configuration in 1930.

Doolittle and Haizlip continued to fly the Shell "R" through the remainder of 1930 and into 1931. Records show the ship in a ground collision with an Army training machine and it was written off by Shell in late 1930. Another source states that Haizlip was flying the airplane and suffered engine failure. But whatever happened, Jimmy Doolittle bought NR482N on March 20, 1931. The racing license originally issued to Shell expired on July 1, 1930, and was reissued for racing until May 1, 1931.

Jimmy Doolittle had a degree in aeronautical engineering and much experience in flying experimental airplanes. He spent many hours aloft in machines that were modified by the men at McCook Field, where Jimmy was stationed in the 1920s. He understood the potential for an airplane like the Travel Air Model "R," so he decided to buy the wreck and rebuild it along his own desires for a speed ship.

Using his personal savings, Doolittle acquired the Travel Air and had it rebuilt and heavily modified by Parks Air College. The fuselage was totally new, the cabane struts were now completely enclosed within deep, rounded fairings that blended nicely into the wings. The original empennage was salvaged and reused.

Another change was in the relation of the wing to the attach points on the fuselage. The new wing configuration caused a redesign of the aileron push-pull tube. It had to be bent slightly to fit the aileron mechanism.

A Pratt & Whitney Wasp Junior of 560 hp was installed. The only other change was in the cockpit. Doolittle had a full-vision canopy and lower side windows put on the ship, and these helped drag reduction and afforded some comfort from the slipstream, too.

The "new" NR482N was ready to fly on July 18, 1931. A group of onlookers had assembled for the momentous occasion. It would be momentous, indeed.

The takeoff was rapid and climb was spectacular — the Pratt & Whitney hurled the ship through the air with all the speed Doolittle had hoped for. A few aerobatic maneuvers were tried with good results. Jimmy then dove the airplane at an indicated airspeed of about 235 mph.

Leveling out at 100 feet altitude, and just emerging from the bottom of the high speed dive, Doolittle suddenly felt the ailerons jerk about and the right wing become heavy.

He didn't know what happened and he wasn't going to stick around to find out! Nosing the crippled ship up to about 400 feet he bailed out, instantly pulling the ripcord when free of the airplane, which was inverted.

No sooner did the parachute open that Jimmy hit the ground. He was still a little stunned, but totally unhurt. However, the modified "R" had buried itself into the ground of East St. Louis and would never fly again.

What caused the accident? The aileron push-pull tube. It had failed.

Last Model "R" went to Italy. R-2005 was licensed 11717 for export purposes. Section of cowl is removed showing further engine detail. (Carl Burnham)

Thus ended the short career of another Travel Air racer. As a crowd gathered around the wreckage, Doolittle searched the surrounding area for his ripcord, considered a good luck charm, and found it. He had made one of the lowest, fastest and most dangerous bailouts on record.

The fourth Model "R" was about to begin its career with Texaco.

Up in New York City the Texas Company had Frank Hawks flying for them. Hawks was setting records with the use of Texaco products, much like Doolittle and Haizlip had done for Shell Oil.

Hawks had been flying since 1917 when he received pilot training as a cadet in the Air Service. He was an instructor during the war and then barnstormed southern California. Hawks also flew down in Mexico.

Frank was hired by Texaco in 1928 and flew their Ford Trimotor to many U.S. Cities, but he got his big "break" when he was asked to fly a Lockheed "Air Express" to New York. The Air Express was a parasol design, with enclosed cabin for passengers and the pilot seated aft and outside.

Frank Hawks set his first record flying the Lockheed between Los Angeles and New York in 18 hours, 21 minute and 59 seconds.

Thirteen months had passed since that journey, and now Hawks stood on Travel Air Field admiring his newest mount . . . NR1313, serial R-2004.

This airplane also had the three fuel tanks fitted in the fuselage and it had the four-piece NACA cowling. Fuel capacity was 109 gallons.

The fuselage contour of the fourth "R" was different from the other three machines. As delivered to Hawks on July 5, 1930, the upper fuselage spine was raised slightly just aft of the cockpit. Power was provided by a 300 hp Wright J-6-9 with a Standard steel propeller.

R-2004 was painted in vermilion and light gray, with the wings solid vermilion and Department of Commerce number was cream trimmed in blue. The fuselage was light gray, with the cowling painted vermilion. The vertical stabilizer was scalloped in vermilion as was the forward fuselage. Horizontal stabilizers were painted vermilion. Four stripes ran from the cowling face all the way back to the empennage. Landing gear was vermilion with cream flashing trimmed out in blue.

Frank Hawks conferred with Clarence Clark about the handling of the ship. Clarence had flight tested NR1313 and pronounced her ready for delivery.

The Texaco logo was painted on the wings and vertical stabilizer in red, green, white and black. "Texaco 13" appeared on the fuselage mid-side in vermilion.

Texaco paid Travel Air $16,900 for the airplane. As it was intended for the exclusive use of Hawks, Texaco let the noted flier install whatever instruments he desired.

NR1313 had the customary grouping of airspeed indicator, altimeter, tachometer and rate of climb/descent, but also featured a cylinder head temperature gauge, turn and bank instrument operated by gyroscope and venturi, a precision chronometer and full set of engine instruments. Three other items were included — a slide rule for calculations, writing pad and Hawks's indispensable co-pilot, Felix the Cat! Tied on the instrument board was a miniature Felix, complete with helmet and goggles.

A compass, artificial horizon and drift indictor were mounted on the cockpit floor. Electric lights were provided for the slide rule and fuel quantity sight tube.

The fuel selector was up on the main instrument panel with detents for "Center," "Left" and "Right" tanks.

All three of the post-Cleveland Model "R" ships had three fuel tanks installed that gave the airplane 109 gallon capacity. Hawks would be glad to have the extra fuel on the long-distance flights he was planning for NR1313.

Clarence Clark had commented that R-2004 was very fast, so an anxious Frank Hawks climbed aboard on July 5 and took off from Travel Air Field.

After a short familiarization flight, Hawks returned for landing. He came in too fast on his first approach and didn't get the little speedster slowed down enough to land.

The second approach went normally, with Hawks slipping his ship in for a nice landing before the crowd that had assembled to watch.

Another flight on July 10 revealed high oil temperatures and cowling adjustments were tried to correct the trouble. Hawks took NR1313 up again on July 11 and again experienced high oil temperatures on the Wright engine. Returning for landing, Hawks was just north of Travel Air Field when the engine failed. Stretching his glide to the limit, Hawks attempted to fly under electrical wires and over telephone lines, but he didn't make it.

The landing gear cleared the electrical wires but snagged the telephone lines, and the Travel Air smashed into the ground nose first at 80 mph. Hawks was knocked unconscious. No fire broke out. Only the gear and cowling/propeller were damaged. Hawks was given medical aid and rest for a few days.

Frank Hawks wanted the ship rebuilt, including some changes. During the rebuild, a 465 hp Wright J-6-9 engine with special supercharger, cylinder heads and finned spark plugs was installed. The fuselage spine was reshaped and another paint scheme applied.

Red and white color now adorned the Travel Air, with broad stripes running along the fuselage. Clarence Clark flew the ship on July 23, 1930. Hawks took off for

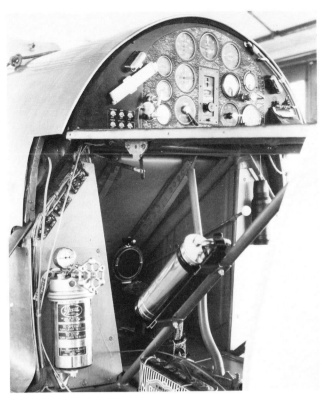

Cockpit of R-105. Slide rule at upper left of panel, fuel sight gauge at upper right. All three final "R" ships, Shell, Texaco and the Italian model had very similar instrument panel arrangements, as the equipment installed by Travel Air was considered essential for intended use of such an airplane. (Beech Aircraft Corporation)

Pittsburgh, Pennsylvania later that day. A special propeller had not arrived at Travel Air in time, so it would be installed at Pittsburgh.

On August 6 Hawks flew across the continent in 14 hours, 30 minutes 43 seconds. Both transcontinental and inter-city records were slashed by Hawks and the Travel Air. August 13 found the two record setters heading east from Los Angeles. 12 hours, 25 minutes 3 seconds after takeoff Hawks put the "R" down at New York City's Curtiss Field . . . two records in one week!

Hawks entered the 1930 Thompson Trophy race, but he stopped in at Travel Air for some work prior to heading for Curtiss Field. He wanted to install the small set of wings on NR1313.

Reliable sources indicate that Jimmy Doolittle had R614K's small set on his NR482N when Hawks came back to the factory. Other sources say the wings were installed on NR1313 and flew in the Thompson race. It appears from study of the records available that Hawks did not have R614K's short span wings in the 1930 National Air Races. Two sets of wings were built for Hawks, as the Travel Air specification sheet for this ship calls out two sets of numbers, one for performance with the small wings, the other with the larger set.

One other possibility exists. When Jimmy Doolittle had to bail out of his rebuilt racer, he stated later that the wings were from an "old ship," and he wasn't too surprised that they failed. He may have obtained the wings from Travel Air that were the original short span set for R614K. (Walter Hunter had R614K's long-span wings installed in 1931 on R614K, and it crashed with those wings.)

In the 1930 Thompson race Hawks had to pull out on the third lap with fuel starvation to the engine, caused by tape over the fuel cap vent. The racing license issued

to Hawks and R-2004 was to expire January 15, 1931 and March 1, 1932. In 1931 NR1313 returned to Travel Air for slight modifications and servicing.

The paint scheme was altered by having a narrow trim line of blue around the fuselage stripes. Position lights were removed for drag reduction.

The fuselage wording was changed to read "Texaco No. 13" and the same phrase was added to the cowling sides.

In 1932 the gear "N" struts were painted white as were the gear "pants." Travel Air's script logo was applied to the forward fuselage.

Many records were broken by Frank Hawks and NR1313. The Travel Air went to Europe in 1931 and at least 12 speed dashes between major European cities showed the British, French and Germans what America was up to in aeronautics. The Italians also saw the Model "R" and General Balbo would soon have his own "R" in Rome.

Frank Hawks had to make another forced landing with the ship in 1932. On April 7 the Wright radial quit and Hawks put the ship down near North Grafton, Massachusetts. He was injured quite badly and required hospitalization for complete recovery.

R-2004 was trucked to the shops and rebuilt only to the point of static display. It was then placed in the Museum of Science and Industry in Chicago, where it hangs today. The "R" is a silent reminder of a famous flier and the ship that he flew. The speed of Hawks and NR1313 gave rise to the phrase "Don't send it by mail . . . send it by Hawks."

Not long after Frank Hawks showed Europe what a Travel Air could do, the Italian government cabled the company in Wichita and placed an order.

The cable was from General Balbo, one of Mussolini's top military men. The price of the "R" was not to exceed $23,000 and delivery was expected as soon as possible.

The Travel Air factory was not shut down at this time, but the Great Depression had wiped out the once flourishing airplane business for the company, and the buildings sat very quiet.

Curtiss-Wright had moved the majority of Travel Air's production to St. Louis, Missouri, where the cabin monoplanes and a new line of biplane models were being built in small numbers.

Walter Burnham was supervisor on the Italian "R" project. It would be his last assignment for the company, and he picked many of the same people for this ship that had built the other four machines.

Ted Cochran, Ed Libby, Howard Baccus and his brother Carl, Ervin "Dutch" Krueger, Andy Bland, Bill Cochran, Pearl Breitweiser, Earl Hyatt and 14 other workers labored together and built the last Travel Air Model "R," serial R-2005. The Department of Commerce issued licence number 11717, but this was probably for export purposes only.

Work began in June of 1931 and was complete by July 15. Clarence Clark had left Travel Air in 1930 to take a flying position with Phillips Petroleum Company in Bartlesville, Oklahoma.

Clark was offered a job flying with Curtiss-Wright in St. Louis but decided to go with Phillips instead. When the day came for a test flight on R-2005, Walter Beech, who was spending time between his office in New York and one in St. Louis, contacted Burnham and wanted an update on the progress of the Italian Job.

It was just about ready to fly, and had been painted very similar to Frank Hawks's NR1313. But no one was available to test hop the airplane and get it ready for acceptance by Italian officials.

Beech called Phillips Petroleum. Walter wanted Clarence to go up to Wichita and fly the last "R."

Billy Parker said he didn't think that was possible, so Clarence declined Beech's request. Beech then called the Wichita Travel Air factory and talked to Newman Wadlow. After discussing the situation with Newman, it was agreed that Wadlow and L.G. "Swede" Larson would share the test flight duties for R-2005.

Larson was another of Travel Air's on-call pilots through the years, and he was very capable of flying the ship, as was Newman.

The Italian "R" first flew on July 19, 1931, with Larson at the controls. Initial test flights were not entirely satisfactory.

Wadlow and Larson began to get flutter from the empennage on one of the early flights. This was reported to engineers who had the cowling removed and another flight made.

The same condition existed. A number of days had gone by since the first flight and still the ship wasn't ready.

Wadlow had a suggestion, though, that turned the trick. He proposed pouring crankcase oil over the fuselage just forward of the horizontal stabilizer. The slipstream would swirl the oil where any aerodynamic disturbance was occurring, thereby exposing the cause of the flutter.

Once airborne the flutter was there. Full throttle runs were made and Newman came back for landing. The Wright clanked to a stop and the engineers huddled around the empennage to see what pattern the oil had left.

Newman's idea had worked. The oil was very swirled in the area adjacent to the fuselage/horizontal stabilizer. Everyone knew it wasn't any fault of the cowling because the flutter was there with or without the cowling on the ship.

A small change had been incorporated into the trailing edge of the wing, altering the airflow coming off the inboard wing section. It wasn't much of a change, but all agreed it was probably the cause.

The fix was completed when the trailing edge was reworked, and the flutter disappeared. Commander Paulo Sbernadori, Italian Air Attache, flew to Wichita with Walter Beech in a Travel Air monoplane. When they left St. Louis, Sbernadori was very sick with ptomaine poisoning, but he insisted on making the trip.

On arrival at Travel Air Field, he consented to pose for pictures but was ushered to the Lassen Hotel for some needed rest. He saw R-2005 and was very elated about the ship. He hoped to fly it the following day, but he didn't. Sbernadori never did fly the "R" at Wichita, but accepted it after a demonstration flight. Newman Wadlow and L.G. Larson put a total of 9.7 flying hours on the ship to make it ready for delivery. Commander Sbernadori praised the airplane and said his government was most happy to receive it.

Within a few days of the demonstration flight the ship was disassembled by Travel Air workmen and placed in special shipping boxes. One box contained the fuselage (with engine) on its gear, completely painted, with stabilizers, propeller, attaching hardware and bracing wires. Wings were carefully packed in another box. The boxes were shipped to New York, then to Italy.

A complete construction/erection manual, engine booklet, logbooks and tool kit were also included. The "R" would go together like a big model airplane.

Despite inquiries, final disposition of the last Model "R" is unknown, but the Italians surely benefitted from its technology.

Clarence Clark and Newman Wadlow both agree that the Model "R" airplanes built by Travel Air were by far the best flying aerobatic and all-around fun ships they ever flew.

Clarence Clark has the distinction of being the one man in aviation history who can claim to have flown four of the five ships constructed.

He also flew them in races. He got to know their distinct mannerisms and still claims they had no bad habits. If the pilot was competent in handling an airplane, he could check out in the "R" without difficulty. But he is also quick to point out that it was no ship for a novice.

The visibility over the nose was not the best, but he never had any trouble seeing on takeoff. Landing was easy, and final approach was flown in a slip, aiding forward visibility.

Takeoff speed was around 60 mph, with brisk acceleration and the climb was best at 100 mph. Cruise was almost an honest 180 mph with final approach flown at 90 mph until the field was made, then reducing airspeed to touch down about 70 mph.

The "R" didn't want to groundloop, either. And it didn't swerve nervously after landing—"rudder walking" was required, but not too much. Once the tail skid dug in the ship slowed down fast and was easy to control. And could that ship climb! It did aileron rolls with ease because the ailerons were feather-light. Elevator pressure was very pleasing. Clarence liked to zoom in low, airspeed hitting 200 mph and pull up into a vertical climb topped off with vertical rolls, pulling the "R" through on her back as stall speed neared, picking up airspeed on the way back down. Yes, it must have been lots of fun.

Herb Rawdon wasn't quite through with the "R" yet, however. He knew the airplane would make a good sport ship, and there was definitely a place in the market for such an offering.

There were plenty of sportsman pilots who wanted just the type of airplane Rawdon could make out of the "R"—a fast, two-place sport ship. Power could come from the Wright or maybe the Chevrolair would be brought up to expectations and that engine could be offered, too. The basic design was flexible enough to allow for stretch, so little difficulty was expected. The "R" could compete against the neat, fiesty looking ships being built for the sportsman class by the Granville Brothers in New England, and the new Alexander Eaglerock Bullet, designed by Al Mooney.

Walter Beech liked the idea enough to propose it to the Curtiss-Wright board of directors and the go-ahead was received in November, 1929.

K.K. Shaul, who was the faithful employee of Travel Air at the comptroller position, informed the press on November 20 that the ship known only as a two-place version of the "R" would be put into production in 1930.

Drawings were made and the lines of the airplane were still as elegant as ever. But the condition of the market did not permit Travel Air to produce this version of the "R."

With orders beginning to shrink, it was the last thing Curtiss-Wright wanted to do—start production of another model.

And with that decision the "Mystery Ship" and all its glory slowly faded from the aviation scene, but not from the memories of those who knew their speed, their genuine high-bred nature and all the majesty that made them unforgettable.

TRAVEL AIR

CHAPTER EIGHT
Inside Travel Air

Buck Hoover was really putting on a show. Everyone in downtown Wichita thought the quasi-cowboy was crazy to try a stunt like breaking the world record for nonstop driving.

Well, that's the way ol' Buck was. Give 'em a wager and he might just take you up on it!

In October, 1928 Buck Hoover was wishing he'd never tried such a fool stunt. Here he was, sitting in a car he had been driving for the last 100 hours. No food, no drink and no sleep! His hands were chained to the steering wheel.

Hoover set a record the night of October 4, 1928 — 101 hours of continuous driving. He stopped his car, the police unlocked his chains and helped Buck from the seat. He was able to stand up pretty well, too, so he was given a bottle of soda pop for his herculean effort behind the wheel. Wichita aviation was in the news, too.

Travel Air and Swallow were growing, expanding companies as were Cessna and Stearman.

When Travel Air moved to East Central Avenue in 1927, their new factory was quite a topic of conversation in Wichita. Clyde Cessna and Walter Beech had outfitted this building with the latest in woodworking equipment, welding gear, tools, and lathes. Most important of all they had laid out the floor plan for efficiency of production.

The $32,000 unit had 21,650 square feet of available floor space. The west end of the building would house the executive and engineering offices, the remainder was dedicated to manufacturing.

Large, multiple glass windows conducted lots of sunlight inside the factory, making work lighting satisfactory for the daytime, and complete electric lights were installed for night work or to supplement the sunlight.

Over 100 workers moved in and began building Travel Air airplanes in June.

Travel Air had progressed from a work space 30 feet by 30 feet in the back of the Kansas Planing Mill to a new, modern factory ready to meet customer demand.

All woods, sheet metal, steel tubing and the hundreds of detail parts and components required to build a Travel Air came to the factory receiving department.

From there each department was supplied with its particular requirement — steel tubing went to wooden racks built in the welding area. Wood was taken to the woodworking departments where the shop had plenty of room for sizing and cutting. A suction fan picked up the wood shavings and debris which were fed to an outside incinerator for burning.

East Central factory, summer, 1928. View looking east. Factory "A" is at right, "B" at left. Frank Ashworth, custodian at Travel Air, lived in house next to "B." Hamburger shop across street from "A" was favorite hangout for pilots, workmen at factory. Note Ford Trimotor exchanging passengers on airfield. (Beech Aircraft Corporation)

Welding of fuselage was done in Factory "A." Jigs were simple but sufficient for the job. (Beech Aircraft Corporation)

A large brick wall separated the wood shop from the paint and dope department.

Here all the doping of wings and fuselages was done. Steel, fireproof doors on sliding rails were furnished in this room in case fire broke out. The nitrate dopes burned furiously when ignited, and special rules were enforced in that department. (Van Schaack nitrate dope was often used by Travel Air, with Berry Brothers "Berryloid" lacquers for finish color coats.)

Welding the fuselages required quite an area, and this important function was accomplished toward the west end of the unit. Crews worked together welding fuselages in sections, passing each finished segment on to the final welding position.

As the fuselage progressed from the west end toward final assembly at the far east end, the turtledeck, fairing strips and sheet metal were added.

Wings were built adjacent to the woodworking department. When the fuselage and wings were completed, doped and painted according to standard or customer ordered colors, the ship was placed on the landing gear and rolled out into final assembly. Here the wings were installed, rigging was accomplished, the engine was installed and serviced for the first flight. When the airplane was ready, Clarence Clark was summoned to

test hop the ship.

By September of 1927, four additional acres were bought from the Booster Building Association and construction of another factory was authorized. Reasons for the expansion can be illustrated by looking at one work week of production in May, 1927. Travel Air built and delivered 15 Model 2000, 5 J-5 Model 4000 and 1 Model 9000 for a total of 21 ships!

Henrion Improvement Company released the second factory unit for occupancy in early January, 1928. The workforce was now 250 men with 100 more to be hired to meet demand. The factory was now split as to its functions.

The original unit, called factory "A" housed the fuselage assembly, dope and paint, stock room "A," upholstering, sheet metal and final assembly.

The second factory, now known as factory "B" housed the woodworking department, wing department, stock room "B" and dope and paint for the wings.

A paved, concrete open court was built between "A" and "B" for the purpose of rolling ships out when assembled, or for moving waiting fuselages outside the factory until ready for further work. This area was also utilized for rigging and engine runup. The general flow of production at Travel Air with these two factories was simple: raw materials entered "A" at the west end and "B" at the east end. The materials then moved toward the center floor area of each building where all components and major assemblies were built. Fuselage with engine and landing gear from "A" met wings from "B" in the open court and were "married" there.

Factory "A" took in raw materials through a large door located at the west end, on the south wall. If a shipment of tubing arrived, for example, it was unloaded and taken by workers to tubing saws where it was cut into predetermined lengths. It was then placed in racks adjacent to the fuselage welders so they could have easy access for the needed pieces.

Landing and flying wires were prepared for assembly in the upper balcony area. Sound-proof walls isolated the offices from factory noise.

Empennage assembly and welding was also done on this upper balcony area.

All the hardware, instruments and detail parts were

Wing department was in Factory "B." Monoplane wings under construction in foreground, biplane wing on rearmost work table. (Beech Aircraft Corporation)

Engine installation, Factory "B," 1928. Model 2000 in foreground, 4000 behind it. Curtiss OX-5 and OXX-6 engines were still plentiful, but less popular with advent of affordable radial powerplants. (Beech Aircraft Corporation)

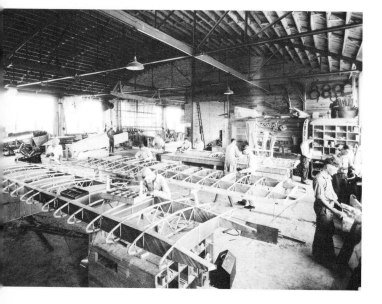

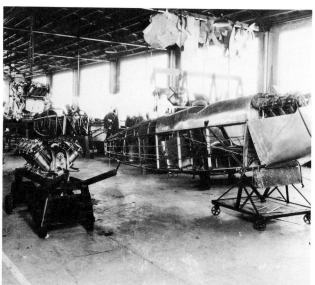

Factory "C" was built in March, 1929. Administration building next to "A" was occupied in January, 1929. Parts and experimental rooms were housed between "A" and "C." Unit "E" is under construction in center. New Keystone "Patrician" airliner is at far right, having stopped at Travel Air Field on a nationwide publicity tour. (Beech Aircraft Corporation)

readily available to the workers. They only had to walk a few steps to get them.

When the empennage assemblies were completed they were taken to the main floor and attached to the fuselage, joining the flow toward final assembly.

The fuselage received all fittings and sheet metal pieces, then proceeded to the upholstering and fabric cover department. ("Flightex" fabric was used most often but other brands were used as well.)

The fabric pieces were already pre-sized and cut to fit each different model. This greatly reduced the time and effort required to cover the airplanes.

When the fuselage left the covering department it went to the dope and paint section. A taughtening coat of dope was sprayed on and then sanded down. Six coats of clear dope were sprayed and three or more finish coats were applied, the last coat was thinned to give the fabric finish a pleasing luster and gloss.

Materials for the wings entered through a receiving door in "B." All lumber went directly to the large millwork area.

Finished pieces went toward the west end of "B" where they entered the wing production flow. Wings were assembled with the ribs and spars, then the complete assembly went across the floor to the dope and paint shop.

On a suspended "island" in the center of "B" wings were varnished and then set aside to dry. The wings were transported down to the floor level for a covering on a system of pulleys and tracks.

If the wings were to be installed on a waiting fuselage, they were taken to the center court area or the west end of "B."

If the wings were to be stored they were placed on an overhead "island" holding area.

Both dope and paint rooms had very good ventilation systems with large fans to draw vapors from the area.

A completely automatic fire protection system was installed in the factories. Fire extinguishers were stationed at key spots within the buildings. Extinguishers were always ready in the court area when ships were started and taxied out for takeoff.

Walter Beech had much to do with the design of the factories along with the input of Bill Snook. Snook was responsible for running the entire facility.

Beech commented once about the factory arrangement: "There is no stoppage of materials from the time they come into the plant until they emerge as a completed airplane."

"We have no stock of raw materials in storage, and no stock of planes on hand."

"We are not paying interest on 'non-motion.'"

Soon after the 1928 financial arrangement with Hayden, Stone and Company, Travel Air built factory "C" to cope with the rising demand for their products.

By spring nearly two million dollars in orders were ready and waiting for the company. A night shift was added with 100 men by February to keep pace with orders, bringing the total workforce to about 350.

A fourth factory unit, called Factory "E" was under construction in February, 1929. It was built directly over the concrete open court.

By enclosing this area, far more speed was attained in getting the ships ready for delivery.

The last factory unit built on the site of Travel Air Field was factory "D." This unit was the same as "A," "B" and "C" in appearance and was built in the spring and summer of 1929.

All five buildings were completely operational by June 12, 1929.

Factory "C" was also used for experimental work and housed construction of both Model "R's."

The company was working on a new monoplane by late 1928. Called the Model 10, it was very similar in appearance to the larger Model 6000. The Model 10 was designed to accommodate four people in a comfortable cabin with good visibility.

Construction was similar to the Model 6000, with the fuselage and empennage of welded steel tubing, and wings of wood using the Gottingen 593 airfoil section. A change in contour of the windshield was made on the Model 10-D, being stepped in front whereas the Model 10-B, the first model to be offered for sale, used a sloped windshield similar in appearance to the Model 6000.

The 10-B had a top speed of 140 mph with the 300 hp Wright J-6-9 radial engine, and a cruise speed of 115 mph. Rate of climb was 1140 feet per minute with a service ceiling of 17,000 feet.

Wingspan was 43 feet 6 inches, height 8 feet 8 inches and overall length 27 feet 4-1/2 inches. Gross weight came out at 3400 pounds with a payload of 510 pounds.

Factory "D" and "E" are completed in this May, 1929, photo. Water tower is nearly finished, hangars and lodging facility across Central Avenue also completed. The entire East Central complex was called "Travel Air City." (Mike Madewell)

Herb Rawdon helped design the Model 10 as a four-place stablemate to the Model 6000 series. The prototype, serial #1008, licensed C8844 carries Wright J-6-9 of 300 hp in this view. Initial version of this airplane was called Model 10-B. (Beech Aircraft Corporation)

Useful load was a respectable 1145 pounds.

The "Dep" dual side by side controls used in the Model 6000 were also used in the Model 10, this design feature being very popular. Seventy gallons of fuel were carried in two wing tanks.

Four wicker seats graced the cabin, and these were often upholstered to match the customer's choice of interior fabrics. Another feature retained from the Model 6000 was the crank-open windows.

Brakes were standard on the landing gear. Color selections were black fuselage with orange stripe, with wings painted orange — green fuselage with orange wings or a blue fuselage with orange wings. Fancy

Left—Curtiss "Challenger" of 185 hp was also fitted to C8844 for certification purposes. Engine was just too weak for good performance, was soon changed to Wright J-6-7. (Beech Aircraft Corporation)

Below—Production version was called Model 10-D, with standard powerplant being Wright R-760 (J-6-7) of 225 hp. Windscreen was revised with stepped design incorporated, changing overall appearance. Records indicate only 11 Model 10 ships were built. (Beech Aircraft Corporation)

Biplane spars were glued and subjected to 20 tons of pressure for 12 hours in this specially-built fixture. (Beech Aircraft Corporation)

Monoplane spars were built and glued under clamping pressure. (Beech Aircraft Corporation)

selections for a 1929 airplane!

The Model 10-B was offered with three engines: the Curtiss 'Challenger' of 185 hp, Wright R-760 of 225 hp and the Wright J-6-9 of 300 hp. This trio of powerplants was intended to suit the needs of potential customers. Herb Rawdon and his assistants were ready for quantity production of the Model 10 by winter, 1929. It was officially introduced in March and enjoyed only slight popularity through the next 18 months. When sales began to sag in the summer of 1929, the Model 10 was one of the early victims.

The ship used for certification was serial #1008. Licensed 8844, the airplane originally had the J-6-9 installed, then the Curtiss. The Wright R-760, or J-6-7, won out as the standard engine. The J-6-9 version, Model 10-B, cost over $12,000. The Model 10-D with the J-6-7 had a price tag of $11,000 initially, but this was reduced to $8,500 by June, 1930.

Only 11 airplanes can be found in the records. Curtiss-Wright later introduced the Model 15 monoplane, with family ties to the Model 10.

With 9 biplane models, 3 monoplane models and 5 factory buildings to construct them in, Travel Air rearranged the production sequence in June, 1929. After the fuselage was welded it received its sheet metal and was covered with fabric. It was rolled on a dolly into the dope room and six coats of clear cellulose nitrate dope were applied. The color coats were sprayed in another room adjacent to the dope area. A "sand coat" was applied first, then two finish coats, the last one being thinned to a 70% thinner, 30% color consistency. This process gave the fuselage and wings a very glossy appearance.

Biplane spars were made of two pieces, routed out for lightness and glued together. The assembly was placed in glue press and subjected to 20 tons of pressure for 12 hours.

Monoplane spars were built up in laminations. Each lamination had the grain running in opposite directions to reduce the warp tendency as much as possible.

Ribs were slipped over the monoplane spars then nailed and glued into position. The monoplane ribs were built up truss but the biplane ribs were web design, with solid compression ribs.

Each department had a system of checks they ran before accepting a piece or part from the previous department. Inspectors were stationed in each factory. Tags were color coded for "OK" or "Rejected." The tags were

not removed until assembly and then assemblies were inspected once again. Quality control was practiced to the extent that very few problems ever surfaced.

C. J. Lucas headed the team of factory inspectors. He gathered reports daily from his inspectors and then reported to Walter Beech. These men did a good job all the years of Travel Air's existence, a job that became more and more difficult as production grew.

Clarence Clark, Monty Barnes, Newman and Truman Wadlow and Pete Hill were the production test pilots. They accepted each airplane from the production department and filled out a sheet that was filed for future reference.

By 1929 Travel Air was opening up the export market, expanding its dealer force and aiming at increased foreign sales. Walter Beech had already succeeded in foreign markets in the past two years selling to customers in Peru, Mexico and other South American countries. But he wanted to expand that market to the utmost.

In November of 1928 Beech sent Ira McConaughey and "Skipper" Howell to Mexico City. Their assignment was to demonstrate the Travel Air Model 6000 to the Mexican government.

Beech knew that Ira could do some selling. While there McConaughey talked with Henry C. Barru, who was acting for the Mexican government. Ira found out that the Mexicans definitely wanted to buy airplanes but they didn't know who to buy them from!

Travel Air wasn't the only one building up an export market. Eddie Stinson was down Mexico way, too, flying his cabin monoplane. Waco was there, and other

View of monoplane spar shows cross-laminations to preclude warping. Mahoghany plywood was glued and nailed to both sides. (Beech Aircraft Corporation)

Every wing built received preservative dipping in special vat. Note anti-slip grating. (Beech Aircraft Corporation)

companies.

Ira took cabinet members up for rides, the airplane performing very well in the high density altitude of Mexico City. When Ira got back to Travel Air he had managed to get the Mexicans interested, but had no firm orders. The demonstrator airplane was left in Mexico City and McConaughey and Howell returned by rail.

Newman and Truman Wadlow also made trips to Mexico City. They demonstrated the Model 6000 and sales were forthcoming from their efforts.

When Curtiss and Wright agreed to combine their or-

ganizations into one, Travel Air was invited to join the group. The merger between Curtiss-Wright went through in August of 1929. Prior to that occasion, Clement Keys and Richard F. Hoyt had worked out the arrangements for an organization called the Aviation Credit Corporation, made up of Wright Aeronautical, Curtiss Flying Service, Keystone/Loening and Travel Air.

The plan was to set up a huge financing company to help promote sales of their products. An amount of 10 million dollars was available for that purpose when the group came together in March of 1929.

Travel Air would benefit from this. It was a good sell-

Model 6000 welding jig was large, complex unit. Teams of skilled welders turned tubing into fuselages under supervision of George Snyder, kneeling with tie on. Such coordinated efforts were necessary to keep pace with the other departments of the factory. Monoplanes were becoming very popular by early 1929. (Beech Aircraft Corporation)

Engines were installed in the east end of Factory "C." Overhead lifts simplified moving engines from one area to the waiting airframe. Six different engines were visible in foreground: Curtiss OX-5, OXX-6 and C-6, Wright-Hispano and Wright J-5, J-6. A-6000-A at right, 6000-B next to it. By summer, 1929, Travel Air was building over 25 ships per week, keeping the workforce very busy. Employment peaked at just over 650 men in 1929.

Above left—A.M. "Monty" Barnes, pilot for Travel Air Transportation. (A. M. Barnes)

Above middle—Ray "Skeets" Barker was one of Travel Air's chief mechanics. Like many good technicians, he learned about the Travel Air from experience, starting back in the early days of the company. (A.M. Barnes)

Above right—Pete Hill managed Travel Air Transportation department. He was a very talented pilot who was respected and liked by those he worked with. He and Walter Beech worked at Arkansas City after World War I, and Hill helped Beech land a part-time job with Swallow in 1921. Pete Hill later flew first flight of Ted Well's Model 17 "Staggerwing" on November 4, 1932. (A.M. Barnes)

Below left—Ira McConaughey flew for Travel Air. He also flew R614K on a number of occasions after the 1929 Cleveland races. (A. M. Barnes)

Below middle—Travel Air's first designated factory representative was Owen G. Harned. He formulated sales policy along with Beech and spearheaded efforts to support worldwide network of distributors. (Beech Aircraft Corporation)

Below right—Ray W. Brown joined the company sales force in 1928. With Harned he further expanded sales efforts from the factory to the field outlets. (Beech Aircraft Corporation)

ing point for the salesmen to use—the customer didn't have to struggle to find financing, as Travel Air had it readily available. It made buying airplanes almost as simple as buying a car.

Travel Air smashed virtually all sales records that same month of March. Three hundred thousand dollars worth of orders from only one month! One year previous the total sales had been $100,000! The hard working sales people like Ray Brown and O. G. Harned were really doing the job, as were the distributors and dealers.

By June, 1929, Travel Air was building 25 airplanes per week. And this was barely holding the line on orders.

When Travel Air exchanged its stock with Curtiss-Wright in August, the value of one share of Travel Air outstanding stock worth $100 in 1925 was now worth $4,000!

The merger was deemed appropriate for the good of the company, in view of the need for more factory space and the financial requirements expected, the board of directors and Walter Beech believed they made the right decision.

The 1928 business deal between Travel Air and Wright Aeronautical produced more than just a change in the bank balance. With sales on the way up the com-

*Engineering office in 1928, with Horace Weihmiller in fore-
ground, Herb Rawdon in rear at left. Compare this setup to any
engineering office found today, and it would look quite sparse
and simple! Yet, from these tables came the Model 6000 and
Model 10, the improved biplanes and the legendary Model "R."
(Beech Aircraft Corporation)*

pany decided to try a different system of distribution.

Ray W. Brown, who had at least 10 years in the aviation business, hired on at Travel Air in October, 1928.
He would be the sales representative covering the area
between Cleveland and Denver, while O. G. Harned was
in charge of the eastern region.

The two men were combination salesman/pilots and
flew Travel Air products to every dealer and distributor in the states. They helped set up sales policies for
those outlets and encouraged sales techniques and
methods.

Brown and Harned were directly responsible to Wal-

*Administration building housed boiler rooms on first floor, exec-
utive and general offices above. Company cars were parked inside garage with double doors. (Beech Aircraft Corporation)*

ter Beech and made regular reports to the president.

Beech recognized that there were many other airplanes flying that were as good as anything Travel Air
made.

He also knew that competition was going to get tough-
er than it already was. Travel Air was determined to remain a leader in the industry, and a new sales plan was
an integral part of that effort.

Walter Beech knew the value of the repeat customer.
It's an old, proven fact that if a buyer is sold a product,
then is treated fairly and with respect in terms of sales
and service, he will very likely come back again when
ready for another purchase. Beech believed in and practiced this philosophy.

It didn't matter what the business was, selling cars,
boats or airplanes, the rule stuck. Travel Air endeav-
ored to do everything in its power to sell and get repeat
sales on its products—treating the customer as king.

Each Travel Air dealer and distributor was required
to complete a monthly sales form, the dealers sending
theirs to the regional distributor. Then the distributor

Above left—K.K. Shaul was comptroller and early employee of Travel Air. His financial wisdom helped bring the company to new heights of success by good management. (Beech Aircraft Corporation)

Above middle—Factory manager William "Bill" Snook was an integral part of Travel Air's five-year success story. He was responsible for the entire production process. (Beech Aircraft Corporation)

Above right—Ralph Nordberg performed public relations/advertising for the company in 1929. (Beech Aircraft Corporation)

analyzed each dealer's performance and needs and sent in his report to the Wichita factory. A complete file was kept on every selling outlet.

Travel Air also monitored service of their ships. No outlets were Travel Air dealers without having Travel Air service available.

Distributors were required to keep a minimum parts supply on hand at all times, both for their own use and for the needs of their dealers.

Regarding parts, the company had experienced difficulty in past years because dealers and distributors ordered wrong parts. This was understandable as there were no parts catalogs up to that time in 1928. Travel Air finally made up a complete listing of all parts used in every model.

Service manuals were not available until the advent of the Model 6000. A manual was prepared for its use, but the biplanes had only a rigging booklet and charts for assembly. These were generally adequate for most mechanics of the era.

Factory bulletins were issued when deemed necessary. These covered improvements in the airplanes that could be incorporated in the field, and other bulletins discussed changes being made and price alterations. All distributors were required to have an airplane 'at the ready' for immediate dispatch of parts. The Travel Air factory had at least one ship on hand all the time for delivery of parts or to bring in technical help. Company advertising was very effective with the buying public. Travel Air did all the national advertising from the Wichita office, but dealers and distributors performed their own retail advertising.

If an outlet ever needed help in any way, or if they wanted assistance in preparing advertising, Travel Air had a man on the payroll to handle that contingency.

Howard W. Harrington and Ralph Nordberg were

Travel Air's advertising men. Both worked hard at helping to put Travel Air at the top of the sales and service list.

One can see from this description that Travel Air was far more than just airplanes. It was people with responsibilities, a respectful attitude for the customer, dedication to a job that wouldn't get done without a great deal of hard work.

The Curtiss-Wright merger finally took Walter Beech away from Wichita. He was elected on October 8, 1929, as president of the Curtiss-Wright Flying Service sales division. He had additional duties as chairman of the sales committee of the Curtiss-Wright Corporation, and also retained the presidency of Travel Air.

Offices were provided Beech in New York City and St. Louis, Missouri.

Ralph Damon of the Curtiss-Wright Corporation was put in charge of operations at the Wichita factory after Beech was no longer able to preside.

Most of the Wichita folks didn't care much for the eastern takeover of "their" factory, but it was eastern money that helped Travel Air grow.

From time to time the men who worked at Travel Air ran into some interesting situations, and Monty Barnes relates this story of how the factory was doing its best to keep the customer satisfied.

During the summer of 1929 the word came down from up front, meaning Walter Beech's office, that every pilot on the line and those on-call were to report to Mr. Beech at once. It sounded very serious—this type of gathering was highly unusual.

Gathered in Walter's spacious office, a few jokes were exchanged and then the subject of the meeting came up.

Beech wanted all Model 2000 airplanes to receive two hours of flying time prior to delivery in addition to original flight test time.

Monty liked that just fine. He was all alone in a brand new Travel Air 2000 with two hours of free flying time. He would climb the Model 2000 up to 6,000 or 7,000 feet and punch through clouds; the white, fluffy cumulus that were always in the summer Kansas sky.

Later on, the two hours per ship program was dropped because it was too time consuming. But Monty Barnes never had an OX-5 "miss a pop" when he was flying. Others weren't so fortunate. Truman Wadlow went down when his OX-5 quit, and he just made it into a meadow south of Travel Air Field. All the pilots helped one another in such situations. Upon seeing an airplane down, the pilot would swoop in low and see who it was. He would fly back to the factory and tell the line chief. Then a truck would be dispatched with a mechanic to repair the problem, usually engine failure.

Monty did have his share of forced landings, though. He remembers when he had total engine failure after takeoff, and the only area available was a 200 ft. stretch directly ahead. He got his ship down without a scratch. The field had a fence on all four sides! No brakes, either, just good piloting.

But sales seemed to be "failing" in the summer of 1929. The stock market was four months from falling flat on its face, but Travel Air suddenly felt a change. It was slow at first, but then gained momentum—downward.

Sales in the month of June, 1928, hit nearly $350,000. By June, 1929, total sales were peaked at $560,000. July through October of 1928 was not too good, with sales decreasing to a low of about $100,000, and the trend was repeated in the same months of 1929.

But the difference between the two years was obvious —in the fall of 1928 sales picked up again, showing a strong upward trend, but the fall of 1929 didn't agree. The slope of the sales chart from June through December looked like a brick had been dropped in mid-air.

It was discouraging, but Beech exhorted the troops in the field to hang on and sell, sell, sell! It was a case of being easier said than done.

Many thought the aviation "boom" was finally over. Sales still took place, but not enough to keep 650 workers on the payroll. Layoffs began soon after the debacle at Wall Street in October. There was sufficient work to keep employees busy, but when sales went down so did the number of employees.

Prices were not reacting that way, however. The Model 2000 sold for $2,785 in January, 1927, went down to $2,750 in January, 1929 and then went up to $3,677.50. That was with a new OX-5, which was getting harder to find by then.

Doctor J.C. Smith (right) and his assistant pose before the Travel Air infirmary. Smith was also personnel manager and chief of safety for the factory. (Beech Aircraft Corporation)

A rebuilt OX-5 could be installed and that lowered the price to $3,152.50, and the OXX-6 of 102 hp and dual magnetos went for $3,452.50 with rebuilt engine and $3,777 with a new powerplant.

The same airplane without either engine cost $2,652.50. Travel Air wasn't ready to cut prices yet. Here's a listing of some other ships and their prices as of November 1, 1929—quite soon after the market started to tumble.

BIPLANES

Model 3000	Less engine—$3,290	
	With rebuilt Wright-Hispano—$4,090	
W-4000	$ 5,646	Warner Scarab
K-4000	$ 5,173	Kinner K-5 of 100 hp
A-4000	$ 6,240	Axelson of 150 hp
C-4000	$ 6,693	Curtiss Challenger of 170 hp
E-4000	$ 6,580	Wright J-6 of 165 hp
B-4000	$ 8,640	Wright J-5C of 200/225 hp

MONOPLANES

Model 6000-B	$13,500	Wright J-6-9 of 300 hp
Model A-6000-A	$18,500	Pratt & Whitney Wasp of 420 hp
Model 10-D	$11,250	Wright J-6 of 225 hp

The total sales of Travel Air Co. at the end of 1928 was $2,069,876.10. The June, 1929 figure was $2,008,366.28. But the June figure only represents sales to June 30. If the slump had not hit at that time, sales would probably have gone higher.

The export market wasn't much better off, either. Sales through those outlets were never as good as domestic figures, but Travel Air did make good progress into those market areas.

Beech helped establish the Aereo Export Company, with its offices at the Orpheum Building in Wichita. Here sales were handled for the West Indies, Central and South America. Anderson, Meyer & Company of New York covered 18 provinces of China, also Manchuria, Mongolia, Chinese Turkestan-Thibet, the island of Hong Kong and some leased territories.

The Canadian government approved Travel Air ships in 1928, and Continental Aero Corporation, Ltd. in Montreal handled all sales for that nation. W. Raymond Garrett of Melbourne took care of Australia and New Zealand.

K. K. Hoffman and E. L. Buckley were the Mexican dealers. South African sales were handled by Calvin Martin of Cape Town, while the Simmons Aircraft Ex-

1981 aerial view of Beech Aircraft factory complex shows Travel Air factory units delineated at left. Runway is still approximately in same location. (Doug Ambler)

Newman Wadlow worked for Pete Hill, flew in the 1929 Ford tour with Ralph Nordberg in Model 6000-B with NACA cowling. (Beech Aircraft Corporation)

port Division of Los Angeles did the sales work for Siberia, India, Siam, the Netherlands, East Indies, Korea, Japan, Greece, Poland, Rumania, and Italy. The Hawaiian Islands and the Philippine Islands were covered by Western Pacific Air Transport, Inc., out of Honolulu.

Travel Air literally covered the globe with a sales network, and much of the credit for the success of this network went to Ray Brown, O.G. Harned and Walter Beech. They set the system up and made it work. The help they received from the respective dealers did the rest.

In the fall of 1929, the domestic sales network was again revamped. New men were brought in to help Beech and Harned, as Ray Brown had departed the company in November.

Under the new system, Travel Air planned to have five zones of responsibility for salesmen from the factory. Walter Beech had laid out the zones in over six weeks of meetings and planning sessions both in New York and Wichita. Everyone of the salesmen got to contribute to the overall scheme. When finished, it looked like this:

Zone 1—O. G. Harned He was to take care of Ohio, Virginia, Pennsylvania, Maryland, Delaware, New Jersey, New York, Maine, New Hampshire, Vermont, Massachusetts and Connecticut.

Zone 2—Doug Davis Davis was based in Atlanta and served southern Texas, Louisiana, Arkansas, Mississippi, Tennessee, Alabama, Florida, North Carolina, South Carolina and Georgia.

Zone 3—Jay R. O'Connell O'Connell was at Anglum, Missouri with responsibilities for east Missouri, Kentucky, Indiana, Michigan, Wisconsin, Minnesota, and the south and east of Illinois.

Zone 4—E. B. Christopher Known to everyone at Travel Air as "Swede," Christopher was in charge of

west Missouri, Oklahoma, north Texas, North Dakota and South Dakota, with the entire territory as far west as the Pacific Coast.

Zone 5—E. K. Campbell "Rusty" Campbell had the smallest region, with Nebraska, Iowa and the northwest part of Illinois.

They had their work cut out for them, and they did the best they could to help and assist the dealer/distributor agents in their respective regions.

Along with the regional shifts, Travel Air also offered more lucrative incentives. The salesman became the most important person at Travel Air. It was up to him to get the orders that would keep the factory in operation —but it couldn't be done without willing buyers. They were few and getting fewer by 1930.

Businesses like Travel Air rallied around President Herbert Hoover as he tried to spark the nation back into productivity and a healthy economy.

But right at the home office in Wichita, layoffs were becoming a thing to be reckoned with. Workers having little time with the company were cut first, then Mr. K. K. Shaul and his ledger books saw the need for more reductions in the workforce.

There were spurts of encouragement from time to time, such as inquiries about airplanes that arrived at the office. Olive Ann Mellor and her assistants had more than 41 letters per day between August and December, 1929. Over 43 people per day visited the factory in the same time period.

One must remember that it wasn't just the salesmen, incentive plans and the like that made Travel Air go, the ladies in the front office had much to do with the success of the company.

Other members of the office in addition to Olive Ann Mellor were Estella Blanton, Madge Doyle, Sylvan Stevens, Merle Van Boskirk, Thelma Geiger and Atlar Meyer.

Thelma Geiger took care of accounts payable. Estel-

Truman Wadlow flew in 1930 Ford tour, using the first Curtiss-Wright "Sedan," Model 6B. (Beech Aircraft Corporation)

la Blanton worked for the sales department as a secretary and stenographer. Sylvan Stevens was the switchboard operator.

Madge Doyle was responsible for the payroll, and she later married Roy Edwards, the chief purchasing agent of the company. He dated Olive Ann, but Madge became Mrs. Edwards in 1930—Olive Ann became Mrs. Beech in the same year.

Merle Van Boskirk was the head secretary and stenographer. She was known as 'Miss Van' about the office, and was selected by Walter Beech as his personal secretary for the New York office. Olive Ann also went to work for the Curtiss organization along with Miss Van Boskirk.

Another office worker was Laura Lee Rawdon, wife of Herb Rawdon.

Atlar Meyer was 'second in command' of the office when Olive Ann was away or unable to work.

A courtesy car was usually available at the factory for transient pilots and guests, and the office girls had a Chevrolet. They used it to run errands and pick up the mail at the downtown post office, and then take the outgoing mail downtown in the later afternoon.

Jack Hicks was a young man who helped at times with the payroll and other office duties. He also ran errands in the car when the girls were busy and he conducted factory tours.

By November of 1930, sales had dropped to new lows. The business pulse of the nation still ran slow. Airplanes and those who built and flew them were early victims of this economic collapse.

As the production fell at the Wichita factory, Curtiss-Wright decided it would be best to move all production to the St. Louis facility. Consolidation of production would save money and hopefully the Wichita facility could be opened again when things looked better. It never happened.

As the Italian Model "R" was being built, most of the great Travel Air factory was empty.

The autumn days of 1932 saw the remaining Travel Air employees given their notices of termination. Hardly any ships were being built.

Fuselages and wings, along with empennage groups and engines were stored in factory "D" and other rooms of the complex.

Still other factory buildings held more parts for once-demanded Travel Air machines . . . some rooms were just empty.

The house Walter Beech built for Frank Ashworth, the custodian and faithful employee at the factory, was now lived in by Roy and Madge Edwards.

Roy Edwards was one of the last employees retained by Curtiss-Wright at the Travel Air location. His job was to sell off all the equipment in the factory. By late 1932 it was all gone. He had obtained the best price he could for all of it, too. He thought about how things had changed—five years before Travel Air didn't have enough equipment, and now it was selling all it had.

The site known as "Travel Air City" ceased to exist in September, 1932.

Example of Travel Air data plate circa 1927 through 1928. Note monoplane in the Travel Air logo. (Frank Strnad)

Example of Travel Air data plate circa 1929, for C-4000 biplane. Monoplane in Travel Air logo was used from 1925 until company ceased to exist. (Frank Strnad)

CHAPTER NINE
The Standard of Aircraft Comparison

Travel Air had always meant a finely crafted airplane for the dollar, but when the company adopted the slogan "Standard of Aircraft Comparison" in September, 1929, it drew the wrath of envy and jealousy from some competitors.

There are many old fliers who will back that slogan up with words of praise that exceed the ones of Travel Air's sales department.

The men of Travel Air Co. felt they had ample justification for use of such a slogan. Reputation, quality, good engineering and lots of records in the books were just a few. Walter Beech liked the sound of it . . . Standard of Aircraft Comparison. He wasn't afraid to publicize what he believed.

The time has come in the story of Travel Air to examine each one of the airplanes that held the banner high for Travel Air Co.

Some were very popular and sold in large numbers while several models were introduced too late for the market or just didn't sell with the same success that others did.

Yet, all were considered the pinnacle of their breed. The company obtained 21 approved type certificates (ATC) in their five years of operation. After the Curtiss-Wright merger in August of 1929, the company came under new control and the designs were altered and renumbered to suit the methods of Curtiss-Wright.

After 1926 every aircraft built for commercial sale had to be awarded the Department of Commerce Approved Type Certificate. Travel Air had built the Model B, Model BW, Model BH, Model CW and the Type 5000 by the time approval was required.

A listing is presented showing all Travel Air models and the date of their approved type certificate, but does not include Curtiss-Wright models. Only original Travel Air airplanes up to December, 1929, are listed. Engines that are listed are those approved for the original type certificate and does not include those approved under the Group Two system, which was a supplement to the parent certificate. Travel Air airplanes that did not receive an approved type certificate are noted in the listing.

MODEL	ENGINE	ATC NUMBER	DATE APPROVED
2000	Curtiss OX-5 or Curtiss OXX-6 90 & 102 HP	30	March, 1928
3000	Wright-Hispano Model A or E 150 & 180 HP	31	March, 1928
4000	Wright J-5 220 HP	32	March, 1928
5000	Wright J-5 220 HP	Not Issued	Not Applicable
6000	Wright J-5 220 HP	100	January, 1929
7000	Wright J-4 or Wright J-5 200 & 225 HP	Not Issued	Not Applicable

Model 6000 fuselage was tube-braced at front, wire-braced from fifth bay aft. Preservative oil was injected into tubing under pressure, then drained. (Beech Aircraft Corporation)

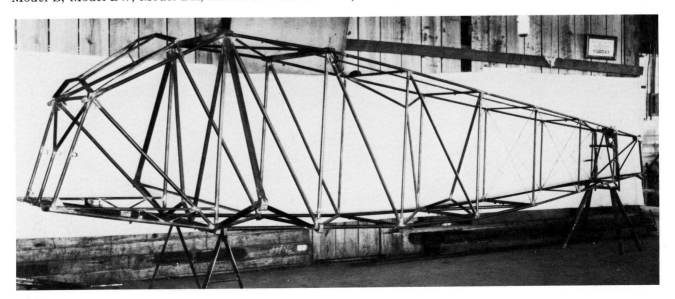

Model 2000/4000 fuselage was welded in two sections. All bi-plane fuselages also received preservative treatment. (Beech Aircraft Corporation)

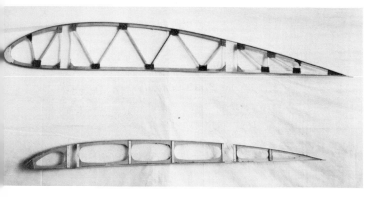

Monoplane rib (top) and biplane rib show differences in construction. Web truss was used on biplane ribs, built-up truss gussets on monoplane version. (Beech Aircraft Corporation)

8000	Fairchild-Caminez 135 HP	37	April, 1928
9000	Siemens-Halske 125 HP	38	April, 1928
SC-2000	Curtiss C-6 160 HP	111	February, 1929
W-4000	Warner "Scarab" 110 HP	112	February, 1929
A-6000-A	Pratt & Whitney R-1340 420 HP	116	February, 1929
6000-B	Wright J-6-9 300 HP	130	March, 1929

Workmen assemble rib on monoplane spars. Note mahogany plywood covering on spar face. (Beech Aircraft Corporation)

B-4000	Wright J-5C 200 to 225 HP	146	June, 1929
BM-4000	Wright J-5C 220 HP	147	May, 1929
A-4000	Axelson R-612 150 HP	148	May, 1929
C-4000	Curtiss "Challenger" 170 HP	149	May, 1929
SA-6000-A	Pratt & Whitney R-1340 "Wasp" 420 HP or 450 HP	175	July, 1929
E-4000	Wright J-6-5 165 HP	188	July, 1929
BC-4000	Curtiss "Challenger" 170 HP	189	July, 1929
K-4000	Kinner K-5 100 HP	205	August, 1929
4-D	Wright J-6-7 R-760 225 HP	254	October, 1929
10-D	Wright J-6-7 225 HP	278	December, 1929
4-P	A.C.E. La-1 140 HP	280	December, 1929

ADDITIONAL NOTES

The Model B-4000 was approved for the installation of speed wings but did not have another Type Certificate issued to cover this change.

The very first W-4000 was actually Travel Air serial #708, X6269. This ship got the approved type certificate for all ensuing airplanes, but a Group 2 approval was required for ships with the Warner "Scarab" built prior to February 16, 1929. These machines had the Travel Air #1 airfoil section and the mass balanced ailerons.

Walter J. Carr installed the first Scarab engine on his Travel Air X3642 and was flown in 1927. This was not a factory conversion.

Only one Travel Air BC-4000 was built, serial #1041, C9821. The airplane was later fitted with floats as the SBC-4000.

Some of the late serial number Travel Air 4-D models were equipped at the factory with Wright R-760 engines of 240 HP.

None of the Model "R" airplanes were issued an approved type certificate, receiving a restricted license for racing on a calendar basis. The two-place version slated to go into production in 1930 would have had a type certificate, and this would have been quite easy for the original "R" ships too, as Herb Rawdon and Walter Burnham designed the airplanes to meet all Department of Commerce airworthiness requirements from the start.

The Model 5000 was not certificated, nor the Model 7000 because of the very limited need expressed for them.

Travel Air obtained Group 2 approvals and these are listed below. Where Curtiss-Wright obtained the approval a note is made.

APPROVAL NUMBER AND DATE ISSUED

1. **2-25/July 6, 1928** — Anzani 10 cylinder radial installed on former Model 2000. This applied only to serial #277 and is

Completed monoplane wing showing fuel tank and quantity indicator at right, cutout for optional landing light and five-point hinge for aileron. (Beech Aircraft Corporation)

sometimes referred to as the "Smith Incubator." French-designed Anzani developed 120 hp; new gross weight of ship 2,180 pounds.

2. **2-26/June 14, 1928** — Serial #510 and #502 with OX-5 engines approved for cotton dusting. Wright J-4 of 200 hp installed at a later date on #501, #502 had Wright-Hispano "E" engine and then Wright J-4 of 200 hp. Both ships in Louisiana area.

3. **2-27/February 23, 1929** — All of the Model 5000 monoplanes were granted this approval for a weight of 3,600 pounds gross, and Wright J-5 radials of 220 hp. The Model 5000 was a 5 PCLM (**P** for place, **C** for cabin, **L** for land and **M** for monoplane) that was never given an approved type certificate. The Group 2 channels allowed relicensing and continued use of this model.

4. **2-28/1929** — Approval for the prototype Model 6000, X4765. Later superceded by approved type certificate #100. This approval included Wright J-5 of 220 hp.

5. **2-35/February 16, 1929** — Approval for all Warner 'Scarab' powered models as W-4000 at 2,276 pounds gross weight. Approved type certificate #112 later superceded this Group 2 permit.

6. **2-42/February 16, 1929** — Model 2000, serial #280 approved for Edo floats at 2,351 pounds gross weight.

7. **2-76/June 11, 1929** — Installation of Pratt & Whitney 450 hp 'Wasp' radial for serial #840, 892, 963, 981, 1079, 1084, 1097, 1098, 2003 as Model A-6000-A, 7PCLM. Approved type certificate #116 was issued for this combination.

8. **2-84/July 2, 1929** — D-4000 "Speedwing" approval for serial #690 and after for installation of Wright J-5 of 220 hp and the "Speedwing" arrangement. Ted Wells owned the first of this model and had the first NACA cowl built by Travel Air on it. Gross weight was 2,650 pounds.

9. **2-138/October 5, 1929** — Model 6000-B were permitted to include an extra seat, making a 7PCLM airplane with 300 hp Wright J-6-9 radial. All serial numbers approved at 4,230 pounds gross weight as S-6000-B.

10. **2-153/December 14, 1929** — Model 6000-B modified for 5PCLM. 300 hp Wright J-6-9 for serial #6B-2028 at 4,230 pounds gross weight. NOTE: Curtiss-Wright serial numbers superceded Travel Air method, hence Model 6B, similar to Model 6000-B.

11. **2-154/November 20, 1929** — Only Model BC-4000 built approved for Edo floats as SBC-4000 at 2,900 pounds gross weight. Curtiss 'Challenger' radial engine of 170 hp.

12. **2-156/1929** — Early approval for E-4000 biplane with Wright J-6-5 of 165 hp. Approved type certificate #188 supercedes 2-156.

13. **2-160/December 4, 1929** — Approval for Model 4P with A.C.E. La-1 radial engine of 140 hp (later known as Jacobs). Only one was built, serial #1332, and approved type certificate #280 was issued on December 12, 1929. Gross weight was 2,388 pounds.

14. **2-167/January 1, 1930** — Model 6000-B, 6 PCLM with 300 hp Wright J-6-9 and 4,230 pounds gross weight. Approved type certificate #130 superceded this approval, but serial #2025 got this approval.

15. **2-169/January 7, 1930** — Approved for Model 4-D, 3 POLB. Wright J-6 radial of 225-240 hp and 2,880 pounds gross weight.

16. **2-178/February 5, 1930** — Model D-4D version, with 240 hp Wright J-6 radial engine. Serial #1340, 1372, 1374, 1376 at 2,650 pounds gross weight.

17. **2-222/June 13, 1930** — Curtiss-Wright approval for D-4000 as 3 POLB with Wright J-5 of 225 hp and 2,650 pounds gross weight. Applied to serial #1391 for this approval.

18. **2-234/July 9, 1930** — Model 6000-B, serial #6B-2012 only with Wright J-6-9 of 300 hp and gross weight of 4,230 pounds.

19 **2-243/July 28, 1930** — Approval for Model 4000 with Wright J-4 of 200 hp for serial #1339 and gross weight of 2,654 pounds.

20. **2-368/July 20, 1931** — Field approval for Tank V-470

Biplane lower wing panel showing aileron push/pull tube, compression and web ribs. (Beech Aircraft Corporation)

Travel Air used shock cord for landing gear after straight axle version was deleted in 1925. Model BH shown here has brakes installed. (Beech Aircraft Corporation)

or V-502 engines (air cooled OX-5) of 115 hp and known as Model 2000-T. Approval held by Milwaukee Parts Corporation and was permitted for all Model 2000 ships under approved type certificate #30.

21. **2-381/1931** — Model B9-4000, either 1 or 3 POLB with 300 hp Wright J-6-9. Applied to serial #1001, 1010, 1103, 1307, 1396, 1397. One of these serial numbers was used by Art Goebel.

22. **2-399/February 3, 1932** — The little biplane built for the Cleveland National Air Races in August, 1929, received this approval as the Model B11D and as a 1 POLB. Wright 240 hp J-6-7, R-760-E radial engine. Serial #1267 was the only ship built, with gross weight of 2,083 pounds. Travel Air applied for this Group 2 approval.

Travel Air produced a total of 35 different models of biplanes and monoplanes during its existence from 1925 to 1931. Of these, 21 models were awarded approved type certificates, with the remainder gaining Group 2 approvals, some approvals being issued at a late date compared to the origin of the airplane itself, such as the Model 5000.

By 1928 and 1929 the popularity of takeoff and landing on water was high on the list of many pilots. Although Travel Air did not build any amphibious or float-equipped ships on its own, it did work with float companies in setting up installations.

These reworked airplanes were then given a Group 2 approval, with the float firms going after approval to aid in getting the business from airframe companies. Here's a sample listing of the most common float installations on Travel Air airplanes.

TRAVEL AIR MODEL	EDO FLOAT MODEL
A-6000-A Monoplane with "Wasp"	#5300 — $3,975
6000-B Monoplane with Wright J-6	#4650 — $3,375
10-D with Wright J-6	#3830 — $2,750
(The Models 10-D or 10-B were not fitted with these floats, but were anticipated in the near future if demand arose.)	
Model 4000 with Wright J-5	#3300 — $2,125
D-4 with Wright J-6	#3300 — $2,125
Model 3000 with Wright-Hispano	#3300 — $2,125
Model C-4000 with Curtiss "Challenger"	#3300 — $2,125
Model A-4000 with Axelson	#3300 — $2,125
Model E-4000 with Wright J-6	#3300 — $2,125
Model K-4000 with Kinner K-5	#2665 — $1,800
Model W-4000 with Warner "Scarab"	#2265 — $1,800
Model 2000 with Curtiss OX-5/OXX-6	#2265 — $1,800

Other float conversions were undoubtedly tried, with or without approval, but these represent the more common ones that were seen in operation. The Model 2000 and Model K-4000 were reportedly anemic in hot weather with floats, especially at high density altitude locations.

Airplanes modified for special use have been around since the Wright Brothers, and the agricultural industry was no exception when it came to airplanes that could apply chemical agents on crops.

Many a Travel Air, when discarded by the original owner for a new ship or at the monetary offer of a buyer, would go into the shop a passenger machine and emerge sometime later a gruff, load-lifting workhorse.

Travel Air saw the market for such a ship in the earlier months of 1929, and decided to engineer a production version of the Model 4000 to fill the "duster" need.

J.R. Woodhull was chief engineer on this project. He began preliminary work in August, and the first airplane was delivered on October 1, 1929, to Lima, Peru.

Designated the Model Z4-D, a Wright J-6-7 of 225 hp was selected to power the airplane. Most of the basic airframe was not re-engineered — but the requirements of a hopper for the chemicals, a feeding and dispensing system were the paramount challenges.

The fuselage was built like any other but was preserved against the corrosive action of the chemicals by use of Lionoil and friction tape that was wrapped around the fuselage tubing as extra protection. This tape was painted with aluminum-pigmented lacquer as a final measure.

All the aluminum fuselage panels were sealed where the dust could enter the pilot's cockpit — a very important precaution as the chemicals were often highly toxic to humans. Two dust-tight baffles were fitted, one in front of the tail skid and another directly behind the cockpit.

A sheep skin sock was placed around the tail skid opening. A smaller sheep skin baffle was fitted where control cables passed through fuselage structure. The hopper was located where the front cockpit would have been and this area was made dust-tight by installation of plywood baffles supplemented with felt sealing strips.

The valve and agitator mechanism and the 24 inch by 3 inch orifice were also sealed with felt material. An extension of the lower cowling covered the control stick

Outrigger/oleo type landing gear for biplanes appeared with Model B-4000 and was necessary to handle higher gross weight. "Aerol" shock struts were often used by Travel Air. This ship has them installed. (Beech Aircraft Corporation)

extension enough to prevent dust entering the cockpit from underneath the fuselage.

Six hundred pounds of chemical agent could be carried in the aluminum hopper that was also reinforced with steel. The hopper was placed on the center of gravity. Loading was accomplished through two hinged doors on top of the cowling. Steps were provided to make loading the hopper easy.

A slide valve with 20 setting increments was adjusted from the cockpit. It only moved three inches total travel, so the 20 positions gave a very good flow adjustment.

The dust was emptied from the hopper through an orifice at the bottom to a wide, venturi-shaped air duct. The duct was exposed to slipstream airflow and the venturi effect helped to pull the dust from the hopper.

To prevent the settled chemical from caking and clogging, a nine-bladed rotating agitator kept the dust churned up. This agitator was driven by an 18-inch propeller blade mounted on the lower right wing. The pitch was set to make rotation easy at slow airspeeds as well as high. Bevel gear and chains ran from the propeller to the agitator, with a 10:1 reduction ratio.

Ball bearings were used for the propeller shaft support and the gear/chain assembly was sealed in a wing/fuselage compartment.

Alemite grease fittings were standard equipment on the gearbox and drive bearings. A structural reinforcement was done to the aft fuselage to make it withstand the extra hard usage anticipated from low-level, high-speed flight operations.

The empennage received attention, too. A single brace strut was fixed to the horizontal stabilizer and fuselage, with wires sufficing for the upper bracing.

Pete Hill tried the early flight tests on the Z4-D and the flour/lime agents were expelled in a very wide, consistent pattern by the hopper and mechanism.

Sixty-one gallons of fuel were carried in the upper wing in two tanks. Gross weight was 3,053 pounds, with a useful load of 1,181 pounds.

Some confusion has existed as to the correct numerical designation of this model, but research has determined the correct number to be Model Z4-D. Cruising range was 480 statute miles.

The first Z4-D was serial #1325 and registered 410N. Travel Air gave the new model a name — "The Cotton Duster," and it is still referred to by that designation.

No approved type certificate data was found, but special Group 2 approval may have been issued due to its special agricultural duties.

The airplane was a good design with much promise,

Milwaukee Parts Corporation obtained Group Two approval for conversion/installation of air-cooled Curtiss OX-5 (Tank V-470 or 502). Known as Model 2000-T, all Model 2000 serial numbers could be converted. (Gordon S. Williams)

and two of the ships were delivered to Peru.

The Z4-D was priced higher than the standard Model 4000 series biplane, costing about $10,000 fully equipped.

TRAVEL AIR
GENERAL CONSTRUCTION DETAILS

Although all of the Travel Air models utilized steel tubing and wood as their primary construction materials, the general methods of how they were built, the changes that were incorporated over the years and improvements made is a worthwhile subject.

FUSELAGE — The very first Travel Air was welded up using commercial grade 1020 steel. Lloyd Stearman knew of other grades, but the availability of this type was a key factor in its use.

Wall thickness was .049 with a tube diameter of 1-1/8 inches, but only from the firewall rearward to the bay just behind the aft cockpit.

From that position the tubing changed to 1 inch diameter with .035 inch wall thickness. This was done to reduce all unnecessary weight where the fuselage was not to be subjected to heavier loads, as was the forward fuselage assembly where the engine was installed.

As production increased and better steel tubing acquired, grade 4130 chrome-molybdenum steel allied with the grade 1025 steel tube were employed for the

Introduced in February, 1929, the Model SC-2000 had 160 hp Curtiss C6, outrigger/oleo landing gear and type "A" wings. (Gordon S. Williams)

92

Paul Braniff bought D-4000, C6239, serial #690 in 1928 with speed wings and specially-faired fuselage and cockpit areas. Group Two approval was issued for others wishing to convert. Engine in this ship is Wright J-5 of 220 hp. C6239 is one of earliest D-4000s built. (Smithsonian Institution Photo No. A47784-A)

forward fuselage and remaining fuselage structure respectively.

Jigs for welding fuselages were made of steel angle welded for proper dimensions with holding fixtures incorporated. The fuselage was welded together starting with the main longerons and brace tubes were added as construction progressed.

The jig could be positioned for ease of welding difficult areas, and the Travel Air procedure of welding the fuselage in two units was helpful. A preservative oil under pressure was run through the finished structure and drained out, the small access hole being sealed.

The fuselage was not heat treated. Other parts were heat treated . . . the control stick, landing gear vees and the tail skid received this process to ensure strength.

Every fuselage was thoroughly inspected in the jig before it was approved to move down the assembly line. Biplane fuselages were easier to build and inspect but the large, bulky monoplane units required a special jig and more workers.

As many as six or eight welders would be working on the big fuselage in order to keep the production schedule.

WINGS — Only the careful selection of spruce wood allowed Travel Air to enjoy its reputation for sturdy, dependable wings. Men trained in the wood business were hired at the factory, adding their expertise to the knowledge of the engineers. These men inspected every shipment of spruce and rejected any that didn't measure up to the Travel Air specification.

Spruce was used because it had long been recognized as the most suitable wood for building important structural assemblies like wing ribs and spars.

The light-weight, straight-grained traits of spruce were desired for the spars, which on the biplanes were of two-piece construction.

Monoplane spars were of three laminations, having opposite grain direction to prevent warping. Each lamination was planed, sanded down for a good glue joint and glued to the other members. A gluing press was used to apply pressure. Mahogany plywood outer cov-

ering on both sides added rigidity and protected the internal laminations.

Ribs were of two different designs. The biplane ribs were built up of spruce webs with 3/16 inch grooved cap strips. Small wood gussets were added adjacent to each web for extra strength. The compression ribs were solid with spruce reinforcing strips on both sides running the full length of the rib. Travel Air used jigs to build these wing ribs quickly and accurately.

The monoplane ribs were quite different than biplane versions. Webs were not used, the ribs being built of truss structure with good rigidity and strength. Monoplane ribs were bigger and required more time to construct. Small plywood gussets were also glued and nailed in place at each rib joint. Heavier cap strips were utilized, too.

When each wing was completed, it was taken to a varnishing station. In the West Douglas factory this was a manual procedure, but the new factory units "C" and "D" eliminated the "choke up" of space, and all wings built after 1929 were dipped in a special vat filled with wood preservative.

Every wing was completely immersed in the vat, then set aside to dry. This procedure greatly accelerated the process and enabled two men to keep pace with 600 others in the production sequence. Grating was provided for sure footing but one worker did slip and fall into the vat over his head! He wasn't seriously hurt, but required some hospitalization.

Travel Air designed three primary types of biplane

Shock cord landing gear, revised cowling, full-length exhaust stacks, improved tail skid were main features of Model 2000 that earlier Model A ships didn't possess all in one package. Note closed coolant radiator shutters. Famous Travel Air Type "A" wings gave biplane docile handling. Over 600 Model A, B and 2000 airplanes were built between 1925 and 1930. (Beech Aircraft Corporation)

Model D4D was a very attractive biplane, with Wright J-6-7 of 225 hp. Type "B" wings and three fuel tanks are shown on this ship. Speed wings could be installed. (Beech Aircraft Corporation)

Last type certificated Travel Air biplane was Model 4P with 140 hp A.C.E. La-1 radial later known as the Jacobs. This is the only example built, ending five years of continuing development of Travel Air biplanes with numerous engines installed. (Peter M. Bowers via Esposito)

wings. Each one had certain requirements for attachment of interplane and cabane struts, center section and rigging of the wings.

Basically grouped, the three wing designs were known as Type "A" with balanced ailerons and no wing tanks, Type "E" with Frise ailerons and no wing tanks, and Type "B" wings had Frise ailerons with a center section fuel tank, plus one fuel tank in each wing. Type "E" wings were introduced in 1927 and 1928, with Type "B" wings showing up in 1929.

The Travel Air airfoil #1 was used on the Type "A" wings. Wing tanks could be installed in either Type "A" or "E" wings. These tanks were usually of 20 gallons capacity each, but larger tanks were available to meet customer requirements. A ship with Type "A" wings without the center section tank carried fuel in a fuselage tank ahead of the front cockpit.

Type "A" wings were the standard setup and are the most well-known version. Rounded wing tips and Frise ailerons were features of the Type "B" and "E" wings. The speed wings had a thinner section and Frise ailerons, with different interplane/cabane struts and rigging requirements.

There were detail changes in the wing construction of the Frise units, these having a plywood web instead of spruce for the ribs.

Speed wings differed, too. They had a semi-built up truss with 3/16 inch x 1/2 inch bracing, with 3/16 inch x 5/8 inch capstrips. This extra strength was required for the anticipated higher airspeeds and load factors with this wing.

Monoplanes used the Gottingen 398 airfoil on the Model 6000 and 6B, with the Gottingen 593 section being chosen for the Model 10B and D. No letter designations were assigned to monoplane wings.

The monoplane used built up truss ribs and Frise ailerons on all models. This combination gave pleasant control feel and good aerodynamic characteristics the customer liked, especially after flying an older machine without such improvements.

METAL FITTINGS — These parts were made of 1026 or 4130 steel, heat-treated as required and given either a cadmium, nickel or chromium plating.

Depth of plating varied, but the cadmium plate was .0003 inch thick with the nickel required to be .0006 inch. Chromium was not used as often.

Every fitting was then given a complete immersion in boiling water to remove any remaining cleaning or plating solutions between laminations or in crevices. This prevented the agents from seeping out later and attacking the finish on the fitting.

Cadmium plated parts were also given a Lionoil treatment for added preservation.

Metal pieces such as cowlings, spinners and upper fuselage decking were given an Oakite bath to remove all residue, and this procedure was sometimes used for fuel and oil tanks.

LANDING GEAR — In this category there were two basic designs. One was the shock cord type, the other the outrigger type. In the first year of Travel Air production, shock cord and straight axle designs were utilized, but the shock cord type was used on all ships after January, 1926.

The shock cord gear attached to the lower, forward fuselage longerons in two ways — by clamps or bolts.

The clamp fittings were installed two inches aft of the forward longeron side fitting, and were installed before the fuselage was covered. The bolt attach method gave the advantage of being able to remove the gear without cutting the fabric around the fittings, as they were easily accessible.

Customer demands for increased load capability required a new, heavy-duty landing gear. The outrigger design was first used on the Model B-4000 of 1929. The fuselage for this model was standard, except for a reinforced forward fuselage and additional mounting fittings.

Bracing tubes ran from the upper and lower longerons on each side to a juncture forward of the lower wing leading edge. An oleo (air and oil) shock strut attached to the tube juncture at the top and the gear vees at the

Travel Air put every improvement possible into the D4D series. These ships were the zenith of biplane development started by Lloyd Stearman back in 1924. (Beech Aircraft Corporation)

C4261, serial #361 was last of Model 7000 built. Four were constructed between 1926 and 1928. Known by the company name of "Pegasus," Wright J-5 of 200 hp gave five-place ship top speed of 107 mph. Compare this airplane with earlier Model CH/CW and the more refined, rounded fuselage and overall appearance of the last example is evident. Complete Department of Commerce stress analysis was completed for "Pegasus" series, but no type certificate was issued. (Walt House)

bottom. The vees were attached to the fuselage at the bottom, center point location and were hinged to rotate.

The outrigger gear was an improvement for Travel Air airplanes, and lent a bit of "bullish" appearance to the ships. The Models B-4000, BM-4000, BC-4000, BE-4000 and B9-4000 utilized the outrigger assembly, as did the Model 4D.

Both monoplane models used a very similar setup, except that heavier capacity oleos were used and they attached to the forward lift strut.

Some of the biplanes with outrigger gear featured a streamlined metal fairing over the oleos for drag reduction.

Rigging the Travel Air was a job for the mechanic, but the company published rigging instructions that were easy to follow.

Lastly, every airplane rigging procedure was slightly different, as each serial number airplane was a distinct ship. Travel Air knew this fact and provided for very minor departures from one airplane to another by giving only the approximate dimensions necessary for rigging.

The interplane/cabane struts on the Model 2000 and the W-4000 were changed after serial #845 when the stagger was modified to 25½ inches with 2 degrees dihedral in the upper wing only.

Closeup showing four cabin windows, assist steps for passengers/pilot. (Beech Aircraft Corporation)

Model 2000 ships serial #449 and before used Model 4000 interplane/cabane struts and featured 28 inch stagger. The wings had to be carefully assembled on the airplanes and then rigged by installing the upper wings first and then the lower wing panels.

Dihedral in the upper wings was accomplished by drawing up the landing wires to tension before the flying wires. Angle of incidence was automatically correct if the interplane strut lengths were correct. Stagger was checked by use of a plumb bob dropped from the upper wing leading edge directly downward and measuring the distance from the leading edge of the lower wing. The stagger on most Travel Air models varied from 24 inches on the D-2000 and DW-4000 with speed wings installed to 30-1/2 inches on the D-3000 and D-4000 with speed wings.

Dihedral was zero degrees on Model 2000 ships with serial #499 to 845, or two degrees to four degrees on the remaining biplane models.

The listing below includes all the known Travel Air (not including Curtiss-Wright) models and their variants, engines installed, type of wings, approximate purchase price and original date of design, when known.

Travel Air numbered their ships consecutively for serial number purposes until the advent of Curtiss-Wright, then a separate serial number system was arranged.

MODEL	ENGINE	WINGS	PURCHASE PRICE	DATE
1st Travel Air	OX-5	A	Unknown	1925
Model A	OX-5/OXX-6	A	$3,500	1925
Model B	OX-5/OXX-6	A	$2,785	1927
2000	OX-5/OXX-6	A	$3,677	11-1-29
2000	OX-5/OXX-6	A	$2,195	1-1-30
SC-2000	C-6	A	$4,000	1929
D-2000	OX-5/OXX-6	Speed Wings	$3,000	1929
3000	Wright-Hispano	A	$4,200	1926
D-3000	Wright-Hispano	Speed Wings	$4,500	1929
4000	Wright J-4	A	$9,800	1926
A-4000	Axelson	A	$6,240	1928
B-4000	Wright J-5	E-B	$8,600	1929
BC-4000	Curtiss R-600	E-B	$6,700	1929
BM-4000	Wright J-5	E-B	$8,600	1929
B9-4000	Wright J-6	E-B	$9,000	1929
BE-4000	Wright J-6	E-B	$6,580	1929
D-4000	Wright J-5	Speed Wings	$9,000	1929
C-4000	Curtiss R-600	A	$6,700	1928
E-4000	Wright J-6	E	$6,580	1929
K-4000	Kinner K-5	A	$5,200	1929
W-4000	Warner R-420	A	$5,646	1928
DW-4000	Warner R-420	Speed Wings	$6,000	1928
4D	Wright J-6	E-B	$8,700	1929
4P	A.C.E. La-1	A	$6,000	1929
6000	Wright J-5	Gottingen 398	$13,500	1928
A-6000-A	P&W "Wasp"	Clark Y-15	$18,500	1928
6000-B	Wright J-6	Clark Y-15	$13,500	1928
10-B	Wright J-6	Gottingen 593	$12,000	1929
10-D	Wright J-6	Gottingen 593	$11,250	1929
R-100	Wright J-6	R.A.F. 34	$17,000	1929
EARLY TRAVEL AIR				
5000	Wright J-5	M-6	$12,000	1926
B6 'Special'	Curtiss C-6	Travel Air #1	$8,000	1925
BH	Wright-Hispano	Travel Air #1	Unknown	1926
7000	Wright J-5	Clark Y	$10,000	1928
BW	Wright J-4	Travel Air #1	Unknown	1926
CW	Wright J-4	Travel Air #1	$9,000	1926

Of all these models the 2000 and the Model 6000-B were the most prolific sellers. This may stem from the fact that both models gave good all-around performance with enough speed, load capability and power to satisfy just about any pilot.

The 4D was also sold in the D-4D configuration with deluxe appointments such as cowling, speed fairings, speed wings and a general drag cleanup.

The following model specifications lists the most common airplanes sold by Travel Air, and is printed using the original style, from 1928-29 factory brochures.

TRAVEL AIR Type 2000
Standard Biplane, Curtiss OX-5
Approved Type Certificate No. 30

S-2000 on floats was a little underpowered, but a small number were equipped and gave acceptable service. (Gordon S. Williams)

SPECIFICATIONS

CAPACITY —
    Pilot and two passengers.

PERFORMANCE WITH NORMAL FULL LOAD —

High speed at sea level	100 mph
Landing speed	42 mph
Normal cruising range (with 42 gal. fuel)	400-420 miles

DIMENSIONS —

Over-all span (tip to tip)	34 ft. 8 in.
Over-all height	8 ft. 9 in.
Over-all length	24 ft. 2 in.
Wing chord (lower)	56 in.
Wing chord (upper)	66 in.
Wing area	296 sq. ft.
Wing section	Travel Air No. 1

POWER PLANT —
    Curtiss OX-5
    90 hp at 1,450 rpm

Fuel consumption at cruising speed	8 gal. per hr.

    Hamilton or Hartzell wood propeller.

WEIGHTS —

Gross weight, fully loaded	2,180 lb.
Weight, empty	1,335 lb.

EQUIPMENT (and other particulars)

COLOR — Fuselage ⎱
    Tail Surfaces ⎰
    Chassis   } Travel Air Blue
    Struts
    Wings —   Aluminum

UPHOLSTERING — Fabrikoid

LETTERING — "Travel Air Mfg. Co., Wichita, Kansas," on fin. Department of Commerce numbers on wings & rudder.

WHEELS — Hayes, wire, 26 x 4.

INSTRUMENTS — Tachometer
    Oil pressure gauge
    Water temperature thermometer
    Altimeter
    Ignition switch
    Choke

LIGHTS — Wings wired for navigation lights. No lights fitted.

CONTROLS — Single, in rear cockpit.
    (Dual control $75.00 extra.)

GAS CAPACITY — 42 gallons.

TANK LOCATION — In fuselage, forward of passenger cockpit.

GAS SUPPLY SYSTEM — Gravity.

OIL CAPACITY — 4 gallons in motor.

WATER CAPACITY — Approximately 5 gallons.

RADIATOR LOCATION — Underslung.

PASSENGERS — Two in front cockpit. Pilot in rear cockpit.

CHASSIS — Rubber shock cord in tension.

Model 3000 was not built in large numbers. Only about 30 can be found in records. Customer furnished Wright-Hispano engine. Serial #798 shown here was sold to J.I. Parker of Kansas

City in October, 1928. Note cabin heat "muff" around left exhaust stack, inlet tube to cabin. (Beech Aircraft Corporation)

TRAVEL AIR Type 3000
Standard Biplane, Hisso
Approved Type Certificate No. 31

SPECIFICATIONS

CAPACITY —
    Pilot and two passengers.

PERFORMANCE WITH NORMAL FULL LOAD —
High speed at sea level	119 mph
Landing speed	46 mph

DIMENSIONS
Over-all span (tip to tip)	34 ft. 8 in.
Over-all height	8 ft. 9 in.
Over-all length	24 ft. 2 in.
Wing chord (lower)	56 in.
Wing chord (upper)	66 in.
Wing area	296 sq. ft.
Wing section	Travel Air No. 1

POWER PLANT —
    This plane is built only when customer furnishes his own power plant.

WEIGHTS —
Gross weight, fully loaded	2590 lb.
Weight, empty	1,640 lb.
Useful load	950 lb.

EQUIPMENT (and other particulars)

COLOR — Fuselage
    Tail Surfaces
    Chassis   } Travel Air Blue
    Struts
    Wings —   Aluminum

UPHOLSTERING — Fabrikoid.

LETTERING — "Travel Air Mfg. Co., Wichita, Kansas," on fin. Department of Commerce numbers on wings and rudder.

WHEELS — Hayes, wire, 750 x 125. mm

INSTRUMENTS — Tachometer
    Oil pressure gauge
    Water temperature thermometer
    Altimeter
    Ignition switch
    Choke

LIGHTS — Wings wired for navigation lights. No lights fitted.

CONTROLS — Single, in rear cockpit. (Dual control, $75.00 extra.)

GAS CAPACITY — 60 gallons.

TANK LOCATION — In fuselage, forward of passenger cockpit, and center section.

GAS SUPPLY SYSTEM — Gravity from center section.

OIL CAPACITY — 5½ gallons.

WATER CAPACITY — Approximately 10 gals.

RADIATOR LOCATION — Underslung.

PASSENGERS — Two in front cockpit. Pilot in rear cockpit.

CHASSIS — Rubber shock cord in tension.

Louise Thaden used this Model 3000, serial #515, licensed 5426 for her endurance attempt. Later fitted with speed wings, it became D-3000 shown here. Radiator was faired into front of cowling, cuffs placed around gear shock cord and fabric installed on wheels for drag reduction. (Peter M. Bowers)

TRAVEL AIR Type 4000
Standard Biplane, Wright Whirlwind J-5C
Approved Type Certificate No. 32

Model 4000, serial #800, licensed 6480, typifies the Travel Air ability to custom-build airplanes for its customers. Note landing lights, double mail pits with covers, revised vertical stabilizer Type "A" wings with fuel tanks; a necessity as the mail pits took away room for the fuel tank. Wright J-5C of 220 hp powered the ship. (Beech Aircraft Corporation)

SPECIFICATIONS

CAPACITY —
Pilot and two passengers.

PERFORMANCE WITH NORMAL FULL LOAD —
High speed at sea level	130 mph
Rate of climb at sea level	1,200 ft. per min.
Service ceiling (climb of 100 ft. per min.)	20,000 ft.
Landing speed	45 mph
Normal cruising range (with 60 gal. fuel)	500-550 miles

DIMENSIONS —
Over-all span (tip to tip)	34 ft. 8 in.
Over-all height	8 ft. 9 in.
Over-all length	24 ft. 2 in.
Wing chord (lower)	56 in.
Wing chord (upper)	66 in.
Wing area	296 sq. ft.
Wing section	Travel Air No. 1
Wing loading	8.1 lb. per sq. ft.
Power loading	12 lb. per hp

POWER PLANT —
Wright Whirlwind J-5C
200 hp at 1,800 rpm
Fuel consumption at cruising speed (1,550 rpm) 12 gal. per hr.
Eclipse hand starter
Intake heater
Hamilton propeller standard equipment.
(Standard steel propeller, $235 extra.)

WEIGHTS —
Gross weight, fully loaded	2,400 lb.
Weight, empty	1,485 lb.

EQUIPMENT (and other particulars)

COLOR — Fuselage ⎫
Tail Surfaces ⎬ Travel Air Blue
Chassis
Struts ⎭
Wings — Aluminum

UPHOLSTERING — Leather

LETTERING — "Travel Air Mfg. Co., Wichita, Kansas," on fin. Department of Commerce numbers on wings and rudder.

WHEELS — Wire, D.H. Type

INSTRUMENTS — Tachometer
Oil pressure gauge
Oil temperature thermometer
Magnetic compass
Air speed indicator
Ignition switch
Primer
Altimeter

LIGHTS — Wings wired for navigation lights. No lights fitted.

CONTROLS — Single, in rear cockpit, stick.

GAS CAPACITY — 60 gallons

TANK LOCATION — 18 gal. in center section.
42 gal. in fuselage forward of passenger cockpit.

GAS SUPPLY SYSTEM — Gravity

OIL CAPACITY — 5 gallons

OIL TANK LOCATION — In front of fuselage below motor.

PASSENGERS — Two in front cockpit. Pilot in rear cockpit.

CHASSIS — Rubber shock cord in tension.

TRAVEL AIR Type A-4000
Three-place Biplane, Axelson 150 hp
Approved Type Certificate No. 148

Model A-4000 featured Axelson R-612 of 150 hp, an improved version of the original "Floco" engine. Type "A" wings were used on early examples, such as serial #1006, licensed NC8842 shown here. (Beech Aircraft Corporation)

SPECIFICATIONS

CAPACITY —

    Pilot and two passengers.

PERFORMANCE WITH NORMAL FULL LOAD —

High speed at sea level	110 mph
Cruising speed	95 mph
Rate of climb	525 ft. per min.
Landing speed	45 mph
Normal cruising range (with 42 gal. fuel)	400-420 miles

DIMENSIONS —

Over-all span (tip to tip)	34 ft. 8 in.
Over-all height	8 ft. 9 in.
Over-all length	24 ft. 8 in.
Wing chord (lower)	56 in.
Wing chord (upper)	66 in.
Wing area	296 sq. ft.
Wing section	Travel Air No. 1

POWER PLANT —

    Axelson, 150 hp at 1,800 rpm

Fuel consumption at cruising speed	8 gal. per hr.

    Wood propeller — stock
    Adjustable metal propeller, $235.00 extra.

WEIGHTS —

Gross weight, fully loaded	2,600 lbs.
Weight, empty	1,600 lbs.
Pay load	425 lbs.
Useful load (2 pass., pilot, baggage, fuel, oil)	1,000 lbs.

EQUIPMENT (and other particulars)

COLOR — Fuselage
    Tail Surfaces
    Chassis   } Travel Air Blue
    Struts
    Wings-   Orange
Or color scheme by arrangement.

UPHOLSTERING — Leatherwove.

LETTERING — "Travel Air" on fin. Department of Commerce numbers on wings and rudder.

WHEELS — and tires 28 x 4

INSTRUMENTS —
    Tachometer
    Oil pressure gauge
    Starting magneto
    Altimeter
    Ignition switch

LIGHTS — Wired for navigation lights. No lights fitted.

CONTROLS — Single, in rear cockpit.
    (Dual control, $75.00 extra.)

GAS CAPACITY — 60 gallons

FUEL SUPPLY SYSTEM — Gravity

PASSENGERS — Two in front cockpit. Pilot in rear cockpit.

CHASSIS — Rubber shock cord in tension.

HEADREST — Standard

TRAVEL AIR Type B-4000
Three-place Biplane, Wright Whirlwind J-5C 200 hp
or Wright Whirlwind Seven 225 hp
Approved Type Certificate No. 146

1929 saw production of the Model B-4000 with stronger wings, higher gross weight and outrigger/oleo landing gear. 8716, serial #1000, is shown here with Type "B" wings having three fuel tanks and Frise ailerons. Landing lights were optional. (Beech Aircraft Corporation)

SPECIFICATIONS

CAPACITY —
Pilot and two passengers.

PERFORMANCE WITH NORMAL FULL LOAD —

High speed at sea level	125-130 mph
Rate of climb, sea level	900 ft. per min.
Takeoff 300 ft.	8 sec.
Service ceiling (Climb of 100 ft. per min.)	14,000 ft.
Absolute ceiling	15,500 ft.
Landing speed	50 mph
Normal cruising range (with 68 gal. fuel)	500-550 miles

DIMENSIONS —

Over-all span (tip to tip)	34 ft. 8 in.
Over-all height	8 ft. 9 in.
Over-all length	23 ft. 7 in.
Wing chord (lower)	56 in.
Wing chord (upper)	66 in.
Wing area	289 sq. ft.
Wing section	Travel Air No. 1
Wing loading	10.1 lbs. per sq. ft.
Power loading	14.5 lb. per hp

POWER PLANT —
J-5C Whirlwind Nine, 200 hp at 1,800 rpm
Fuel consumption at cruising speed
(1,550 rpm)   12 gal. per hr.
Eclipse hand starter
Intake heater
Steel propeller standard equipment

WEIGHTS —

Gross weight, fully loaded	2,900 lbs.
Weight, empty	1,885 lbs.

EQUIPMENT (and other particulars)

COLOR — Fuselage ⎫
   Tail Surfaces ⎪
   Chassis   ⎬ Travel Air Blue
   Struts   ⎪
   Wings-   ⎭ Orange

UPHOLSTERING — Brown Spanish Leather

LETTERING — "Travel Air" on fin. Department of Commerce numbers on wings and rudder.

WHEELS — Wire - 30 x 5 tires
Brakes — Bendix

INSTRUMENTS — Tachometer
Oil pressure gauge
Oil temperature gauge
Magnetic compass
Air speed indicator
Switch
Primer
Altimeter

NIGHT FLYING EQUIPMENT — Complete with landing lights, 12 volt battery and two flares, $500 additional.

LIGHTS — Wired for navigation lights. No lights fitted.

CONTROLS — Single stick in rear cockpit.

GAS CAPACITY — 68 gallons

TANK LOCATION — 26 gal. in center section. 42 gal. in wing tanks.

GAS SUPPLY SYSTEM — Gravity

OIL TANK LOCATION — In front of fuselage below motor

PASSENGERS — Two in front cockpit. Pilot in rear cockpit.

CHASSIS — Oleo

TRAVEL AIR Type B9-4000
Three-place Biplane, Wright Whirlwind Nine 300 hp
Approved Type Certificate (none listed)

B9-4000 was a special version of B-4000 model, equipped with 300 hp Wright J-6-9, Type "B" wings and this example, serial #1001, had tailwheel installed. Group Two approval applied to only six serial numbers for this model. Some used Type "E" wings. (Beech Aircraft Corporation)

SPECIFICATIONS

CAPACITY —
  Pilot and two passengers.

PERFORMANCE WITH NORMAL FULL LOAD —

High speed at sea level	135 mph
Landing speed	50 mph
Rate of climb, sea level	1,500 ft. per min.
Take-off time, no wind, sea level	7 sec.
Take-off in feet	275 ft.
Landing run (no brakes)	400 ft.
Climb to 5,000 ft.	4 min.
Climb to 10,000 ft.	11 min.
Service ceiling	18,000 ft.
Absolute ceiling	20,000 ft.
Cruising speed	115 mph

DIMENSIONS —

Over-all span (tip to tip)	33 ft. 0 in.
Over-all height	8 ft. 9 in.
Over-all length	23 ft. 2½ in.
Wing chord (upper)	66 in.
Wing chord (lower)	56 in.
Wing area	289 sq. ft.
Wing section	Travel Air No. 1

POWER PLANT —
  J-6 Whirlwind Nine-300 hp
  Steel propeller.

WEIGHTS —

Gross weight, fully loaded	2,800 lbs.
Weight, empty	1,885 lbs.
Pay load 340 lbs. Useful load (2 passengers, pilot, baggage, fuel, oil)	915 lbs.

EQUIPMENT (and other particulars)

COLOR — Fuselage ⎫
  Tail Surfaces ⎬ Travel Air Blue
  Chassis   ⎪
  Struts   ⎭
  Wings—Orange, or color scheme by arrangement.

UPHOLSTERING — Brown Spanish Leather.

LETTERING — "Travel Air" on fin. Department of Commerce numbers on wings and rudder.

WHEELS — 30 x 5 tires. Brakes—Bendix.

INSTRUMENTS —
  Tachometer
  Oil pressure gauge
  Starting magneto
  Compass
  Altimeter
  Ignition switch
  Airspeed indicator
  Oil temperature gauge

LIGHTS — Wired for navigation lights. No lights fitted.

CONTROLS — Single, in rear cockpit. (Dual control, $75.00 extra.)

GAS CAPACITY — 60 gallons

FUEL SUPPLY SYSTEM — Gravity.

PASSENGERS — Two in front cockpit. Pilot in rear cockpit.

CHASSIS — Oleo.

STARTER — (Series No. 16 Eclipse.)

TRAVEL AIR Type C-4000
Three-place Biplane, Curtiss Challenger 170 hp
Approved Type Certificate No. 149

In 1928, a Curtiss "Challenger," 170 hp six-cylinder radial was installed in serial # 754 for testing. Model became C-4000. Note speed cuffs around landing gear shock cord. Type "E" wings shown here were popular, but some pilots preferred Type "A" wings on this model. (Beech Aircraft Corporation)

SPECIFICATIONS

CAPACITY —
    Pilot and two passengers

PERFORMANCE WITH NORMAL FULL LOAD —

High speed at sea level	125-130 mph
Rate of climb, sea level	800 ft. per min.
Service ceiling (Climb of 100 ft. per min.)	14,000 ft.
Landing speed	45 mph
Normal cruising range (with 60 gal. fuel)	550-660 miles

DIMENSIONS —

Over-all span (tip to tip)	34 ft. 8 in.
Over-all height	8 ft. 9 in.
Over-all length	24 ft. 6 in.
Wing chord (lower)	56 in.
Wing chord (upper)	66 in.
Wing area	296 sq. ft.
Wing section	Travel Air No. 1
Wing loading	8.8 lb. per sq. ft.
Power loading	15.3 lb. per hp

POWER PLANT —
    Challenger 170 hp at 1800 rpm
    Fuel consumption at cruising speed (1,550 rpm) 10 gal/hr.
    Bosch Booster
    Wood propeller standard equipment (Standard propeller $235 extra.)

WEIGHTS —

Gross weight, fully loaded	2,600 lbs.
Weight, empty	1,600 lbs.

EQUIPMENT (and other particulars)

COLOR — Fuselage
    Tail Surfaces
    Chassis   } Travel Air Blue
    Struts
    Wings-Orange, or color scheme by arrangement.

UPHOLSTERING — Brown Spanish Leather

LETTERING — "Travel Air" on fin. Dept. of Commerce numbers on wings and rudder.

WHEELS — and tires 28 x 4.

INSTRUMENTS —
    Tachometer
    Oil pressure gauge
    Starting magneto
    Altimeter
    Ignition switch

LIGHTS — Wired for navigation lights. No lights fitted.

CONTROLS — Single, in rear cockpit. (Dual control $75.00 extra.)

GAS CAPACITY — 68 gallons.

FUEL SUPPLY SYSTEM — Gravity.

PASSENGERS — Two in front cockpit. Pilot in rear cockpit.

CHASSIS — Rubber shock cord in tension.

HEADREST — Standard.

TRAVEL AIR Type E-4000
Three-place Biplane, Wright Whirlwind Five 165 hp
Approved Type Certificate No. 188

Model E-4000 was very a popular ship. Wright J-6-5 of 165 hp gave good performance, low maintenance. E-4000 was best seller of 4000 series biplanes, experiencing a marked jump in sales in 1929. (Beech Aircraft Corporation)

SPECIFICATIONS

CAPACITY —
Pilot and two passengers.

PERFORMANCE WITH NORMAL FULL LOAD —

High speed at sea level	122 mph
Cruising speed	103 mph
Rate of climb, sea level	700' per min.
Service ceiling (Climb of 100 ft. per min.)	13,000 ft.
Landing speed	46 mph
Normal cruising range (with 67 gal. fuel)	690 miles

DIMENSIONS —

Over-all span (tip to tip)	33 ft.
Over-all height	8 ft. 11 in.
Over-all length	24 ft. 1 in.
Wing chord (lower)	56 in.
Wing chord (upper)	66 in.
Wing area	289 sq. ft.
Wing section	Travel Air No. 1
Wing loading	9.3 lbs. per sq. ft.
Power loading	16.4 lbs. per hp

POWER PLANT —
J-6 Whirlwind Five, 165 hp at 1,800 rpm

WEIGHTS —

Gross weight, full loaded	2,700 lbs.
Weight, empty	1,640 lbs.

EQUIPMENT (and other particulars)

COLOR —Fuselage
Tail Surfaces
Chassis   } Travel Air Blue
Struts
Wings-Orange, or color scheme by arrangement.

UPHOLSTERING —Brown Spanish Leather.

LETTERING —"Travel Air" on fin. Dept. of Commerce numbers on wings and rudder.

WHEELS —and tires 28 x 4.

INSTRUMENTS —
Tachometer
Oil pressure gauge
Starting magneto
Altimeter
Ignition switch

LIGHTS — Wired for navigation lights. No lights fitted.

CONTROLS — Single, in rear cockpit.
(Dual control, $75.00 extra.)

GAS CAPACITY — 67 gallons.

FUEL SUPPLY SYSTEM — Gravity.

PASSENGERS — Two in front cockpit. Pilot in rear cockpit.

CHASSIS — Rubber shock cord in tension.

HEADREST — Standard.

TRAVEL AIR Type K-4000
Three-place Biplane, Kinner 100 hp
Approved Type Certificate No. 205

Model K-4000 used 100 hp Kinner K-5 radial. Economical and fun to fly, K-4000 was popular enough to sell about 8 ships, but it never caught on big. Extension of fuselage to accomodate weight and balance changes is evident in this view of C8841, serial #1005. (Beech Aircraft Corporation)

SPECIFICATIONS

CAPACITY —
  Pilot and two passengers.

PERFORMANCE WITH NORMAL FULL LOAD —

High speed at sea level	105 mph
Landing speed	43 mph
Rate of climb, sea level	500 ft. per min.
Takeoff time, no wind, sea level	11 sec.
Takeoff in feet	300 ft.
Landing run, no brakes	200 ft.
Climb to 5,000 ft.	14 min.
Climb to 10,000 ft.	35 min.
Service ceiling	10,000 ft.
Absolute ceiling	12,000 ft.
Cruising speed at 1,750 rpm	90 mph
Normal cruising range (with 42 gal. fuel)	400-420 miles

DIMENSIONS —

Over-all span (tip to tip)	34 ft. 8 in.
Over-all height	8 ft. 9 in.
Over-all length	24 ft. 8 in.
Wing chord (lower)	56 in.
Wing chord (upper)	66 in.
Wing area	296 sq. ft.
Wing section	Travel Air No. 1

POWER PLANT —
  Kinner, 100 hp at 1,800 rpm

Fuel consumption at cruising speed	8 gal. per hr.

  Wood propeller — stock.
  Adjustable metal propeller, $235.00 extra.

WEIGHTS —

Gross weight, fully loaded	2,300 lbs.
Weight, empty	1,400 lbs.
Pay load	440 lbs.
Useful load (2 pass., pilot, baggage, fuel, oil)	900 lbs.

EQUIPMENT (and other particulars)

COLOR — Fuselage
  Tail Surfaces } Travel Air Blue
  Chassis
  Struts
  Wings-Orange, or color scheme by arrangement.

UPHOLSTERING — Brown Spanish Leather.

LETTERING — "Travel Air" on fin. Department of commerce numbers on wings and rudder.

WHEELS — and tires 28 x 4.

INSTRUMENTS —
  Tachometer
  Oil pressure gauge
  Starting magneto
  Altimeter
  Ignition switch

LIGHTS — Wired for navigation lights. No lights fitted.

CONTROLS — Single, in rear cockpit.
  (Dual control, $75.00 extra.)

GAS CAPACITY — 42 gallons.

FUEL SUPPLY SYSTEM — Gravity.

PASSENGERS — Two in front cockpit. Pilot in rear cockpit.

CHASSIS — Rubber shock cord in tension.

HEADREST — Standard.

TRAVEL AIR Type W-4000
Three-place Biplane, Warner Scarab 110 hp
Approved Type Certificate No. 112

Warner "Scarab" of 110 hp powered Model W-4000. This model was quite attractive and sales proved it. Type "A" and "E" wings were fitted, and speed wings were available if desired. (Beech Aircraft Corporation)

SPECIFICATIONS

CAPACITY —
  Pilot and two passengers.

PERFORMANCE WITH NORMAL FULL LOAD —
High speed at sea level	105 mph
Landing speed	43 mph
Normal cruising range (with 42 gal. fuel)	400-420 miles

DIMENSIONS —
Over-all span (tip to tip)	34 ft. 8 in.
Over-all height	8 ft. 9 in.
Over-all length	24 ft. 7 in.
Wing chord (lower)	56 in.
Wing chord (upper)	66 in.
Wing area	296 sq. ft.
Wing section	Travel Air No. 1

POWER PLANT —
  Warner-Scarab 110 hp at 1,800 rpm
  Fuel consumption at cruising speed   8 gal. per hr.
  Wood propeller — stock.
  Adjustable metal propeller, $235.00 extra.

WEIGHTS —
Gross weight, fully loaded	2,300 lbs.
Weight, empty	1,400 lbs.
Pay load	440 lbs.
Useful load (2 pass., pilot, baggage, fuel, oil)	900 lbs.

EQUIPMENT (and other particulars)

COLOR — Fuselage
  Tail Surfaces
  Chassis   } Travel Air Blue
  Struts
  Wings—Orange, or color scheme by arrangement.

UPHOLSTERING — Brown Spanish Leather.

LETTERING — "Travel Air" on fin.
  Dept. of Commerce numbers on wings and rudder.

WHEELS — and tires 28 x 4.

INSTRUMENTS —
  Tachometer
  Oil pressure gauge
  Starting magneto
  Altimeter
  Ignition switch

LIGHTS — Wired for navigation lights. No lights fitted.

CONTROLS — Single, in rear cockpit.
  (Dual control, $75.00 extra.)

GAS CAPACITY — 42 gallons.

FUEL SUPPLY SYSTEM — Gravity.

PASSENGERS — Two in front cockpit. Pilot in rear cockpit.

CHASSIS — Rubber shock cord in tension.

TRAVEL AIR Type 6000
Six-place Cabin Monoplane, Wright Whirlwind J-5C 200 hp
Approved Type Certificate No. 100

S-6000-B was another float conversion that worked out better than S-2000. This is serial #999, licensed NC8885, flown by Robert S. Fogg, Concord, N.H. (Beech Aircraft Corporation)

SPECIFICATIONS

CAPACITY —
    2 pilots, 4 passengers, and 150 lbs. of baggage, or pilot and 1,000 lbs. mail or express.

PERFORMANCE WITH NORMAL FULL LOAD —

High speed at sea level	120 mph
Cruising	105 mph
High speed at 10,000 ft.	110 mph
Rate of climb at sea level	700 ft. per min.
Service ceiling	10,000 ft.
Landing speed	50 mph
Normal cruising range (78 gallons fuel)	725 miles

DIMENSIONS —

Over-all span	48 ft. 8 in.
Over-all length	30 ft. 6 in.
Over-all height	9 ft.
Wing chord	78 in.
Wing area	282 sq. ft.

POWER PLANT —
    200 hp Wright Whirlwind J-5C motor.

WEIGHTS —

Gross weight	4,000 lbs.
Weight empty (fully equipped)	2,350 lbs.
Pay load	1,000 lbs.
Useful load	1,650 lbs.

EQUIPMENT (and other particulars)

COLOR —
    Travel Air Blue.
    Interior Finish — Option of Velour, Whipcord or two-tone Fabrikoid.
    Cabin furnishing — 4 removable wicker chairs. Windows plate glass, raised and lowered by auto-type crank lifts.
    Wheels — 30 x 5 with 32 x 6 tires.
    Brakes — Bendix.
    Heater.

LETTERING — "Travel Air Mfg. Co., Wichita, Kansas," on fin. Department of Commerce numbers on wings and rudder.

LIGHTS — Instrument lights, navigation lights.

CONTROLS — Dual "dep" side by side.
    Rudder pedals.
    Separately controlled brake pedals.

INSTRUMENTS —
    Tachometer
    Oil pressure gauge
    Oil temperature gauge
    Magnetic compass
    Air speed indicator
    Bank and turn indicator
    Switch, primer
    Altimeter

FUEL CAPACITY —
    78 gallon tank in wing roots
    Fuel, gravity feed.
    Oil capacity, 8 gallons.

TRAVEL AIR Type 8000
Standard Biplane, Fairchild-Caminez
Approved Type Certificate No. 37

The prototype Model 8000 resulted from marriage of Model B airframe and new Caminez radial engine of 120 hp. Four cylinder radial turned 1,000 rpm, had large diameter propeller that required high ground clearance. Only three Model 8000s were built, as the Caminez engine did not prove popular. (Courtesy Mal Holcomb Collection)

SPECIFICATIONS

CAPACITY —
 Pilot and two passengers.

PERFORMANCE WITH NORMAL FULL LOAD —
High speed at sea level	110 mph
Landing speed	43 mph
Normal cruising range (with 42 gal. fuel)	450-500 miles

DIMENSIONS —
Over-all span (tip to tip)	34 ft. 8 in.
Over-all height	8 ft. 9 in.
Over-all length	24 ft. 2 in.
Wing chord (lower)	56 in.
Wing chord (upper)	66 in.
Wing area	296 sq. ft.
Wing section	Travel Air No. 1

POWER PLANT —
 Fairchild-Caminez, 135 hp at 1,000 rpm
 Fuel consumption at cruising speed   7.5 gal. per hr.
 Hamilton or Hartzell wood propeller.
 Eclipse Starter.

WEIGHTS —
Gross weight, fully loaded	2,300 lbs.
Weight, empty	1,475 lbs.
Pay load	360 lbs.

EQUIPMENT (and other particulars)

COLOR — Fuselage
 Tail Surfaces
 Chassis   } Travel Air Blue
 Struts
 Wings —   Aluminum

UPHOLSTERING — Fabrikoid

LETTERING — "Travel Air Mfg. Co., Wichita, Kansas," on fin. Department of Commerce numbers on wings & rudder.

WHEELS — 750 x 125 mm.

INSTRUMENTS —
 Tachometer
 Oil pressure gauge
 Altimeter
 Ignition switch
 Choke

LIGHTS — Wings wired for navigation lights. No lights fitted.

CONTROLS — Single, in rear cockpit.
 (Dual control $75.00 extra.)

GAS CAPACITY — 60 gallons.

TANK LOCATION — In fuselage, forward of passenger cockpit.

GAS SUPPLY SYSTEM — Gravity.

OIL CAPACITY — 5 gallons.

PASSENGERS — Two in front cockpit. Pilot in rear cockpit.

CHASSIS — Rubber shock cord in tension.

TRAVEL AIR Type 6000-B
Six-place Cabin Monoplane, Wright Whirlwind Nine 300 hp
Approved Type Certificate No. 130

Model 6000-B was Wright-powered "Limousine of the Air." Monoplanes were closing the gap on biplane sales by early 1929, pilots preferring to shed their helmet and goggles for the comfort of an enclosed cabin. Shown is NC9084, serial #865, owned by Phillips Petroleum Company. (Phillips Petroleum Company)

SPECIFICATIONS

CAPACITY —
   2 pilots, 4 passengers, and 150 lbs. baggage,
   or equivalent.

PERFORMANCE WITH NORMAL FULL LOAD —

High speed at sea level	130-135 mph
Rate of climb, sea level	800 ft. per min.
Takeoff time, no wind, sea level	12 sec.
Takeoff in feet	500 ft.
Landing run (no brakes)	700 ft.
Climb to 5,000 ft.	8 min.
Climb to 10,000 ft.	16 min.
Service ceiling	16,000 ft.
Absolute ceiling	18,000 ft.
Cruising speed	110 mph
Landing speed	60 mph

DIMENSIONS —

Over-all span	48 ft. 6½ in.
Over-all height	9 ft. 0½ in.
Over-all length	31 ft. 2 in.
Wing chord	78 in.
Wing area	282 sq. ft.

POWER PLANT —
   J-6 Whirlwind Nine Engine, 300 hp

WEIGHTS —

Gross weight, fully loaded	4,230 lbs.
Weight, empty, fully equipped	2,700 lbs.
Pay load, with night flying equipment	815 lbs.
Useful load	1,530 lbs.

EQUIPMENT (and other particulars)

COLOR — Black fuselage with orange fuselage stripe and orange wings or green and orange or blue and orange.

INTERIOR FINISH — High grade Broadcloth.

CABIN FURNISHING — 6 steel frame removable wicker chairs upholstered to harmonize with cabin interior.
   Windows — plate glass, raised and lowered by auto-type crank lifts.

WHEELS — 32 x 6 with 36 x 8 tires.
   Brakes — Bendix.
   Heaters located on both sides of front of cabin.
   Rest Room — $195 extra.

LETTERING — "Travel Air" on fin. Department of Commerce numbers on wings and rudder.

LIGHTS — Instrument lights, navigation lights.

NIGHT FLYING EQUIPMENT — Complete with landing lights, 12 V. battery and two flares, $500.00 additional.

CONTROLS — Dual "dep" side by side.
   Rudder pedals.
   Separately controlled brake pedals.

INSTRUMENTS —
   Tachometer
   Oil pressure gauge
   Oil temperature gauge
   Magnetic compass
   Clock
   Air speed indicator
   Bank and turn indicator
   Switch, primer
   Altimeter

FUEL CAPACITY — 82 gal. tank in wing roots.
   Fuel, gravity feed.
   Oil capacity, 7 gallons.

GENERAL

Cabin insulation is very effective in insulating against heat and cold. Heaters can be regulated to maintain constant cabin temperatures. Flights have been made to a height of 15,500 ft. above sea level in which the outside temperature registered 35 degrees F. below zero while the cabin temperature was perfectly comfortable without wraps, 60-65 degrees F. Insulation is very effective in deadening sound and conversation can be engaged in normal tone of voice.

This airplane is stable, laterally, directionally, and longitudinally and is easy to land.

TRAVEL AIR Type SA-6000-A
Six-place Cabin Monoplane, Pratt/Whitney Wasp 420 and EDO floats
Approved Type Certificate No. 175

SA-6000-A with 450 hp "Wasp" proved to be a rugged, dependable workhorse. Forward entry door on right side was feature of SA-6000-A. Only two of this model were sold, this one being CF-AFK in Canadian service. (Beech Aircraft Corporation)

SPECIFICATIONS

EQUIPMENT (and other particulars)

COLOR — Standard production color, black fuselage with orange fuselage stripe and orange wings or in green and orange or blue and orange.

INTERIOR FINISH UPHOLSTERY — Standard — Blue or taupe Chase Velmo Cut Mohair or fine quality of broadcloth. Special quality of broadcloth or mohair $200.00 extra.

CABIN FURNISHING —
  Chairs — Six steel frame removable wicker chairs upholstered to harmonize with cabin interior.
  Rest room in rear of cabin $195.00 additional.
  Windows — Plate glass raised and lowered by autotype crank lifts. Shatterproof glass in front of pilot's compartment.

PONTOONS — Edo.

HEATERS — Located on each side of front of cabin.

LIGHTS — Instrument lights, navigation lights.

NIGHT FLYING EQUIPMENT — Complete with landing lights, 12 V. battery and two flares, $500.00 additional.

LETTERING — "Travel Air" on fin and nose of fuselage.

CONTROLS — Dual "dep" side by side.
  Rudder pedals.

INSTRUMENTS —
  Tachometer
  Oil pressure gauge
  Oil temperature gauge
  Magnetic compass
  Clock
  Air speed indicator
  Bank & turn indicator
  Switch, primer
  Altimeter

FUEL CAPACITY — 130 gal. tank in wing roots.
  Fuel, gravity feed.
  Oil capacity, 8 gallons.

TRAVEL AIR Type 10-B
Four-place Cabin Monoplane, Wright Whirlwind Nine (J-6) 300 hp
Wright Whirlwind Seven (J-6) 225 hp
Approved Type Certificate No. 278

Model 10-B was replaced in production by 10-D, but 8844, serial #1008 led the way for certification with 300 hp J-6-9. (Beech Aircraft Corporation)

SPECIFICATIONS

CAPACITY —
  Pilot and three passengers

PERFORMANCE WITH NORMAL FULL LOAD —
High speed at sea level	140-145 mph
Landing speed at sea level	55 mph
Rate of climb, sea level	1,140 ft. per min.
Takeoff time, no wind, sea level	11 sec.
Takeoff in feet	500 ft.
Landing run (no brakes)	700 ft.
Climb to 5,000 ft.	6 min.
Climb to 10,000 ft.	16 min.
Service ceiling	17,000 ft.
Absolute ceiling	19,000 ft.
Cruising speed	115 mph

DIMENSIONS —
Over-all span (tip to tip)	43 ft. 6 in.
Over-all height	8 ft. 8 in.
Over-all length	27 ft. 4½ in.
Wing chord	74 in.
Wing area	239 sq. ft.

POWER PLANT — J-6 Whirlwind Nine, 300 hp
  Steel propeller.

WEIGHTS —
Gross weight, fully loaded	3,400 lbs.
Weight, empty	2,255 lbs.
Pay load	510 lbs.
Useful load (2 pass., pilot, baggage, fuel, oil)	1,145 lbs.

NOTE: This Travel Air Monoplane will also be offered with J-6 — Whirlwind Seven — 225 hp engine as soon as engines of that hp are available.

EQUIPMENT (and other particulars)

COLOR — Black fuselage with orange fuselage stripe and or-orange wings or green and orange or blue and orange.

INTERIOR FINISH — Four removable wicker chairs upholstered to harmonize with cabin interior.
  Windows — Plate glass, raised and lowered by auto-type crank lifts.

WHEELS — 30 x 5 with 32 x 6 tires.
  Brakes — Bendix.
  Heater.

LETTERING — "Travel Air" on fin. Department of Commerce numbers on wings and rudder.

LIGHTS — Instrument lights, navigation lights.

CONTROLS — Dual "dep" side by side.
  Rudder pedals.
  Separately controlled brake pedals.

INSTRUMENTS —
  Tachometer
  Magnetic compass
  Air speed indicator
  Starter (Series No. 16 Inertia)
  Oil pressure gauge
  Oil temperature gauge
  Switch, primer
  Altimeter

FUEL CAPACITY — 70 gallon tank in wing roots.
  Fuel, gravity feed.
  Oil capacity, 8 gallons.

TRAVEL AIR Type Z4-D
Cotton Duster Biplane, Wright Whirlwind Seven 225 hp

600 pounds of chemical was carried in forward hopper. Special anti-corrosive paint and tape were applied on fuselage tubing, cockpit was sealed from toxic dust. (Beech Aircraft Corporation)

SPECIFICATIONS

POWER PLANT — Wright R-760 at 2,000 rpm 225 hp
    7 cylinder radial air cooled
    Fuel capacity, 61 gallons
    Oil capacity, 6 gallons

WEIGHT —

Gross	3,053 lbs.
Empty	1,872 lbs.
Useful load	1,181 lbs.
Pay load	600 lbs.
Wing loading	10.5 lbs. per sq. ft.
Power loading	13.6 lbs. per hp

PERFORMANCE —

High speed	128 mph
rpm	2,000
Cruising speed	107 mph
rpm	1,700
Fuel consumption	14 gal./hr.
Cruising range	480 miles
Rate of Climb	850 ft. per min.
Best climbing speed	75 mph
Service ceiling	15,000 ft.
Absolute ceiling	16,500 ft.
Stalling speed	50 mph

Pete Hill flies the Z4-D with flour/lime dust. Calcium arsenate was one of the chemical agents actually used to kill insects attacking crops. (Beech Aircraft Corporation)

The first Z4-D, serial #1325, ushered in the era of specialized agricultural aircraft. Venturi air duct spread chemical evenly. Propeller at left powered hopper agitator. (Beech Aircraft Corporation)

Many Travel Airs were converted for crop dusting. With front cockpit removed and Wright radial or other suitable powerplant, these airplanes soldiered on into the 1930s and 40s. One Group Two approval permitted using the OX-5 for power. (Fran Rourke)

TRAVEL AIR Type R
Racing Monoplane
No Approved Type Certificate

L.G. Larsen flies R-2005 high above the Kansas plains. First flight was July 19, 1931. Newman Wadlow also shared flight test duties on this ship. (Beech Aircraft Corporation)

SPECIFICATIONS

DIMENSIONS —
Span	29 ft. 2 in.

(The Texaco, Shell, and Italian "Rs" had 30-foot, 6-inch span.)

Length	20 ft. 2 in.
Height	7 ft. 9 in.
Wing Chord	60 in.

AREAS
Wing	125 sq. ft.

(Except Texaco, Shell, and Italian airplanes, with 140 sq. ft.)

Ailerons	12.3 sq. ft.
Horizontal stabilizers	23.5 sq. ft.
Vertical stabilizers	9.8 sq. ft.

WEIGHTS
Empty weight	1,485 lbs.

(NR1313 was heaviest of all 5 ships, weighing 1,880 lbs. empty.)

Gross weight	1,950 lbs.

(NR1313 weighed 2,742 lbs.)

Useful load	465 lbs.

(This figure varied on all 5 airplanes; each was unique.)

Wing loading	15.5 lbs./sq. ft.

(NR1313 with small wings 22 lbs./sq. ft., large wings 18.2 lbs./sq. ft.)

Power loading	4.6 lbs./hp

(NR1313 had 5.75 lbs./hp)

ENGINES — Wright J-6 series, as originally installed by Travel Air.

PERFORMANCE
High speed	230 mph

(Both NR1313 and NR482N were capable of higher speeds than this.)

Cruising speed	185 mph

(This varied with each ship.)

Rate of climb, sea level	3,200 ft./min.
Maximum dive speed	300 mph
Landing speed	70 mph

SPECIFICATIONS

TRAVEL AIR TYPE SC-2000

Length — 24 ft. 2 in.
Height — 9 ft. 2 in.
Wing Span, Upper — 34 ft. 8 in.
Wing Span, Lower — 28 ft. 8 in.
Wing Chord, Upper — 66 in.
Wing Chord, Lower — 56 in.
Wing Area, Upper — 178 sq. ft.
Wing Area, Lower — 118 sq. ft.
Total Wing Area — 296 sq. ft.
Airfoil — Travel Air No. 1
Empty Weight — 1,659 lbs.
Useful Load — 941 lbs.
Gross Weight — 2,600 lbs.
Payload with 60 gal. fuel — 370 lbs.
Payload with 42 gal. fuel — 480 lbs.
Maximum Speed — 120 mph
Cruising Speed — 102 mph
Landing Speed — 48 mph
Rate of Climb — 850 ft. per min.
Service Ceiling — 15,000 ft.
Fuel Capacity — 42 or 60 gal.
Oil Capacity — 5 gal.
Cruising Range — 400-575 miles
Fuel Consumption — 10 gal. per hr.
Powerplant — Curtiss C6A, 160 hp

TRAVEL AIR TYPE 4-P

Length — 24 ft. 6 in.
Height — 8 ft. 11 in.
Wing Span, Upper — 33 ft.
Wing Span, Lower — 28 ft. 10 in.
Wing Chord, Upper — 66 in.
Wing Chord, Lower — 56 in.
Wing Area, Upper — 171 sq. ft.
Wing Area, Lower — 118 sq. ft.
Total Wing Area — 289 sq. ft.
Airfoil — Travel Air No. 1
Empty Weight — 1,531 lbs.
Useful Load — 857 lbs.
Payload — 392 lbs.
Gross Weight — 2,388 lbs.
Maximum Speed — 115 mph
Cruising Speed — 97 mph
Landing Speed — 45 mph
Rate of Climb — 700 ft. per min.
Service Ceiling — 12,000 ft.
Fuel Capacity — 42 gal.
Oil Capacity — 6 gal.
Cruising Range — 485 miles
Powerplant — A.C.E. La. 1, 140 hp

TRAVEL AIR TYPE 7000

Length — 26 ft. 5 in.
Height — 8 ft. 11 in.
Wing Span, Upper — 42 ft.
Wing Span, Lower — 31 ft. 7 in.
Wing Chord, Upper — 72 in.
Wing Chord, Lower — 60 in.
Wing Area, Upper — 246 sq. ft.
Wing Area, Lower — 137 sq. ft.
Total Wing Area — 383 sq. ft.
Airfoil — Clark "Y"
Empty Weight — 2,140 lbs.
(with night flying equipment)
Useful Load — 1,579 lbs.
Payload — 1,100 lbs.
Gross Weight — 3,719 lbs.
Maximum Speed — 107 mph
Cruising Speed — 90 mph
Landing Speed — 48 mph
Rate of Climb — Unknown
Service Ceiling — Unknown
Fuel Capacity — 60 gal.
Oil Capacity — 5 gal.
Cruising Range — 375 miles
Powerplant — Wright J-5C, 200 hp

TRAVEL AIR TYPE BC-4000

Length — 24 ft. 6 in.
Height — 9ft. 1 in.
Wing Span, Upper — 33 ft.
Wing Span, Lower — 28 ft. 10 in.
Wing Chord, Upper — 66 in.
Wing Chord, Lower — 56 in.
Wing Area, Upper — 171 sq. ft.
Wing Area, Lower — 118 sq. ft.
Total Wing Area — 289 sq. ft.
Airfoil — Travel Air No. 2 upper span
　　　　Travel Air No. 1 lower span
Empty Weight — 1,793 lbs.
Useful Load — 1,007 lbs.
Payload — 392 lbs.
Gross Weight — 2,800 lbs.
Maximum Speed — 122 mph
Cruising Speed — 104 mph
Landing Speed — 50 mph
Rate of Climb — 720 ft. per min.
Service Ceiling — 12,500 ft.
Fuel Capacity — 67 gal.
Oil Capacity — 6 gal.
Cruising Range — 600 miles
Powerplant — Curtiss "Challenger," 170 hp

TRAVEL AIR TYPE 5000

Length — 30 ft. 5 in.
Height — 8 ft. 9 in.
Wing Span — 51 ft. 7 in.
Wing Chord — 78 in.
Total Wing Area — 312 sq. ft.
Airfoil — M-6
Empty Weight — 2,160 lbs.
Useful Load — 1,440 lbs.
Payload — 750 lbs.
Gross Weight — 3,600 lbs.
Maximum Speed — 123 mph
Cruising Speed — 108 mph
Landing Speed — 55 mph
Rate of Climb — 750 ft. per min.
Service Ceiling — 13,600 ft.
Fuel Capacity — 75 gal.
Oil Capacity — 6 gal.
Powerplant — Wright J-5C, 230 hp
(Other versions of the J-5
were also used, and
horsepower varied.)

TRAVEL AIR TYPE 9000

Length — 24 ft. 4 in.
Height — 9 ft.
Wing Span, Upper — 34 ft. 8 in.
Wing Span, Lower — 28 ft. 8 in.
Wing Chord, Upper — 66.75 in.
Wing Chord, Lower — 55.75 in.
Wing Area, Upper - 178 sq. ft.
Wing Area, Lower - 118 sq. ft.
Total Wing Area — 296 sq. ft.
Airfoil — Travel Air No. 1
Empty Weight — 1,475 lbs.
Useful Load — 825 lbs.
Payload — 360 lbs.
Gross Weight — 2,300 lbs.
Maximum Speed — 112 mph
Cruising Speed — 93 mph
Landing Speed — 42 mph
Rate of Climb — 700 ft. per min.
Service Ceiling — 12,000 ft.
Fuel Capacity — 42 gal.
Oil Capacity — Unknown
Powerplant — Siemens-Halske
(Ryan) R-517, 125 hp

TRAVEL AIR TYPE 4-D

Length — 23 ft. 4 in.
Height — 9 ft. 1 in.
Wing Span, Upper — 33 f t.
Wing Span, Lower — 28 ft. 10 in.
Wing Chord, Upper — 66 in.
Wing Chord, Lower — 56 in.
Wing Area, Upper — 171 sq. ft.
Wing Area, Lower — 118 sq. ft.
Total Wing Area — 289 sq. ft.
Airfoil — Travel Air No. 1
Empty Weight — 1,837 lbs.
Useful Load — 1,043 lbs.
Payload — 428 lbs.
Gross Weight — 2,880 lbs.
Maximum Speed — 130 mph
Cruising Speed — 110 mph
Landing Speed — 52 mph
Rate of Climb — 980 ft. per min.
Service Ceiling — 14,000 ft.
Fuel Capacity — 67 gal.
Oil Capacity — 6 gal.
Cruising Range — 520 miles
Powerplant — Wright J-6-7, 225 hp.
or Wright J-6-7, 240 hp

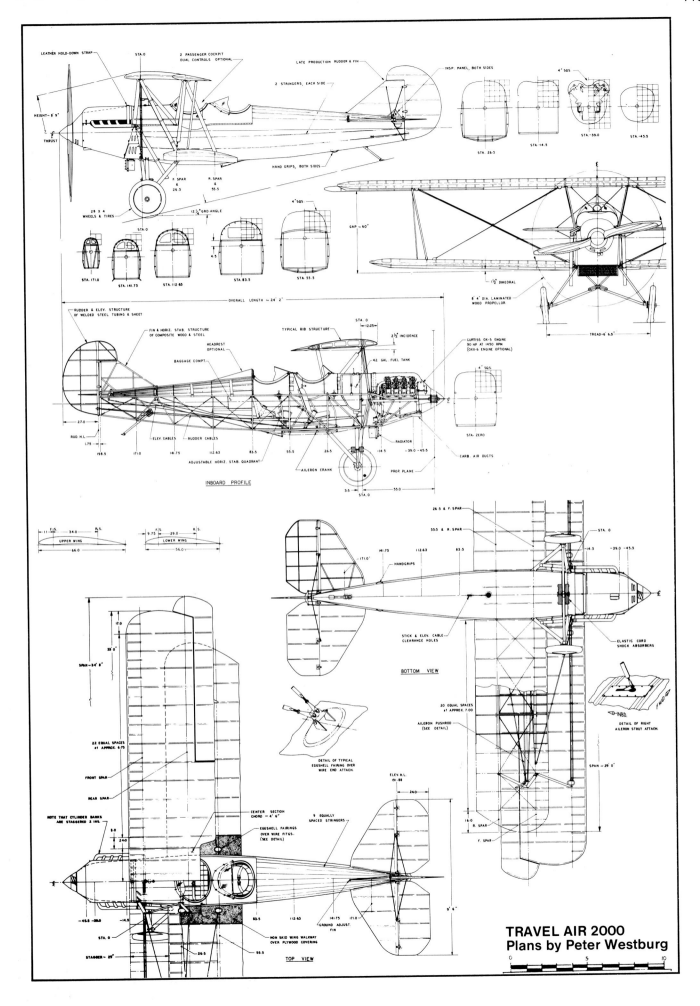

TRAVEL AIR 2000
Plans by Peter Westburg

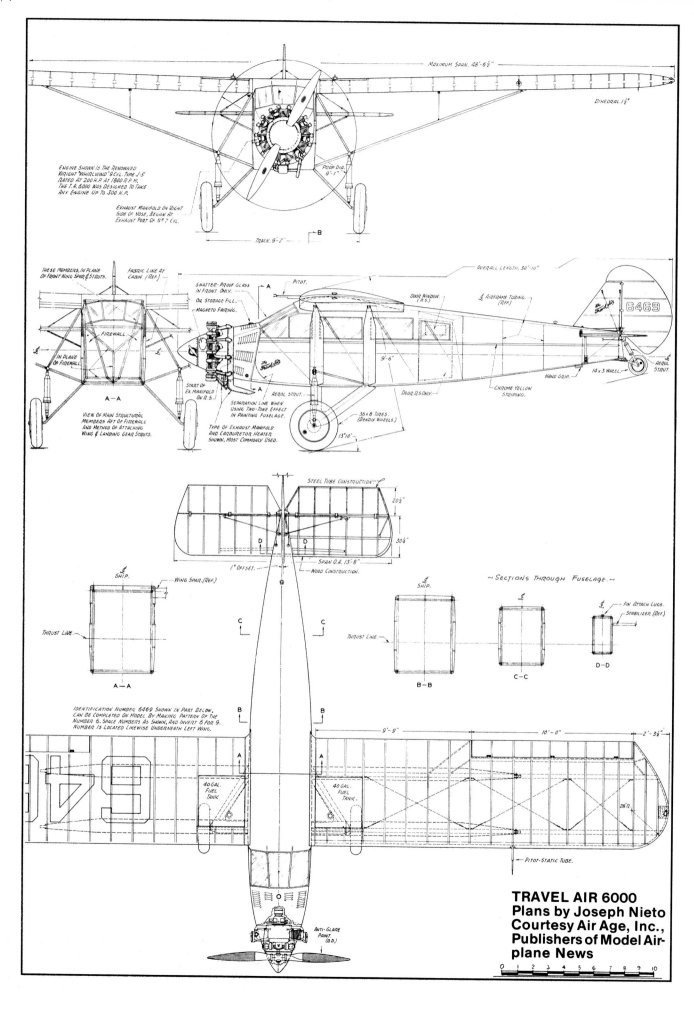

MAXIMUM SPAN. 48'-6½"

DIHEDRAL. 1½°

ENGINE SHOWN IS THE RENOWNED
WRIGHT WHIRLWIND 9 CYL. TYPE J-5
RATED AT 200 H.P. AT 1800 R.P.M.
THE T.A. 6000 WAS DESIGNED TO TAKE
ANY ENGINE UP TO 300 H.P.

PROP DIA.
9'-1"

EXHAUST MANIFOLD ON RIGHT
SIDE OF NOSE, BEGAN AT
EXHAUST PORT OF N° 7 CYL.

B

TRACK. 9'-7"

THESE MEMBERS, IN PLANE
OF FRONT WING SPAR & STRUTS.

FABRIC LINE AT
CABIN (REF.)

PITOT.

OVERALL LENGTH. 30'-10"

SHATTER-PROOF GLASS
IN FRONT ONLY.

A

DOOR WINDOW.
(R.S.)

€ AIRFRAME TUBING.
(REF.)

OIL STORAGE FILL.

MAGNETO FAIRING.

6469

FIREWALL

IN PLANE
OF FIREWALL

A

9'-6"

HAND GRIP.

A—A

START OF
EX. MANIFOLD
ON R.S.

AEROL STRUT.

14 x 3 WHEEL.

AEROL
STRUT.

VIEW OF MAIN STRUCTURAL
MEMBERS AFT OF FIREWALL
AND METHOD OF ATTACHING
WING & LANDING GEAR STRUTS.

SEPARATION LINE WHEN
USING TWO-TONE EFFECT
IN PAINTING FUSELAGE.

TYPE OF EXHAUST MANIFOLD
AND CARBURETOR HEATER
SHOWN, MOST COMMONLY USED.

36 x 8 TIRES
(BENDIX WHEELS.)

13'-10"

DOOR. R.S. ONLY.

CHROME YELLOW
STRIPING.

STEEL TUBE CONSTRUCTION

20½"

30¼"

1° OFFSET.

SPAN O.A. 13'-8"

WOOD CONSTRUCTION.

D   D

€
SHIP.

WING SPAR. (REF.)

€
SHIP.

~ SECTIONS THROUGH FUSELAGE. ~

€

FIN ATTACH LUGS.

€

STABILIZER. (REF.)

THRUST LINE.

THRUST LINE.

A—A

B—B

C—C

D—D

IDENTIFICATION NUMBER 6469 SHOWN IN PART BELOW,
CAN BE COMPLETED ON MODEL BY MAKING PATTERN OF THE
NUMBER 6. SPACE NUMBERS AS SHOWN, AND INVERT 6 FOR 9.
NUMBER IS LOCATED LIKEWISE UNDERNEATH LEFT WING.

B   B

C   C

A   A

9'-9"

10'-0"

2'-3½"

40 GAL.
FUEL
TANK.

40 GAL.
FUEL
TANK.

28'2"

PITOT-STATIC TUBE.

ANTI-GLARE
PAINT.
(O.D.)

**TRAVEL AIR 6000
Plans by Joseph Nieto
Courtesy Air Age, Inc.,
Publishers of Model Air-
plane News**

0 1 2 3 4 5 6 7 8 9 10

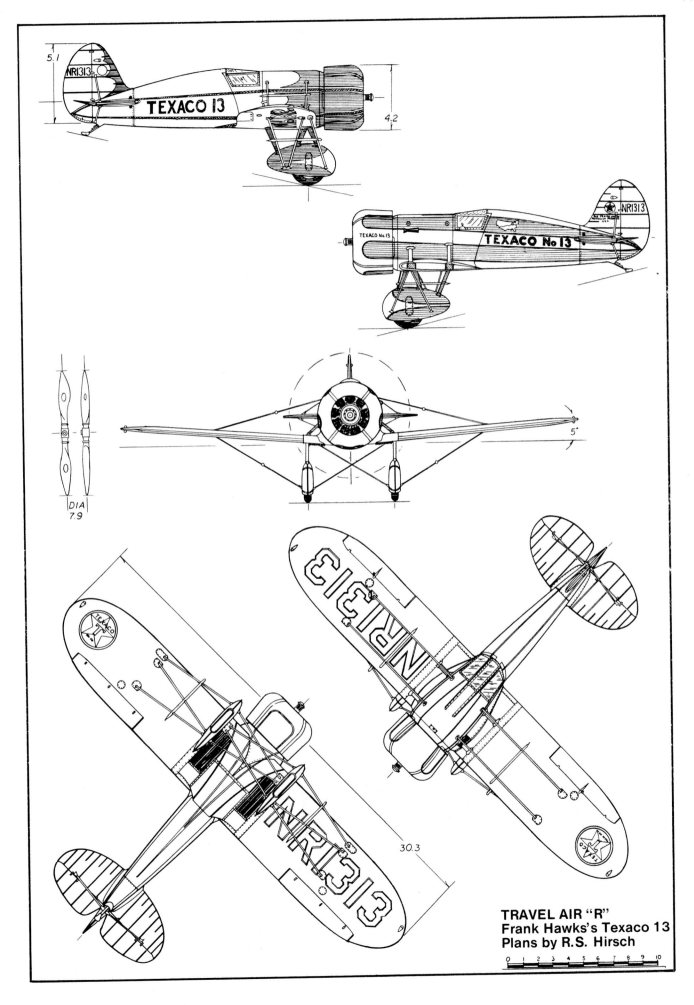

TEXACO 13

NR1313

5.1

4.2

NR1313

TEXACO No.13

TEXACO No 13

DIA
7.9

5'

NR1313

30.3

NR1313

TEXACO

TRAVEL AIR "R"
Frank Hawks's Texaco 13
Plans by R.S. Hirsch

0 1 2 3 4 5 6 7 8 9 10

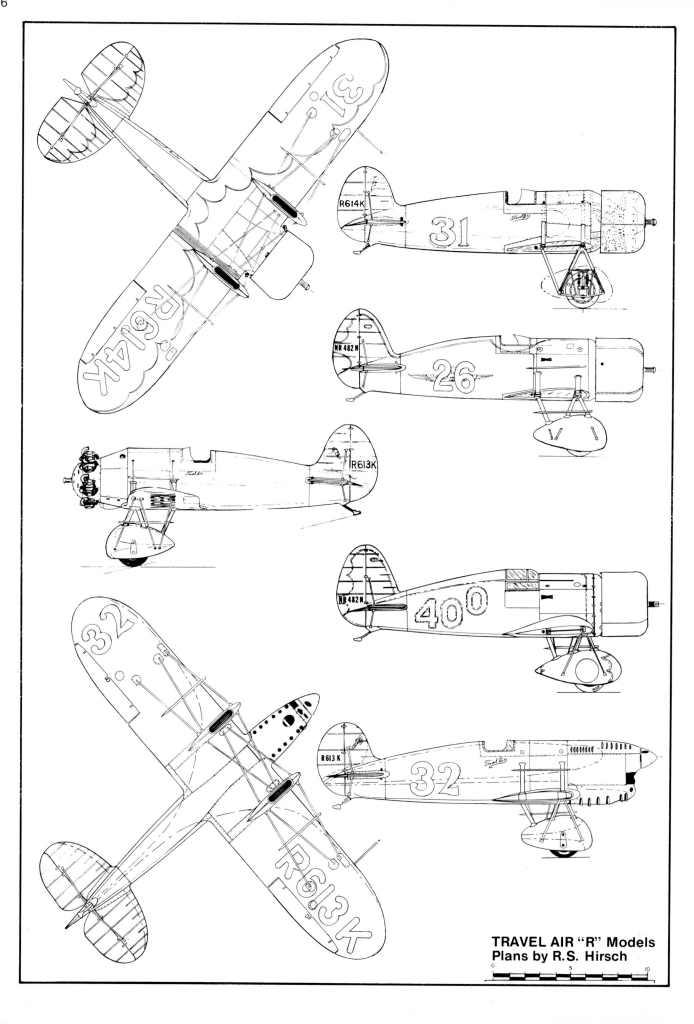

TRAVEL AIR "R" Models
Plans by R.S. Hirsch

CHAPTER TEN
Travel Air Potpourri

In the years of its existence, Travel Air grew from six men in downtown Wichita to 650 men on East Central Avenue — from two airplanes per month to 30 ships per week!

The site of Travel Air's factory still sees many exciting things happen. Like the day in 1979 when the near tranquility of turboprops was broken by the roar of Jim Younkin's replica Model "R."

People gathered. Heads turned, searching with eyes hoping to see the source of all that noise. There it was! Coming around in a long, descending turn the distant image was gathering speed.

Louder and closer the ship came, but what was it? Still too far away to be sure. "Look, it's . . . it's a 'Mystery Ship'!

Ears were covered by hands as the red and black rider of the sky flashed by. Right down on the deck it was . . . throttle wide open . . . flying wires screaming their protest along with the engine. What a sight!

Up, up into the blue of its birth the Travel Air flew. Her master banked the messenger of the past around in a hard left climbing turn, the little ship clawing at the air with her wings and propeller.

Then, the roar subsided to a cacophony of exhaust noises, the big radial relaxing as the throttle was closed. With the grace of a winged memory the ship came around . . . easing into position on final approach.

Over the fence, throttle closed . . . coming out of the slip for landing. A gentle touchdown in prairie grass, tail coming down, speed gone. She was home again . . . it felt good to be there.

In a matter of minutes the airplane was surrounded by visitors, all of them perusing her beautiful lines and reaching out slowly to touch her skin, as if she were gold.

Many had never witnessed such an airplane before. Some were totally unaware of the history and 'roots' the craft before them represented.

Some were awed by the mere existence of such a flying machine. Others poked their heads into the cockpit to see what her internal beauties might hold.

All agreed she was something of a legend . . . not even the layman was unmoved. Travel Air had reached ahead 50 years and touched the respect of modern pilots and workers. She was the legacy Herb Rawdon and Walter Burnham created.

Travel Air Field had seen a day like this once before, back in August of 1929. And the prairie grass that inhabited the sod on East Central could tell quite a number of stories if it could speak. Perhaps it can . . .

Charley Landers ran out of the hangar to see what was

Lloyd Stearman (center) poses with the first Stearman biplane, the C-1, in Venice, California. George Lyle on left, Fred Hoyt on right. (The Boeing Company via Jack Wecker)

The first Beechcraft, 1932. NC499N, designated Model 17R was equipped with 420 hp Wright "Whirlwind." Top speed was 201 mph. Ted Wells and Walter Beech had created a classic. (Beech Aircraft Corporation)

going on. That OX-5 Model B had made two or three passes across the field, so he must be trying to get somebody's attention.

W.B. Emery from Bradford, Pennsylvania eased the Travel Air around for another trip across the airport. He and Mr. Fisher had flown from Bradford to bring the biplane in for a major servicing appointment.

However, on takeoff from Kansas City's Richards Field a wheel had been lost. It fell off the axle. All the way to Wichita Emery thought about what he should do when he got to Travel Air Field.

He was doing the right thing coming down to Wichita — that way if he cracked up the ship the factory was there to rebuild it. Landers was now outside watching Emery as he brought his ship around for the fourth time. Landers saw the problem as the Travel Air swooped by and waved his arm in response.

He got Clarence Clark and the two men fetched a new

wheel and tire from the hangar. Clarence got in the Model B and Charley whirled the propeller. With the Curtiss engine popping out loud, Landers jumped in the front seat and off they flew.

Emery took his ship away from the field so there would be no danger to other traffic. Clark caught up with him and eased the Travel Air biplane into a position above and slightly to the side of Emery.

Mr. Fisher had not flown much before, and here he was flying in a one-wheeled airplane with two guys about to collide with him! Perhaps he should have stayed in Bradford, he thought to himself.

But Bill Emery was a good pilot. He looked up as Clark and Landers eased in a little closer. Charley was tying a rope to the wheel and then he placed it over the side of the biplane.

Emery signalled Mr. Fisher to get the wheel when Landers lowered it down. What! Get the wheel! Wait a

Stearman Aircraft Company returned to Wichita in 1927. One of the first ships built was the C-2, shown here. (The Boeing Company via Jack Wecker)

Lindbergh stands next to Model 6000-B he flew. His flight in 1927 sparked fantastic growth for American aviation. (A. M. Barnes)

minute, he was not here for that sort of crazy stunt!

But Emery prevailed. It was get that wheel or they would crack-up on landing. The airstream made it difficult to line up the wheel so Fisher could get it. He was almost standing up in the front cockpit, but Landers' rope just wasn't adequate.

Charley needed a longer rope. Back to the field they went and picked up another length. In a matter of minutes the two Travel Airs were in formation... wings high above the Kansas countryside.

Landers tried to lower the rope again. No success... it was just too hard to get the lightweight wheel/tire down to Mr. Fisher. They would have to go on in and land on the good tire.

It causes one to think what Mr. Fisher would have done with the item if he had received it. Only one possibility exists... Bill Emery expected his passenger to leave the cockpit, crawl from the lower wing down to the landing gear and install the wheel!

Forty minutes had been consumed in this aerial exercise, and Mr. Emery's OX-5 had just about consumed all its fuel, so the decision was made to take'er on in.

Flying at near stall speed, Emery touched down with great skill and the other tire did not blow or run off the rim, as many tires were prone to do in those days.

As airspeed decreased, the wingtip caught the grass and the Travel Air curved around in a gentle groundloop.

That was it. Down safe and sound. Mr. Fisher was just glad to be down! The ship was repaired very soon after the mishap and was back in the air.

Those were exciting days, indeed. All who lived through them say they wouldn't trade them for anything.

In March, 1928, when the Travel Air Transportation Company went into business. Walter Beech wanted the organization to keep busy, flying charters to just about anywhere, giving 'joyrides' and providing a ship for quick trips here and there.

Three airplanes were always to be at the ready. One never knew who might be around the factory that needed a ride. Lots of people were at the factory every day, and some may be inclined to go for a hop, perhaps for the first time.

A.M. 'Monty' Barnes was one of the pilots on the flightline for such needs. If Newman Wadlow was busy or not available, and Pete Hill couldn't take the flight, one of the other pilots, like Barnes, would get the call.

One winter day, after walking into the transportation office located in factory "B," Monty answered the phone. It was Walter Beech. "Barnes, get your flying suit on. As you know, Art Goebel is here and wants to catch the transcontinental plane east out of Kansas City early this afternoon. So I want you to fly him up to Kansas City."

Monty understood and hung up the phone. A Model 2000 was already being warmed up outside the hangar. As usual, when Mr. Beech spoke, people jumped.

Model 6000-B, serial #962, licensed NR8139 was used by Charles Lindbergh for his Mexico trip, later by Truman and Newman Wadlow in their flying service. Note name "Romancer" on fuselage, derived from Lindbergh's courting of Ann Morrow in Mexico. Ship is configured as tanker in this view, to refuel another airplane in endurance attempt. (Beech Aircraft Corporation)

Travel Air's baseball team were Industrial League champs in 1929. Coach Roy Edwards stands at center. (Dean Edwards)

Donning his usual flying suit of quilted construction, Monty headed for the office door. "Barnes, that suit won't cut the mustard." It was Pete Hill speaking from across the room.

"You'll freeze to death in that suit. You had better go over to the stock room and buy one of those fur-lined suits with bear fur and double zippers. It cost $200 retail, but since you work for the factory, they will sell it to you for cost." Monty listened, but didn't buy the fur-lined suit.

Barnes went to the flightline and found Walter and Art. The Model 2000 was just about ready, and Monty noticed that Goebel wore only a thin, reddish fabricoid suit with a blanket lining.

It was only two degrees above zero outside, and Monty wondered if that was all Art was going to put on. Apparently it was, for Goebel climbed into the front cockpit of the Travel Air and Monty took the back seat.

In the air and headed for Kansas City, Barnes realized they had a 15 mph headwind from the northeast at ground level, but it seemed to be swinging around to the northwest at 1500 feet altitude. Monty decided to stay at that height.

About 65 miles out of Kansas City the headwind again appeared, and the groundspeed of the Travel Air went down.

Up in the front cockpit, Art Goebel was suffering terribly. Monty could tell because Art would turn around and gesture for Barnes to go faster.

Monty replied that he would, but Barnes was feeling the full brunt of the icy wind, too. He was wishing he bought that fur-lined flying suit, but poor Goebel was sitting up front in a 1/4 inch thick outfit.

Every time Monty stirred in the back cockpit to get another comfortable position, Art would turn around and give him a worried look. Goebel felt the airplane shudder slightly and was wondering if the old OX-5 was about to quit for the day. Yet, the engine ran strong and true.

Finally, Kansas City Airport came into sight. Barnes eased the Travel Air down and taxied up to the terminal building. Art got out and went to his hotel for a good warming up. Monty had the ship refueled and headed home.

Art Goebel had missed his plane and for the next three weeks he was flat on his back in a Kansas City hospital with a very serious case of pneumonia.

Monty Barnes didn't see Goebel again for ten years. The next time he did was when Goebel came through Wichita on a skywriting job. He walked into Monty's office and the two shook hands in greeting. Not expecting Goebel to remember him, Monty said "I don't know if you will remember me." But Art replied, "My God, man, will I ever forget you? The last time I flew with you, you put me in the hospital for three weeks!"

Incidentally, ten years earlier Monty bought that fur-lined flying suit right after he returned from flying Art Goebel. It cost him $106, but he used it for many years and never regretted its purchase.

Walter Herschel Beech was an ambitious man. Born in Pulaski, Tennessee on January 30, 1892, Walter was a farm boy, and he wasn't afraid to admit it.

After Travel Air had sold 50% of its business to

The "Aerovane" next to East Central Avenue and Travel Air factory, 1928. Unit was designed to orient airmen as to city, wind direction and true north. (Beech Aircraft Corporation)

Truman Wadlow flew this Model 6-B with wheel fairings and Townend ring in 1930 Ford tour. Ship was serial #6B-2037, called Curtiss-Wright "Sedan." (Beech Aircraft Corporation)

Hayden, Stone and Company, Beech told the press "I'm just a country boy. Go get a picture of me when I first came to Wichita. I've made out good, and I'm not afraid to say so." And he wasn't. Years earlier Walter told his brother, Richard Beech, that he wasn't going to farm. There had to be something more outside of Pulaski, Tennessee.

One day, as the two young boys hoed weeds in the cotton fields, Walter stopped, leaned on his hoe and said, "I'll be damned if I'm gonna do this the rest of my life!"

He didn't hoe weeds long after that statement was made. Beech acquired mechanical skills from his familiarity with farm equipment and then he joined a truck manufacturer and spent some time in Europe as a representative.

World War I found Walter in the Army serving as an engine mechanic at a base in Waco, Texas. He may have been exposed to flight at that point, because very little is known about his flight experience prior to World War I.

Claims that Beech soloed a Curtiss "Pusher" biplane on July 11, 1914, have not been accepted, as there were no witnesses to the flight. He may have flown, but this lack of evidence about the 1914 flight, coupled with the fact that Matty Laird remembers Beech as being a pilot of "limited experience," seems to point to a later date.

Beech was, however, a pilot with Pete Hill and Errett Williams in Arkansas City by 1920, and he is remembered as being quite energetic and eager to get things done for aviation. John Robson, who lived in Arkansas City and worked with Beech at the Williams-Hill Aircraft Company, recalls that he and Walter Beech were watching pigeons one day in downtown Arkansas City. The birds were eating popcorn that had been spilled on the sidewalk. Although it was of no interest to Robson, Beech commented that he saw a definite point of interest in the wing action of the birds.

He got some paper and drew the motions of the wings as the pigeons flew back and forth, picking up popcorn.

To be sure the birds stayed long enough to make his sketches, Walter had John go back in the store and buy some more popcorn and continue to throw it on the sidewalk.

After Beech was satisfied that he had all necessary details down in pictures, he set about designing a modification to the empennage of the JN-4 he flew.

Beech's idea was to put a "V" style tail on the Curtiss. The two men built the pair of vertical surfaces in a small workshop under the local Ford dealer's garage in

"Smiling Thru," a Model 6000-B, serial #2012 in the Curtiss-Wright system, was owned by Automatic Washer Company. It was specially equipped with 12-volt auxiliary power unit to demonstrate washers to prospective customers. Three washers could be carried in the cabin after all seats were removed. (Beech Aircraft Corporation)

Curtiss-Wright took the Model 6000 and modified this example into the Model A-6-A, with eight seats, 420 hp "Wasp" and revised empennage/windscreen. (Beech Aircraft Corporation)

Equador bought this attractive Model B-4000 in 1929 for primary training duties. (Beech Aircraft Corporation)

122

Edgar B. Smith poses before his Standard biplane. Smith took many photographs of Wichita aircraft over the years. (Earle Sayre)

downtown Arkansas City. It was the same shop used by the Williams-Hill company to rebuild airplanes and overhaul engines.

The modification was completed and installed on the airplane. It consisted of two surfaces, similar in appearance to horizontal stabilizers, bolted at an upward angle to the fuselage. They were attached just forward of the normal empennage. There was no motion of any kind to the surfaces.

When Walter flight-tested the airplane he told Robson it flew better than ever that way, and the "V" surfaces were a successful change. Walter really thought he discovered something.

Nothing more was done with the project, but it does illustrate how Walter Beech pursued an idea and was not hesitant to innovate. Travel Air would benefit from his innovative character and will to succeed.

It has been stated that Walter Beech did not endorse 'stunting' as a means of furthering the aviation business. The letter he wrote to one aviation publication in August, 1929, does a very good job of explaining Walter's position (and therefore Travel Air Co.'s position) on the subject. It is reproduced in its entirety, and makes for some interesting reading.

"If aviation is to become a means of transportation and is to be taken out of the realm of the spectacular so that the businessmen of the country will have an appreciation of its possibilities, and an acceptance of it as a means of safe and quick transportation, it seems to me that all manufacturers who are honestly interested in the furtherance of aviation will be very much against any stunting and circus flying at future aeronautical expositions.

"Although we are often asked to take part in acrobatic demonstrations and races and meets, we turn these offers down because we do not believe them to be for the best interests of aviation. We will not enter competition of this kind, and if it is necessary to continue with the airplane business to keep in step with programs of this nature, I am looking forward to the day when I can resign from airplane activities. The writer believes that the airplane circus days are over, and

these competitive races should be put on with the thought in mind that we are selling aeronautics to the general public who must be sold on the safety of aircraft, and not to a few who want nothing but speed.

"If you agree with the position we have taken, we know that you can, through your good magazine, help foster the cause of sanity and safety in aviation, and we will be very grateful to you for anything you can do to promote this cause."

"A few weeks ago hundreds of thousands of people watched the endurance planes breaking the world's record at St. Louis.

"By far the majority of them were interested from a standpoint of this demonstration of safety, but in a great measure considerable effectiveness was lost because of numerous planes stunting and doing acrobatics in an endeavor to amuse the crowds, when in reality the crowd was interested and amused in seeing and being convinced that an airplane could stay aloft this great length of time without adjustments of any kind.

"Your comments on this situation would be interesting."

It was signed . . . Walter H. Beech, President, Travel Air Company. Such was the opinion of Walter Beech, an opinion he carried forth to his own company some three years later.

The spirit of invention and the will to build the best airplanes in the world led Walter Beech to leave Curtiss-Wright in 1932 and return to Wichita.

Ted Wells was the only Travel Air engineer that went to St. Louis with Curtiss-Wright. Beech and Wells had some similar ideas on what kind of airplane could be built to sell in the dark days of the Great Depression.

Ted had been working on a reverse stagger biplane of very attractive lines. He wanted to develop the design and see if the Curtiss-Wright people were interested.

Louise Thaden was an important sales/demonstration pilot for Beech Aircraft Company, too. She and Blanche Noyes won the 1936 Bendix race, first women to do so, in their C17R. (Beech Aircraft Corporation)

They were not in the least bit interested, and when Walter Beech wasn't interested in remaining as another member of a big organization, he, Olive Ann Beech, and Ted Wells put an airplane company together.

Beech had the money and Wells had the design. From this fortuitous duo came the Beechcraft Model 17. Technically, the Model 17 was just another biplane, but the negative stagger of the wings gave rise to the term 'staggerwing.'

On November 4, 1932, the first Model 17 flew with Pete Hill at the controls. By 1937 Walter Beech and his wife Olive Ann were back in the old Travel Air factory. The sounds of woodworking machines, fabric being doped and the thunder of big bore radial engines had returned to the prairie.

Walter Beech died on November 29, 1950. He had left a permanent impression on all aviation and its history, one that began in a farm field and would never be forgotten.

There are many people today who speak of Beech Aircraft Corporation as though it were a continuation of Travel Air Co. This is far from the truth. Travel Air was the seasoning and learning environment for Walter Beech and those who worked with him, like Clyde Cessna and Lloyd Carlton Stearman.

But had the Travel Air firm never existed is is doubtful that Beech Aircraft Corporation would have come into being.

What Walter Beech learned about the aviation business, he learned from the ground up at Swallow and Travel Air. Over five years at Travel Air gave Beech invaluable experience. It also placed him in contact with people and places that would render their business at a later date.

And it cannot be forgotten that Travel Air was more than just a company. It was also a place to build the Model 17. Had the Travel Air factory complex not been there, who knows where Walter Beech would have gone to build Ted Wells' airplane.

Some of Travel Air's customers were young, like 17-year-old John Gubbins (left) with salesman "Swede" Christopher. (Beech Aircraft Corporation)

But, what happened to other men at Travel Air?

Owen G. Harned, who helped Walter Beech put together the first big nationwide sales organization in 1927 and 1928, stayed with Travel Air and then Curtiss-Wright until 1931. He then quit the aviation business.

Ray W. Brown was the other arm of sales at Travel Air in 1928 and 1929. He grew up in Illinois and Hutchinson, Kansas, and learned to fly at Call Field in 1918, where he became a Second Lieutenant.

He came with Travel Air in 1928 and assisted in the formation of the regional and local marketing areas for the company. Leaving in the fall of 1929, Brown joined the Detroit Aircraft Corporation as sales manager and then did a stint with Parks Air College, a division of Detroit Aircraft.

Pete Hill worked for Travel Air until it closed down in

Billy Parker of Phillips Petroleum was a fine pilot and his company bought Travel Air airplanes from 1927 through 1930. Model BW shown here was 'Nu-Aviation' fuel test ship in 1927. (Phillips Petroleum Company)

In June, 1929, Art Goebel (center) bought 10 Model 2000 biplanes for his Kansas City flying school. O.A. Mellor and Ray Brown go through the official paperwork for the sale. (Beech Aircraft Corporation)

124

After their marriage, Charles and Ann Lindbergh visited Wichita and landed at Travel Air Field. They were flying in a specially built Curtiss Falcon biplane with "Conqueror" engine. (Beech Aircraft Corporation)

O. A. Mellor and Walter Beech were married in 1930. Here the couple pose with Curtiss-Wright Model 15-C with "Challenger" of 185 hp. (Beech Aircraft Corporation)

1932 and then he worked for Beech Aircraft Company and did the initial test flights on the Model 17. He remained in aviation and was operating a business in the northwest United States when he died in September, 1980.

Richard "Dick" Beech was Walter's brother. He was not in aviation as deeply as Walter, but he worked as a foreman both at Travel Air and Beech Aircraft Company.

Charles A. Lindbergh took a trip to Mexico in 1929 and flew a Model 6000-B having left his own ship in Kansas City. The purpose of the trip was to visit Ann Morrow, daughter of Ambassador Dwight Morrow.

The airplane, 6000-B serial #962, was damaged in Mexico City, repaired and flown back to Wichita. Originally this ship was sold to Central Air Lines, a short-haul, feeder airline with its base in Wichita. The line operated from Travel Air Field, where it had built a large, modern hangar in 1929. Travel Air was involved with the venture financially.

Newman and Truman Wadlow took over the facilities with the help of Walter Beech in 1931. Beech had enough confidence in his two former employees to co-sign a note for $25,000, and they ran a business there until 1934.

The new name of the company was Wadlow Brothers Flying Service. The twins had flight and ground school courses that could take a neophyte from private license to the transport pilot ticket.

Hollywood cowboy actor, Ken Maynard, flew this Model 4000 with Wright engine. (Beech Aircraft Corporation)

They used Model 6000-B ships and converted one to a 420 hp "Wasp" powered A-6000-A, plus a complement of biplanes. The boys had Lindbergh's 6000-B and decided to name it the 'Romancer.'

Both Newman and Truman 'romanced' their wives-to-be in the ship, and advertised it as a convenient accommodation for courting. Marriages were also possible within the Travel Air's spacious cabin.

Unfortunately, the brothers didn't remain in business very long, as the Depression was deepening and flying was slowly winding down.

Newman and Truman both went on to have distinguished flying careers. Truman flew with Clarence Clark again at Phillips Petroleum's aviation division after World War II.

Travel Air was one of the early companies to try out the 'Aerovane,' built by Aerovane Utilities Corporation of New York. It was an airway marker intended to be placed on the right hand side of every highway leading into a town or city.

The unit was designed to be a combination wind direction indicator, compass bearing indicator and have the name of the town or city over which the aviator was flying.

The first Aerovane was installed just to the west of Travel Air's factory "A" in June, 1928, on the south edge of Central Avenue. A structural steel pole was 25 feet high and 6 inches in diameter. At the top a wind sock three feet long was installed. Eight feet below the sock a horizontal, flat arrow 13-1/2 feet long and painted a chrome yellow for visibility, carried the name of the town or city toward which it was pointing lettered in black.

On the tail of the arrow a black, three-foot square had a small, white arrow pointing toward true north. Both of the arrows were fixed.

Marvel Crosson flashes her winning smile from the cockpit of Union Oil Co. Model 4000. C.F. Lienesch flew ship for company. Crosson was killed in the 1929 Women's Air Derby flying a Travel Air. (Roger Tengwall)

Below the large arrow a rectangular sign, eight feet by three feet in size, was used for road information of use to automobile travelers.

Suspended from this sign on either side of the supporting pole were two circular panels, each one 42 inches in diameter. These panels could be rented by local merchants, thereby paying for the cost and installation of the Aerovane. The unit was of help to the wayward flier, as a quick glance from an altitude low enough to read the Aerovane would provide instant data on true north, town name and direction, as well as wind direction.

The only drawback to this idea seemed to be very important — the pilot had to know where the Aerovane was! Despite its 25-foot height, the Aerovane could be easily missed by a pilot if he was not watching carefully. Placing them next to roadways and metropolitan streets was to have been a key factor in making the Aerovane visible.

The Aerovane placed at the Travel Air factory had a bullish statement on the large signboard: "Wichita, Kansas, Aviation Center of the United States."

As a final feature, the Aerovane had provisions for night lighting, should the town or city desire to have it installed.

Travel Air's Aerovane disappeared by the time Walter Beech returned to start Beech Aircraft Company.

After the Women's Air Derby of 1929, Travel Air sold the winning airplane to an eastern buyer. Louise Thaden had to part company with her beloved D-4000, still equipped with the NACA cowling, Wright J-5, speed wings and completely enclosed shock cord 'cuffs' on the landing gear.

Truman Wadlow was assigned to fly Louise's former derby airplane back east. This particular machine was serial #1266 and was licensed NR671H, with Wright J-5 serial #8980.

Truman had to put the ship down in a forced landing, and it flipped over on its back. Very little damage was done and repairs were quickly made. It took a couple of weeks to deliver that ship, but Truman finally made it.

Another airplane Truman got to deliver was not a Travel Air. The Butler 'Blackhawk' was a clean, very attractive biplane built in Kansas City. Truman picked the ship up there and flew it all the way to California for Hoot Gibson, famous movie star.

By July, 1929, Travel Air was slowly building up to the unheard rate of 50 airplanes per week. Nearly half of the ships being delivered in the late summer were cabin monoplanes, namely the 6000-B with a few A-6000-A machines filling out the order books.

That's a very high number of airplanes. The company never sustained a production rate that high, but were working toward it and may have made the goal if time had permitted.

Travel Air did make its success known, however, when it reached certain milestones in production. The same month of July, 1929, saw the Travel Air factory claim a total of 1/4 of all registered or identified airplanes in the United States as being their products.

About 5,030 total ships were registered, but eliminating the 1,389 war surplus machines, Travel Air had built about 25% of the remaining number.

At the same time this claim was being put forth, the company also hit the press with the news that Travel Air just produced and delivered over 1,000 ships since its beginning, only 4-1/2 years earlier.

Al Jacobs, an engineer from Philadelphia, went to Travel Air in September, 1929 with his new engine — the Fischer and Jacobs radial. It was installed in a Model 4000 airframe and Al Jacobs flew it home for testing. The Department of Commerce had already approved the powerplant and production was expected to get underway sometime in the fall of the year. No approved type certificate was ever issued for this original combination, however.

Mr. Jacobs wasn't alone. Arthur Chevrolet was back at Travel Air in the spring of 1930. His firm ordered a biplane and hung another Chevrolet engine on it, the engine being of similar design as the D-6 used in R-2002 in 1929.

Chevrolet's pilot French Livezy flew the ship to an altitude of 16,000 feet, with the airplane reaching 8,000 feet in eight minutes. After this second 'marriage' of a Travel Air airframe and Chevrolet engine, nothing more was heard about further plans or possible production models.

The track record for the Travel Air factory as of July, 1929, showed 307 airplanes during the first six months of the year. Their total worth was $2,000,000. This 180-day effort represented one of the last production peaks for the company, although production remained fairly high, the trend was downward by the late summer and early fall.

It's also interesting to note that Travel Air managed to do all the construction of those 307 ships while the new factories "D" and "E" were being built.

One of the largest orders Travel Air ever got came from Tom Hardin of Texas Air Transport. Hardin sought Travel Air to "build me whatever you think I ought to have" and then he put together an airline down in Texas.

Eight different routes were anticipated, using the Model 6000-B monoplanes outfitted for passenger work. This frequently included toilet facilities in the aft cabin, vomit tubes and possibly Group 2 approval for one or two extra seats.

Texas Air Transport ordered 15 6000-B and 10 biplane ships, and Hardin took delivery of the first 6000-B on January 19, 1930. The biplanes went to the Dallas sales office of the company, while the monoplanes went to work hauling passengers as fast as they could be delivered. Hardin paid $13,500 for each of the monoplanes.

Walter Burnham and Herb Rawdon stuck it out with Travel Air until 1931. Burnham left the company to fulfill an assignment to Tri-State College at Angola, Indiana, where Burnham was to design and construct a wind tunnel.

Burnham accomplished that task and then picked up his degree in aeronautical engineering, too. He was head of that department by 1934, and remained at Tri-State until 1937. He joined another airplane firm and taught classes for a technical institute on the side. Walter Burnham retired from The Boeing Co. in 1965, then becoming a consulting engineer.

Herbert Rawdon was born on December 30, 1904. He grew up working on the farm, tending long hours in the fields with his father. High school was completed in only three years. Then Rawdon was in college working on his engineering degree. He joined Travel Air in the days of West Douglas, and was recognized by Beech and Weihmiller as an engineer of promise and expertise in design.

Herb Rawdon helped build the "Woolaroc" and "Oklahoma" with Burnham and Weihmiller, and in later Travel Air days he built up the engineering department to one of high respect by other manufacturers.

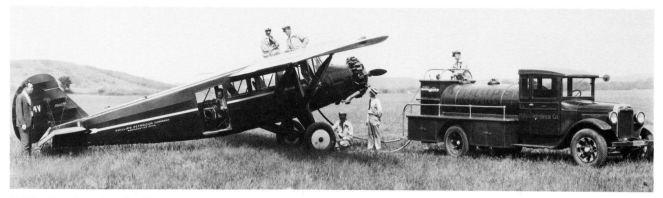

Phillips Petroleum bought this specially equipped Model 6000-B camera ship in January, 1929. Elmer Sark operated camera, "Cap" Gray was pilot. (Phillips Petroleum Company)

A "Wichita Fokker" stands ready to meet the enemy. Many weary Travel Air biplanes were converted to inline engines such as the Ranger for movie work as psuedo-Fokkers. General resemblance between a Fokker D-VII and the Travel Air is centered mostly in fuselage/empennage area. (Gordon S. Williams)

Rawdon is best remembered for his efforts with Burnham on the Model "R," but he is also credited with the Model 10 design and a few others, one being the co-design with Ted Wells of the Curtiss-Wright Model 12 "Sport Trainer." Burnham and Rawdon are deceased.

Travel Air was not all airplanes, either, and Walter Beech was not all business and no pleasure. Beech loved to watch wrestling and boxing duals, so much so that he decided to have a little action right at the Travel Air factory.

In 1928 Mr. Beech had a boxing ring built, complete with poles and ropes, for entertainment of the workers. A large, overhead electric light lit up the ring, and rows of shipping crates were turned on their sides to serve as seats for the spectators.

If any employees had a dispute and wanted to fight it out, no problem . . . just step right outside and into the ready-made ring. Don some boxing gloves, if desired, and have at it!

When a person walks into the factory on East Central Avenue today, there is a magnetism pervading the entire area where Travel Air once was . . . and still is.

On a quiet night, when all the workers have gone and only the silence remains behind, a walk through the halls of the old Travel Air buildings is a journey back in time.

The bricked-in windows stand in remembrance of the days when bright Kansas sunlight shown through them, bathing the busy factory in worker's light.

Though in existence only five years, Travel Air became one of the greatest airplane manufacturing companies the world has ever known. Its legacy is a lasting tribute to American aviation in the 1920s, and to the people who made Travel Air "The Standard of Aircraft Comparison."

The following books provided information that assisted in the preparation of this publication.

1. Shamburger, Page and Christy, Joe—*Command The Horizon*, 1968, A.S. Barnes and Company, Inc. and Castle Books.

2. Allard, Noel E.—*Speed, The Biography of Charles W. Holman*, 1976, Burgess-Beckwith Company.

3. Forden, Lesley—*The Ford Air Tours*, 1973, The Nottingham Press.

4. Byttebier, Hugo T.—*The Curtiss D-12 Aero Engine*, 1972, Smithsonian Institution Press.

5. Juptner, Joseph P.—*U.S. Civil Aircraft, Volumes 1, 2 and 3*, 1962, 1964 and 1966, Aero Publishers, Inc.

6. Van Meter, Sondra J.—*The Primary Contribution of E.M. Laird To The Aviation Industry Of Wichita*, 1962, Sondra J. Van Meter.

7. Nevill, John T.—*The Story of Wichita*, 1930, Aviation Magazine.

8. Eagle and Beacon, The Wichita, 1924 through 1931, Newspapers and supplements thereto.

9. Aviation and Aero Digest Magazines, 1922 through 1931.

10. Shamburger, Page and Christy, Joe—*The Curtiss Hawks*, 1972, Wolverine Press, Inc.

11. Von Thaden, Louise McPhetridge—*High, Wide and Frightened*, 1973, Air Facts, Inc.

12. Banks, F.R. (Rod), Air Commodore—*I Kept No Diary*, 1978, Airlife Publications.

13. Rice, M.S.—*Guide To Pre-1930 Aircraft Engines*, 1972, Hector Cervantes, Inc. and Aviation Publications.

14. Zimmerman, John—*Aerospace: Wichita Perspective*, 1966, John Zimmerman.

15. Jablonski, Edward and Thomas, Lowell—*Doolittle—A Biography*, 1976, Doubleday & Company